KEY TEXT
REFERENCE

D1429311

YOUNG BRITISH MUSLIMS

YOUNG BRITISH MUSLIMS

IDENTITY, CULTURE, POLITICS AND THE MEDIA

• • •

NAHID AFROSE KABIR

Edinburgh University Press

© Nahid Afrose Kabir, 2010

Edinburgh University Press Ltd
22 George Square, Edinburgh
www.euppublishing.com

Typeset in 10/12.5 Sabon by
Servis Filmsetting Ltd, Stockport, Cheshire, and
printed and bound in Great Britain by
CPI Antony Rowe, Chippenham and Eastbourne

A CIP record for this book is available from the British Library

ISBN 978 0 7486 4133 8 (hardback)

The right of Nahid Afrose Kabir to be identified as author of this work
has been asserted inaccordance with the Copyright, Designs and Patents
Act 1988.

Published in association with the HRH Prince
Alwaleed bin Talal Centre for the Study of
Islam in the Contemporary World, University
of Edinburgh. For further details of the centre
see www.alwaleed.ed.ac.uk

CONTENTS

TABLES AND FIGURES

Tables

Figures

ABBREVIATIONS

BBC	British Broadcasting Corporation
BNP	British National Party
CRE	Commission for Racial Equality
FOSIS	Federation of Student Islamic Societies
GFK	Growth from Knowledge
MCB	Muslim Council of Britain
MINAB	Mosques and Imams National Advisory Board
MP	Member of Parliament
NOP	National Opinion Poll
ONS	Office for National Statistics
PBUH	Peace Be Upon Him
PE	Physical Exercise
SNP	Scottish National Party
UK	United Kingdom
ULUISOC	Universities of London Union Islamic Society

GLOSSARY

Abaya	A loose black robe from head to toe; traditionally worn by Muslim women
Ahl-i-Hadith	Tradition of Prophet Muhammad [PBUH] and the Quran
Alim	Islamic scholar
Burqa	Loose outer garment worn by Muslim women
Chilla	Retreat for 40 days for spiritual self-reformation
Dar-al-Harb	Territory of war
Dar-al-Islam	Territory of peace
Eid-ul-Adha	Muslim religious celebration
Eid-ul-Fitr	Muslim religious celebration
Fatwa	Religious ruling
Fiqh	Jurisprudence
Hadith	Teachings or tradition of Prophet Muhammad [PBUH]
Hajj	Pilgrimage to the Muslim holy place of *Ka'bah* in Mecca performed in the prescribed tenth month of the Islamic calendar
Halal	Slaughter of animals in Islamic way
Haram	Forbidden in Islam
Hijab	Head scarf
Hudud	Limits set by Allah
Imam	Prayer leader of a mosque
Jihad	Religious struggle of Muslims
Jihadi	An individual who participates in a *jihad*
Jilbab	Long coat
Ka'bah	An important shrine of the Islamic world in Mecca
Kalima	First Islamic declaration of belief
Khalifah	Caliph

Khilafah	Caliphate
Kurta	Muslim shirt
Madrasah	Islamic school
Makrouh	Dislike or undesirable
Nasheed	Devotional Islamic songs
Niqab	Face veil
Purdah	Concealing clothing worn by women which prevents them from being seen by men
Ramadan	Month of fasting
Rasul	Messenger or Prophet sent by Allah with Divine Ordinance
Salaam	Muslim greeting
Salat	Muslim prayer
Sawm	Fasting
Shahada (Kalima)	First Islamic declaration of belief
Shaheed	Martyrs
Shariah	Islamic way
Shariah law	The code of law derived from the teachings of the Quran and the teachings and tradition of Prophet Muhammad [PBUH]
Sunnah	Teachings or tradition of Prophet Muhammad [PBUH]
Taliban	Students
Topi	Muslim men's cap
Ulama	A group of legal Muslim scholars
Ummah	Islamic community transcending all national boundaries
Umrah Hajj	Pilgrimage to the Muslim holy place of *Ka'bah* in Mecca performed at any time of the year (other than the prescribed time of Hajj)
Zakat	Alms giving
Zina	A major sin

ACKNOWLEDGEMENTS

For the information contained in this book I am indebted to the Muslims who most generously agreed to be interviewed and, in some cases, gave me permission to mention their names when quoting them. I sincerely thank the students and staff of the Islamic and State schools who helped me to make this study a success. The various youth centres in Britain have also been very supportive. Thanks to the imams who participated in this survey. I am grateful to Dr Muhammad Abdul Bari, the Secretary General of the Muslim Council of Britain; Mr Saleem Kidwai, General Secretary of the Muslim Council of Wales; Shaykh Ibrahim Mogra, the Chair of the Interfaith Relations Committee of the Muslim Council of Britain in Leicester; and Mr Sadiq Khan, Labour Member of Parliament for Tooting, London, for their insightful comments. I also express my thanks to the members of the Federation of Student Islamic Societies for supporting this study.

I express my grateful thanks to Mr Dilwar Hussain, Head of the Policy Research Centre, the Islamic Foundation, Leicester; Mr Philip Lewis, author of *Young British and Muslim*; Mr Jani Rasheed, Head of Diversity and Cohesion, Education Bradford; and Ms Rehana Minhas, Director of Equality and Diversity, Education Leeds for their support. Dr Max Farrar, Professor of Community Engagement, Leeds Metropolitan University deserves a special mention for agreeing to be the contact person in Britain if participants/ interviewees had any concerns regarding this research project. Many thanks to Mr Steve Bell and Dr Tony Gaskew who have most graciously extended their support. Mr Steve Bell has allowed me to publish his cartoon in the book and Dr Tony Gaskew, author of *Policing Muslim American Communities*, has provided constructive comments for the book.

I sincerely thank Ms Helen Dorfman, Principal and Ms Cath Brookes, Deputy Principal of Burntwood School, London for arranging an interview appointment with Mr Sadiq Khan, Labour Member of Parliament for Tooting. Thanks are also due to Dr Sadaf Rizvi and Councillors Mrs Lutfa Begum and Ms Rania Khan for providing interview contacts. I express my gratitude to Dr Abu Sayeed Rahman and Mrs Dilruba Rahman for their kind hospitality when I was in London. I am also grateful to Mr Tarek Kalam for his kind support of the survey. Thanks are due to Sheelah Trefle Hidden for supporting this study while I was in Britain. Dr Yasmin Khan and Ms Amira Alam in Cardiff also deserve a special mention here for their kind hospitality. I express my thanks to the Edinburgh University Press, and their editorial team, Mr James Dale, Mr Eddie Clark and Ms Nicola Ramsey, for assisting me in the publication process.

In Australia, I express my sincere gratitude to the British-born scholar Dr Mary Kooyman who dedicated many hours to editing my drafts and making constructive comments. I thank my colleagues Professor Leila Green for encouraging me to do this study, and Dr John Hall for his valuable advice. I extend my warm appreciation for the constant support of my family, especially my husband Dr Mohammad Ismat Kabir and our three sons, Sakhawat, Naoshad and Mahtab Kabir, for allowing me to concentrate on the project and make several trips to Britain while they looked after each other in my absence. Of course, the caring nature of my husband helped me concentrate on my research work and write this book.

This project was funded by an Early Career Researcher Grant, and Faculty Small Grant Scheme, School of Communications and Arts, Edith Cowan University, Perth, Australia, in 2008.

FOREWORD

There is an avalanche of books seeking to address and illuminate what many dub since 9/11, Madrid and 7/7, Europe's 'Muslim question'. However, the number of works which incorporate the views of young Muslims themselves so as to understand their hopes and fears, struggles and perplexities of growing up in contexts frequently suspicious of Islam and Muslims, can still be counted on one hand. Dr Kabir's work adds significantly to our knowledge of how young British Muslims between 15 and 30 years old make sense of and manage their multiple identities – ethnic, religious, cultural and local.

The author brings to this task a number of key assets. She is an academic who has already published on Muslims in Australia, where she and her husband have lived for sixteen years. She is a Muslim herself, part of the educated Bangladeshi elite: she has lived in Pakistan for some years and speaks Urdu, as well as spending ten years in the Middle East. The book is thus enlivened by a comparative perspective and rooted in a deep knowledge of the Muslim world. She also has a real desire to enable Muslim minorities and wider society to discover ways of living together that draws on the best in all communities.

Another valuable feature of this study is that its in-depth interviews with more than 200 young people are drawn from five major cities: Bradford, Cardiff, Leeds, Leicester and London. While a majority of respondents have roots in the South Asian communities, other more marginalised voices such as Yemeni and Somali are also audible. Another welcome feature of the work is the space given to the perspectives of young women.

The study is structured to elicit their views about a number of key issues, including whether and to what extent they share a sense of 'Britishness'; what they think of the media coverage of their communities; and their responses to the furore generated by comments made by Jack Straw, MP for Blackburn, about the face veil – *niqab* – and the *Shariah*, following the lecture delivered by the Archbishop of Canterbury.

While exploring their attitudes to such issues, the author does not neglect issues internal to the Muslim communities; in particular, the cultural and religious constraints which are felt as burdensome by many and which also impact their ability to engage all aspects of wider society. There are candid comments about the ill-informed stereotypes many Muslim religious leaders and parents exhibit with regard to aspects of British society and its institutions, not least a penchant for conspiracy theories.

What comes across from the comments marshalled here is both the common sense and capacity for self-criticism of many of these young people; they are frequently able to rise above the particularities, ethnic and sectarian, of their upbringing and the indignities of a post-7/7 world, where increasingly Muslims are seen through a narrow security lens. The book is a perfect antidote to those who can only see Muslims as 'threat'. Unsurprisingly, on a range of contested issues there is little consensus among them. This book makes clear that on a range of issues they are probably as confused as many of their non-Muslim peers!

Philip Lewis
Department of Peace Studies, University of Bradford
Author of *Young British and Muslim* (2007)
July 2009

To my father (late Nurul Matin) for his vision, and mother (Dil Afrose Matin) for her inspiration.

INTRODUCTION: MY RESEARCH OBSERVATIONS

During my research visits to Britain in 2008, I interviewed a number of young Muslims aged 15–30 years, and some Muslim adults, 30 years and over, in London, Leicester, Bradford, Leeds and Cardiff. I was fascinated to hear their life stories and how they defined their sense of belonging. They all looked visibly Asian, some were noticeably Muslims because of their Islamic dress codes, and many (to my ear) sounded English. However, as I went north to Yorkshire, the interviewees' accents got stronger and sounded more like the resident Yorkshire people. The respondents' life stories reflected their fears and concerns as Muslims, but they also showed an appreciation of and gratitude for their 'home', Britain. They were living at a time when the Muslims' peace-loving reputation had been tarnished by the 7/7 London tragedy. However, all participants of this study expressed their identity articulately and in different ways. For example, in April 2008, when I met the Malawian, East African-born Shaykh Ibrahim Mogra of Gujrati-Indian background and asked him about his identity, he replied:

> I live in Britain, Britain is my home. This is where I raise my family, they go to school here. And I work in this country, I earn my livelihood in this country. I practise my religion in this country, this is home. So I am British. I do struggle with the idea of me being English because in my mind somehow I think English-ness is to do with the race where you have to be white Anglo-Saxon. We all come under the banner of being British, but when you talk about English or Scottish or Welsh, I'm still struggling with that one, I haven't yet convinced myself that I am English because I'm brown you see. But yes, British definitely, so whenever I'm in Europe and abroad, I was in Sydney for a conference, I am very British when I'm there. And when I go to Scotland to give lectures or something, then I'm very English because of the old English/Scottish rivalry.

So you can see that with the passing of time I am also beginning to accept that I am English. My wife and children are certainly English as they were all born in this beautiful country. The question is, does British and English society accept me and my family as one of them? Integration is a two-way street. (Interview, Leicester, 14 April 2008)

I kept wondering about Shaykh Ibrahim Mogra's sense of British identity because he looked very Muslim in appearance, with his beard, *jilbab* (long Islamic dress) and a *topi* (Islamic cap) on his head. Shaykh Mogra has been living in Britain for the last 24 years, and received his degree in Theology in Lancashire in northern England. Thereafter, he studied at the Al Azhar University in Egypt for two years and completed his Masters degree at the School of Oriental and African studies in the University of London. At the time of interview, he was working in Leicester. He was also very involved in Muslim community affairs, interfaith activities and had a voice in the media. Shaykh Mogra mentioned the dynamics of identity between the English, Scottish and Welsh. I sensed this feeling of 'territorial oneness' among young Muslim interviewees in Wales, who prided themselves on their Welsh identity. I also read about Muslims in Scotland who strongly felt Scottish as opposed to other identities such as British (discussed in Chapter 1). Then I met the British-born Member of Parliament for Tooting, London, Sadiq Khan (of Pakistani background) at the Houses of Parliament in Westminster and asked him about his identity. Mr Khan replied:

One of the customary mistakes we make is to say that we have one identity. I believe we have multi-identities so you know I'm a man, I'm a parent, I'm a husband, I'm a Londoner, I'm a Tootinite, I'm British, I'm Muslim, I'm Asian, I can carry on. You know one of the riches of our city, our community, one of the reasons why Olympics will take place here, one of the reasons why our economy continues to boom, one of the reasons why we are the city in the country which India invests most in, for example, and one of the cities and countries where China invests most in, where most countries invest in, is because we have diversity and we are comfortable in multiple identities. (Interview, London, 22 May 2008)

Being the MP for Tooting, I assume he represented all the people in his constituency in Parliament. He has certainly integrated well into British society and that was expressed in his interview comments. So I assume that for Sadiq Khan all the criteria — integration, achievement and recognition from the wider society — impacted on his identity. Mr Khan felt proud to be British and constantly referred to London as 'our city'. This is further illustrated by Dilwar Hussain, Head of the Policy Research Centre, based at the Islamic Foundation, Leicester, of Bangladeshi background who talked about the different dimensions of identity:

At home, I may like rice and curry and the Bangladeshi dimension becomes more important. In religious terms, the Muslim dimension becomes more important, so, depending on where you are, different facets of your identity are emphasised.

I feel very much that this [Britain] is my country; that I belong to and it belongs to me. There is a sense of ownership and a sense of connection. It's about where you feel an emotional attachment – and I do love this country. I love the culture here, the openness. I've travelled across Europe and luckily with a British passport you can go and live almost anywhere in the world. But I choose to live here. I wouldn't live, unless I really had to, somewhere else; I feel settled and rooted here. (Interview, Leicester, 12 April 2008)

Hussain's cultural dimension comes into operation when he is at home, in mosques or with other Muslims because he feels Muslim, but overall he feels very connected to Britain. These three adult interviewees, aged 30–50 years, have lived in Britain for a long time and spoke of their sense of connection to Britain. The last two respondents, Sadiq Khan and Hussain, come from relatively big families and their parents came to Britain as immigrants. Like many other newly arrived immigrants, they had to face some of the challenges of resettlement. Khan and Hussain both grew up in their respective cultural environments, but integrated with the wider community through their educational institutions and part-time work. All three respondents have lived in Britain when there were race-relations issues with the non-white people (Asian and African-Caribbean), riots in Brixton, London, riots in Bradford, and the Salman Rushdie Affair and the burning of his book, *The Satanic Verses*. However, they overcame those tense periods, as they received acceptance from the mainstream British people, and perhaps at that time the British media were not so heavily focused on the Muslim question.

Aim of the book

In this book, I examine the life stories of some young Muslims, aged 15–30 years, and see how their identity is formed within the family, cultural and wider societal environments. This book attempts to understand the identity of young British Muslims through various constructs: their migration history, family settlement, socioeconomic status, culture, education, community and wider society gleaned from responses to the following research questions:

- How do British Muslim youths and young adults define their identity and imagine their life as Muslims in a Western, secularised, traditionally Christian society?
- What are the difficulties in the context of the family, in being raised at home within a Muslim tradition that, to some extent, differs from the social life and mores dominant in Western societies?

- What is the role of socioeconomic factors in the youths'/young adults' identity construction?
- How do Muslim youths and young adults define their 'national identity', and their sense of belonging? What factors have impacted on their definition?
- How do the Western media help in constructing an Islamic identity that is distinct from and irreconcilable with citizenship in the UK?
- How did Jack Straw's *niqab* and the Archbishop of Canterbury Dr Rowan Williams' *shariah* law debates impact on their identity?
- What are the methods for 'a humanitarian way forward'?

Some scholars have already written about Bangladeshi and Pakistani kinship, and how it impacts on identity. But they have restricted their research to one city: for example, Birmingham (Cressey 2006) and Manchester (Werbner 2002), or one community – the Pakistani Muslim families in Oxford (Jacobson 1998; Shaw 2000) and the Bangladeshi (Sylheti) community in London's East End (Dench, Gavron and Young 2006). My research has taken a broader approach by surveying five British cities in order to compare the flexibility and rigidity of certain cultures, such as the Bangladeshi-Muslim and Pakistani-Muslim cultures. I will see if the same cultural environment prevails or whether people have moved on. I also take into consideration other ethnic groups, such as the Somali and Yemeni Muslims, in this study. Furthermore, I investigate whether any of the wider community issues, such as unemployment (Ansari 2004: 210; Choudhury 2005: 74) and the media representation of Muslims (Poole 2002; Ahmed 2005: 114–15; Poole and Richardson 2006; Kabir and Green 2008) are impacting on the respondents' identity. And by discussing the recent *niqab* and the *shariah* law debate, I explore the religious dimension of their identity. I also observe whether Muslim women are more privileged compared to their male counterparts, and in what way gender issues are taken into consideration. Overall, under the current geopolitical environment, Muslim communities' cultural and religious restrictions, the mainstream media representation of Islam and law-enforcement agencies' rules and regulations (anti-terrorism laws), this book examines how young Muslims position themselves and define their single, double and multiple identities.

Organisation of the book

This book, *Young British Muslims: Identity, Culture, Politics and the Media*, contains a brief introduction and eight chapters (including conclusion). Chapter 1: The identity debate discusses different identity theories, and identifies contemporary British Muslim issues along with current geopolitical events laced with appropriate social identity theories. In other words, it sets the scene of the book. Chapter 1 also discusses the research methodology and researcher's experience in collecting the data. Chapter 2 gives an overview of Muslim history in Britain, in particular focusing on Muslim immigration history in five cities: London, Leicester, Bradford, Leeds and Cardiff, where the fieldwork was carried out consecutively. Chapter 3 examines the cultural dimension of identity within the Muslim community, and explores whether young Muslims feel positively about it, and how it shapes their identity. Chapter 3 also focuses on Muslim women's issues. Chapter 4 discusses the national identity of the respondents – their sense of belonging to Britain, their country of origin, and to their religion. Chapter 5 examines how the British media are shaping the young Muslim's identity. Chapter 6 discusses the *niqab* debate that was initiated by Jack Straw, and what impact this debate had on young British Muslims. Chapter 7 examines the comment of Archbishop of Canterbury Dr Rowan Williams on the *Shariah* law, and how it impacted on the identity of young British Muslims. The final chapter, the Conclusion, finishes with an investigation of the role of leaders in the Muslim community and their relationship with Muslim youth, and suggests a 'humanitarian way forward'.

THE IDENTITY DEBATE

Defining Muslims

It is generally believed that Muslims share all aspects of Islamic culture – names, dress code and eating and drinking habits – and that they are a distinct non-Christian cultural group, separate from the mainstream British population. However, Muslims in Britain are ethnically diverse and heterogeneous in language, skin colour and culture. The only element they have in common is their religion. Nevertheless, most Muslims feel a strong affiliation with the broader Islamic community (*ummah*) and have a constant desire for greater Islamic political unity within the 'Abode of Islam' (*dar-al-Islam*). The centrepiece of unity among Muslims is the Quran – the very word of Allah (God). The Quran provides the same message for all Muslims, although interpretations of that message differ across the various Muslim groups and because of the different levels of meaning to the text.

   Muslims' devotional practice rests on what are known as the five pillars of Islam:

Kalima (or *shahada*). *Kalima* is an open declaration of faith. It has to be said in Arabic, '*La ilaha il-lal-lahu, Muhammadur Rasoo-lul-lah*', and means: 'I testify (confess) that there is no God but the one God and that Muhammad is the Messenger of God.'
Salat. This is the communal prayer that has to be performed five times each day – in the morning (before sunrise), at noon, in the afternoon, at sunset and at night – facing the *Ka'bah*, an important shrine of the Islamic world in Mecca. Before performing the *salat*, the believer must be in a state of purity, and therefore needs to carry out a series of ritual ablutions. The *salat* may be performed wherever the Muslim happens to be, though some prefer to pray in mosques.

Zakat. This is alms giving. Muslims are expected to pay 2.5 per cent of their net income to other members of the same faith who are less well off or in need.

Sawm. This is fasting. During *Ramadan*, the ninth month of the Islamic calendar, Muslims must refrain from eating, smoking, drinking and sex between the hours of sunrise and sunset.

Hajj. The fifth pillar is the pilgrimage or visit to Mecca to pray around the *Ka'bah*, on *Zil Hajj*, the twelfth month of the Islamic calendar. Every Muslim should, if health, financial means and safety of the routes allow, undertake this pilgrimage at least once in his or her lifetime. People who have performed *hajj* are called *hajjis* (see also Nasr 2002: 129–42; Tohon 2010: 27–46).

In addition to the five pillars, Muslims must not eat certain foods, such as pork, or drink alcohol. Muslims slaughter animals according to the teachings of the Quran, which is called *halal*, and devout Muslims eat *halal* meat. Some women choose to wear the *hijab* (headscarf) and *abaya* or *burqa* (loose outer garment) to pay due respect to the teachings and tradition of Prophet Muhammad [PBUH], known as the *hadith* or *sunnah*. In some Muslim countries, such as Saudi Arabia, the wearing of the *hijab* is mandatory, whereas in other countries, such as Bangladesh, it is a matter of personal choice (see also Nasr 2002: 195–7). Muslims have two important festivals each year: *Eid-ul-Fitr,* which is celebrated immediately after the month of fasting, *Ramadan:* and *Eid-ul-Adha,* the feast celebrated after *hajj* on the tenth day of *Zil Hajj.* To mark the pilgrimage to Mecca, Muslims all over the world celebrate the Feast of Sacrifice in *Eid-ul-Adha.* Sheep are ritually slaughtered to commemorate Prophet Ibrahim's [PBUH] willingness to sacrifice his son. This meat is partly for one's own consumption and the rest is given to friends and distributed among the poor and needy. About 87 per cent of all Muslims in the world are Sunnis and about 13 per cent are Shi'ite (Nasr 2002: 65). There are further divisions among the Sunnis and Shi'ites (see Chapter 3), though all believe in the five pillars of Islam.

In the remainder of this chapter, I first examine identity theory, and apply this theory towards an understanding of Muslim identity. Second, I consider whether 'Britishness' has any impact on or conflict with Muslim identity. Third, I explore the Scottish identity question. Fourth, I look into the debate on 'Muslim identity' raised by Channel 4. Fifth, I investigate the geopolitical factors that could influence British Muslims' identity. Finally, I provide an overview of my research methodology.

Examining the concept of 'identity'

Identity is the condition of being oneself (and not another). Arguably it is a process that is fluid and is shaped according to circumstances and opportunities.

Identity may depend on the family one is born into, the culture and religion one belongs to, the community in which the family lives, the values learnt from near and dear ones, and the experiences of one's surroundings. Identity is both individual and group oriented. Group identity recognises similarity, or shared belonging, and the differences that form the rhetoric of 'us' and 'them'. As Gilroy (1997: 301–2, cited in Jenkins 2008: 21) puts it:

> Identity is always particular, as much about difference as about shared belonging . . . Identity can help us to comprehend the formation of the fateful pronoun 'we' and to reckon with the patterns of inclusion and exclusion that it cannot help but to create. This may be one of the most troubling aspects of all: the fact that the formation of every 'we' must leave out or exclude a 'they', that identities depend on the marking of difference.

It is generally believed that identity embodies individuals, though individuals are also constituted collectively. In identification, the collective and the individual can occupy the same space. For example, a British Muslim may connect himself to the Muslim community as well as to the wider British community. Through group identification, a British Muslim may connect himself to the criteria that are minimally common with the groups to which he belongs. For example, with the Muslim community he may identify himself with his Muslim name or eating habits, and with the wider British community he might identify himself with his place of birth (British-born), common English language and sports (e.g. being a Manchester United fan). Jenkins (2008: 133) believes collectivity means having something in common, whether 'real' or 'imagined', trivial or important, strong or weak. Group identification (as for individual identification) leads to a community feeling, which encompasses notions of similarity and difference – 'us' and 'them'. This focuses attention on the boundary, which is where the sense of belonging becomes most apparent. And when there is a national crisis, such as the 7/7 London bombings, there is a clear notion of 'us' and 'them'. Some British Muslims collectively felt that on this occasion they (us) were treated as the 'Other' by the wider community (them). Cohen (cited in Jenkins 2008: 134) observes:

> This sense of difference . . . lies at the heart of people's awareness of their culture and indeed, makes it appropriate for ethnographers to designate as 'cultures' such arenas of distinctiveness . . . people become aware of their culture when they stand at its boundaries. (Cohen 1982: 2, 3)

Cohen envisages that identity is a cultural marker that can classify an in-group and an out-group person. For example, as a researcher of Muslim background I was considered an in-group person by the respondents of this research because we shared aspects of Islamic religion and culture. I do not wear the Islamic attire (*hijab, jilbab* or *burqa*), but I dress modestly, and my background and name indicate that I am one of 'them'. Insofar as they included me, the participants privileged our similarities rather than our differences.

The term 'social identity' references an individual's multiple identities, especially the degree of overlap between groups of which a person is simultaneously a member. For example, some respondents of this research identified themselves as British Pakistani Muslims, which meant they considered themselves British because they were born and raised in Britain, Pakistani because they spoke Urdu (Pakistan's official language) and Muslims because they celebrated *Eid* (a Muslim religious celebration). Tajfel's theory of 'social identity' (1978) provides the basis for a systematic investigation of the relationship between an individual's self-definitions and his/her perceptions of the social categories to which he/she belongs. Tajfel (cited in Jacobson 1998: 10) writes that there are three components of group membership: first, cognitive (knowledge that one belongs to a group); second, evaluative (assumptions about the positive and negative value connotations of group membership); and third, emotional (emotions towards one group and towards others who stand in particular relation to it). For example, when the Archbishop of Canterbury Dr Rowan Williams spoke about *shariah* law for Muslims, group membership between the Muslim community and the wider British community became distinct, and the debate between 'us' and 'them' was activated (discussed further in Chapter 7). Other scholars (Turner 1984; Turner et al. 1987, cited in Jenkins 2008: 112–13) note that 'social identity theory' and its offshoot 'self-categorisation theory' address the complexity of social identities. Jenkins (2008: 112–13) provides a thumbnail sketch of the complexities:

> Society is structured categorically, and organised by inequalities of power and resources. It is in the translation of social categories into meaningful reference groups that 'social structure' influences or produces individual behaviour. Social identity theory focuses on how categories become groups, with the emphasis on inter-group processes.
>
> Individuals, in using stereotypical categories to define themselves, thus bring into being human collective life. Individuals will self-categorise themselves differently and the contingencies with which they are faced.

Social identity theory, particularly the last point – that individuals self-categorise themselves differently and the contingencies with which they are faced – could be illustrated by the view of British-born Dilwar Hussain of Bangladeshi background (Hussain 2007: 37–8) that some external factors are impacting on the formation of Muslim identity today, namely foreign policy, social exclusion and Islamophobia. On the contemporary positive or neutral scale, Hussain (2007: 37–8) notes that there are other sources that could impact on Muslim identity, such as theological resources, parental culture and the wider British culture. Two historical points could also shape Muslim identity: 1) the encounter with colonialism and post-colonial movements. For example, a Pakistani or a Bangladeshi Muslim may find Western occupation of Afghanistan or Iraq as a legacy of the British colonial past. So the debate could appear as 'they' [the West] have been against 'us' [Muslims]; 2) the reaction to the fall of the Caliphate in 1924 and the restorationist movements that tried to re-establish some sort of Muslim political identity. For example, some British Muslims have endorsed the ideology of *Hizb ut-Tahrir* (Hamid 2007; Husain 2007). In 2007, when I asked a member of *Hizb ut-Tahrir* (Party of Liberation) about its ideology, he said:

> The role of *Hizb ut-Tahrir* is to work within the Muslim world in order to reconstruct the Islamic life and this cannot be achieved except by the re-establishment of the Islamic Caliphate. This struggle is not necessarily limited just to the Muslim world: fundamentally this struggle is embodied in the notion of a battle of ideas and the battle to win the hearts and the minds of the people and so necessarily, it's a global phenomenon. (Interview, Sydney, 7 February 2007)

Hizb ut-Tahrir has not been banned in the United Kingdom since it is considered to be a non-violent organisation. However, the British-born Dilwar Hussain (2007) was concerned that for a second-generation or third-generation British Muslim growing up in Britain today, most of the external influencing factors were overtly political and based on negative events, such as the Iranian Revolution, the Rushdie Affair, Bosnia, Algeria, the Gulf War and 9/11, which have 'led to identities being skewed in a strongly politicised direction. This has only been exacerbated by the identity politics of Muslim community protests in more recent years' (Hussain 2007: 37).

Speaking of 'Muslims and Identity', Modood (2007: 137) observes that British Muslim identity is formed as a result of pressures from the 'outside' and 'inside', which has a powerful geographical dimension. The emergence of a British Muslim identity and activism has been propelled by a strong concern for the plight of Muslims elsewhere in the world, especially where this plight is seen in terms of anti-imperialist emancipation and where the UK government is perceived to be part of the problem. British Muslims' political activity, charitable fundraising, the delivering of humanitarian relief, and sometimes the taking up of arms (in connection with Palestine, Kashmir, Chechnya, Kosovo, Afghanistan and Iraq) appear to be a protest against the British government (Modood 2007: 137). As a consequence, British Muslims have been perceived by some British people as disloyal and the Muslims themselves have experienced deepening tensions, with dual loyalties and alienation from the government, which was initially seen as a supporter of British Muslims (Werbner 2004a; cited in Modood 2007: 138). As discussed earlier in the context of social identity theory, identities may become sharpened by perceived inequality in power and resources; for example, some British Muslims viewed British foreign policy as detrimental to the well-being of the Muslim *ummah* (imaginary Muslim state transcending all national boundaries) during the Iraqi war.

Discourse on British identity or 'Britishness'

'Britishness' refers to the sense of national identity of the British people. In the wake of the 7 July London bombings, Britain entered into a new phase of defining British national identity and citizenship. Parekh (2007: 134) observes, 'Being British basically means three things: commitment to Britain and its people, loyalty to its legal and political institutions, and respect for the values and norms that are central to its way of life.' Arguably, these three conditions are essential obligations for all British citizens. Johnson (2007: 30) notes the principles ascribed to being British are almost entirely consistent with those that people apply to notions of citizenship. In seeking to define Britishness, according to Johnson (2007: 30), one should look for something that can unify people and tie communities together. In that context, one should see it as a manifestation of collective identity and perhaps an overarching bridging tool.

Julios (2008) states that since the late nineteenth century the monarchy, the Union, the Church of England and Parliament have become the essence of Britishness. Underlying them all was the obvious English language – perhaps Britain's greatest export and the Empire's ultimate tool of cultural domination. More recently, in the period following the Second World War, immigrants who succeeded in learning the English language and in embracing British customs quickly became immersed in society. Now in the twenty-first century, politicians have begun to perceive that integration is also crucial to 'British identity'. In January 2006, Gordon Brown, as the Chancellor of the Exchequer, urged Labour supporters to 'embrace the Union flag', and placed emphasis on a 'united shared sense of purpose' (BBC 2006a, 'Brown Speech Promotes Britishness'). Chancellor Brown said promoting integration had become even more important since the London bombings.

Later, in December 2006, as part of his 'Our Nation's Future' lecture series, Prime Minister Tony Blair pointed out that active British citizenship depended on an integrative and collective identity that entails respect for British common values, rights and responsibilities, as opposed to one's individual cultural identity:

> When it comes to our essential values – belief in democracy, the rule of law, tolerance, equal treatment for all, respect for this country and its shared heritage – then that is where we come together, it is what we hold in common; it is what gives us the right to call ourselves British. At that point no distinctive culture or religion supersedes our duty to be part of an integrated United Kingdom. (Blair 2006)

Tony Blair emphasised that English language skills should be the focal point of Britain's national identity:

> We should share a common language. Equal opportunity for all groups requires that they be conversant in that common language. It is a matter of both cohesion and of justice that we should set the use of language as a condition of citizenship. In addition, for those who wish to take up residence permanently in the UK, we will include a requirement to pass an English test before such permanent residency is granted. (Blair 2006)

In 2008 the government introduced the English-language test for individuals wishing to come to or remain in the United Kingdom to work, train or study.

Notions of inclusion, integration, knowledge of a common language and common values can be heard in the voice of Faiza (fictitious name), a 17-year-old British-born Muslim girl of Pakistani origin. When I asked Faiza, 'What are the qualities of a good citizen and how would you display them? I mean, how do you feel you are a British citizen?', she replied:

> A good citizen I think is someone who would go out every day, whether they're going to a Muslim girls' school or whatever, they'd come out and they'd look round and they would have no prejudice. If they saw an old lady carrying some bags, whether she is black, white or mixed race, they'd go out of their way to help someone. Even if it's not helping someone, just a bit of community spirit you know? Say hello or give *salaam* [Muslim greetings] to your neighbours, or even a friendly Hi, or a wave to someone. I think that's being a really good citizen. With regard to a British citizen, you know making that extra effort in your community, maybe setting up community sessions, attending community sessions, not necessarily the Muslims ones, set up things like Neighbourhood Watch and stuff like that, just making that extra effort. (Interview, Britain, October 2008)

Faiza defined her identity as:

> I'm a British Muslim because that's what I am. My citizenship is British. My religion is Islam. I practise Islam when I go out, I cover myself up with full veil, that includes *jilbab* [long coat], *hijab* [head scarf] and *niqab* [face veil] and sometimes it's a bit difficult with it being in such a secular country and lately with everything happening in the media, but I have no problem saying I'm a British Muslim.

Faiza further explained her connection to Britishness:

> In my heart I feel this is my home. I would never say that Pakistan was my home because we go there to visit family and friends, but that's not where you've been

brought up, you know this is your home. You know from when you were young, your first language, it might have been your mother-tongue, my mother-tongue was English actually to be honest, then I learnt Hindko [Pakistani dialect] afterwards when I was about 3, 4. But even that has the influence on you in the sense that English was your first language. Britain is your home: your family is here, your friends are here, everything is here. When you go back home to Pakistan or even to another country, that's your holiday; you're going to visit people; you could never settle anywhere else.

I was somewhat surprised by Faiza's expression of Britishness. Faiza wore a *niqab* when she went out, which could be regarded by some people (both Muslims and non-Muslims) as a barrier to communication, but she was adamant of her British citizenship, rights and responsibilities, believing that Britain was a multicultural country, which accepted all cultures. Faiza said that the *niqab* was her personal choice (and not imposed by her family and school) of Muslim identity.

Faiza's first school (primary school) was a Christian school, and her secondary school was Islamic. Presumably, the British values of inclusion, communication and respect for other cultures were cherished in both. Faiza was a third-generation Pakistani-British girl. Her grandparents and parents, the latter quite young when they moved to the United Kingdom, were born in Pakistan. As I interviewed Faiza, I became impressed with her ability to articulate her connection to Britain, but I wondered whether Faiza's commitment to wearing the *niqab* might pose a barrier. However, when I asked Faiza about her future career, she stated she would compromise her *niqab* if the need arose, while continuing to wear some form of Islamic attire (*hijab* and *jilbab*). In Chapter 6 there are further discussions on the recent *niqab* debate, sparked by former Labour Foreign Minister Jack Straw's comment in 2006.

The Scottish identity question

If British identity consists of inclusion, integration, knowledge of a common language and common values (as mentioned by the politicians and also acknowledged by the participant Faiza), why it is that many Scottish people cherish their exclusive Scottish identity (as opposed to British)? In the context of Scotland, Douglas (2009: 11, 19) observes, 'Identity is both a complex and a fascinating phenomenon. At a basic level, identity is about who we are, and who and what we identify with. However, identity is also about who we want to be, and how we wish to be seen by others.' In other words, identity is 'a state of mind', including what we aspire to be. Sociologists Keily et al. (2001: 36, cited in Douglas 2009: 18) identified ten 'identity markers' which people use to claim or attribute identity: place of birth, ancestry, place of residence, length of residence, upbringing and education, name, accent, physical appearance, dress and commitment to place. So it is not surprising that many Scottish people have a distinct identity that is based on markers such as their ancestry, and memories and values shaped by Scottish history.

However, research (Hopkins 2004, 2007a; Mir 2007) on Muslims in Scotland has found that many young Muslims feel strongly connected to Scotland despite not having this shared ancestry or history. In 2001 the Muslim population in Scotland was almost 43,000, with a younger age profile than mainstream Scottish people. Greater Glasgow, Edinburgh and Dundee are home to the largest Muslim communities in Scotland (Hopkins 2004: 258). In his research on seventy young Scottish Muslim men of diverse backgrounds (aged 16–25), Hopkins (2007a: 61–81) found that apart from two who identified as English and one as Welsh, all the young men spoke of their affiliation as Scottish. In asserting their national identities, the respondents utilised markers of birthplace, length of residence, commitment to place, education, upbringing and accent. Some participants identified themselves as Muslim and Scottish.

The association of respondents in the Hopkins study with Scottishness was also linked with sports – football in particular. Since the late nineteenth century 'fitba' (football) has been a Scottish national game, and in matches between England and Scotland especially, Scottish nationalism comes to the fore (Kowalski 2004: 75). Rugby has also acquired an overtly 'national patina' and the Scottish Rugby Union has capitalised on this by adopting 'Flower of Scotland' as its national anthem instead of 'God Save the Queen' (Kowalski 2004: 79).

As mentioned above, according to Hopkins (2007a; 2007b), young Muslim men were more inclined to express their Scottishness and their masculinity with football than with other sports. However, some identified themselves within a broad multicultural, multi-faith vision of Scottishness, and others expressed their multiple identities, such as Scottish-Muslim-Punjabi. Hopkins (2007a) also noticed the participants' Scottish accent and the use of Scottish vocabulary and idioms. Drinking Irn-Bru (a popular Scottish soft drink) and having an appreciation of Scotland's natural environment and people were also markers of Scottishness (Hopkins 2004). Mir (2007) found that the identities of the young and professional suburban Pakistanis in Glasgow were in line with the middle-class Scottish suburbanite identity (as proud home-owners who sent their children to good schools) rather than with a distinctly Pakistani marginalised identity. In this case the place of residence, upbringing and education influenced the Scottish identity factor.

In my brief travel experience to Edinburgh in 2008, I found the Scottish identity factor very obvious. When I visited Edinburgh Castle I bought a ticket with a Bank of England banknote and received change in Scottish currency. The moment I entered the castle I saw a man wearing a Scottish kilt, and on visiting the Parliament it was made very clear that the Scottish people have an exclusive identity. As I walked along Princes Street and the historic Royal Mile I saw the cashmere stores selling kilts. When I visited St Giles' Cathedral in the Royal Mile, I was told that it had been Edinburgh's religious focal point for several centuries, and it is also sometimes regarded as the 'mother church of Presbyterianism'. Scottish identity could also be identified through their speaking English with a lowland Scots accent. Yet the Scottish identity factor among some Muslims could be related to their place of birth, length of stay, sports and integration with the mainstream Scottish people. For example, Osama Saeed, born and raised in Glasgow, is a member of the Scottish National Party (a left-leaning nationalist party advocating secession from the United Kingdom). However, as the SNP's candidate for Central Glasgow he lost out in the 2005 UK general election, then lost again in his second bid in May 2010.

Since the 9/11 Twin Towers attacks, the 7/7 London bombings and the 30 June Glasgow Airport terrorist act, some Muslims in Scotland are viewed as the 'Other'. Hopkins (2007a; 2007b) examined how global events impacted on the lives of young Muslim men in urban Scotland and showed how global events shaped these young people's political actions locally, such as tactical voting and protesting in marches. In the next subsection I examine the placement of Muslims on a broader level – in contemporary British society.

Channel 4: 'What Muslims Want'?

On 7 August 2006, Channel 4 *Dispatches* broadcasted a documentary, 'What Muslims Want', based on a Growth from Knowledge National Opinion Poll (GFKNOP) survey of British Muslims in the aftermath of the 7/7 London bombing (see GFKNOP Social Research 2006). The GFKNOP survey revealed that British Muslims do not form a single homogenous community. In response to questions, such as whether Muslim children should attend state or Muslim schools, whether they should attend single-sex schools, whether Muslim women should wear the *hijab*, whether it is better to live under *shariah law* or British law, Muslims were deeply divided.

Almost the only issue that Muslims seemed to agree on was the importance of Islam. On the question of 'Britain: My country or their country?', 49 per cent responded 'Britain: My country'. However, men were more likely to say this (53 per cent men against 45 per cent women); and older Muslims were more inclined to align themselves with Britain (55 per cent of those aged 45 and over; 44 per cent of 18–24-year-olds). Furthermore, Muslims who preferred to live under the British legal system felt more British than those who preferred to live under *shariah law* (56 per cent against 38 per cent) (GFKNOP 2006).

On the question 'Belonging to Britain vs belonging to Islam', two in five Muslims in Britain (38 per cent) indicated that nation and religion were not mutually exclusive, as they felt they belonged to both Britain and Islam 'very strongly'. However, 14 per cent of those who said that they belonged to Islam very strongly did not feel a very strong sense of belonging in Britain. On the question of integration, 70 per cent of Muslims who said that they would prefer to live under *shariah law* would also prefer to send their child to an Islamic school (this compared to 30 per cent of those who would prefer to live under British law) (see GFKNOP 2006).

Obviously, some of the Muslim responses were of concern to the mainstream British viewers. For example, following the documentary one blogger wrote:

> British law is not compatible with Islamic law (*shariah* law). Among other things, Islamic law stipulates the stoning of homosexuals and adulterers, and cutting off the hands of thieves. British people as a whole do not want to live under this type of law. British law also upholds freedom of speech, which is also not compatible with Islamic law.
>
> Britain is a multicultural, tolerant society, and all faiths and nationalities are welcome to come and live here, as long as they are prepared to integrate peaceably under our law. But this means that Muslims who choose to live in Britain must respect British law. As such, they should be working to integrate into British society; and they should not be working for the overthrow of British law and the imposition of Islamic law . . . (Channel 4 2006, 'What Muslims Want')

In the above comment, the implication is that 'our' British laws are superior to Islamic laws, and when 'they' (the Muslims) come to 'our' country they must integrate under 'our' law. This rhetoric of mainstream British 'superiority' was echoed by other bloggers. Some bloggers quoted verses from the Quran saying that it was incompatible with the teachings of the Bible, and that Muslims and terrorism are synonymous. Some even stated that when compared to Muslim terrorists the IRA were not real terrorists. One blogger held that Jewish people (and other ethnic minorities) were better than Muslims as the former express gratitude to the Queen in their prayers.

There were some bloggers in the Channel 4 *Dispatches* discussion who brought back the social identity theory. Social identity theory asserts that group membership creates in-group self-categorisation in ways that favour the 'in-group' against the 'out-group'. In this context, the mainstream British bloggers perceived themselves as an 'in-group' against the 'out-group' (Muslims). The wider British community whose identity is modelled on an English-speaking white Anglo-Saxon Protestant ideal felt threatened that their core values of 'Britishness', such as British laws, would be undermined by Islamic law (*shariah* law). This concern transformed them into an 'in-group' versus the 'out-group', the 'Muslim other'. As late as 2008, the Washington-based Pew Research Center's global attitude survey found that about one person in four in Britain thought poorly of Muslims ('Poll finds rising antipathy towards Jews and Muslims in Europe', *New York Times*, 18 September 2008: 7).

The point in this case is that British Muslims were lumped into a homogenous category, though, as argued above, Muslim identity has much variability: for some, it is a simple matter of community membership and heritage; for others, it is about self, compassion, respect, tolerance, justice and the life hereafter, or a spiritual association with the *Ummah*. Some Muslims are social, outgoing, devout, introvert, and some are politically conscious (see also Modood 2007: 134). The social identity theorist Tajfel (1981, cited in Jenkins 2008: 152) argues that stereotyping is a collective process, involving the creation and maintenance of group values and ideologies, and the positive valorisation of the in-group. Jenkins (2008: 152) observes that stereotypes are extremely condensed symbols of collective identification. Attribution, the attempt to understand others, particularly the motivations of others, by inference from the limited information provided by their verbal and non-verbal behaviour, is also at work within stereotyping.

Geopolitical factors and Muslim identity

Even before the 7/7 London tragedy, a poll commissioned by the *Guardian* newspaper showed that 33 per cent of Muslims wanted more integration into mainstream British culture, whereas the same poll showed that 26 per cent of British Muslims felt integration had gone too far (cited in Thorne 2004). The head of the Muslim Council of Britain's Imams and Mosques Committee, Shaykh Ibrahim Mogra, admitted, 'We have pockets [of British Muslims] who . . . feel that even integration is a threat to their way of life' (cited in Thorne 2004). For example, some Muslim parents worry that their children will pick up un-Islamic behaviour from their English peers. At the same time, moderate Muslims worry that the British media's focus on the few 'bad apples' creates a false, sinister image of all Muslims (Thorne 2004).

News of Islamic terrorism started reaching the West from the late 1970s, beginning with the Iranian Revolution in 1979, when Ayatollah Khomeini described the US as the 'Great Satan'. It was followed by the Iranian hostage crisis from 1979 to 1981, when 51 American hostages were held at the US consulate in Tehran by some Iranian students; the seizure of the Grand Mosque in Mecca in 1979; the Lockerbie bombing in 1988; Ayatollah Khomeini's *fatwa* against Salman Rushdie in 1989; Saddam Hussein's occupation of Kuwait in 1990, followed by the 1991 Gulf War; the rise of the Al-Qaeda terrorist network; the Taliban; and the Jeemah Islamiyah. Whereas these separate incidents brought disaster to the US and its allies, they were reported in such a way that the impression was of an ever-encroaching threat from the common enemy of Islam. This obviously began to impact negatively on Western perceptions of Muslims.

Other incidents involving Islamic extremists reinforced this perception: the 1993 World Trade Center bombing; the 1996 Khobar Twin Towers bombing in Saudi Arabia; the US Consulate bombing in Somalia in 1998; the USS *Cole* attack in 2000; the destruction of the Buddhist statues by the Taliban, and the capture of eight aid workers (including two Australians) in 2001; the September 11th Twin Towers attacks in 2001; and the Bali tragedy in 2002. The news of the Moscow hostage crisis and the death sentence by stoning of the convicted Nigerian woman Amina Lawal in 2002 were other disastrous news items from the Muslim world. Since 2001, there have also been several attacks on Australian interests by alleged Jeemah Islamiyah members in Indonesia. The 2003 Istanbul and Riyadh bombings, the 2004 Madrid bombing, the Australian Embassy bombing in Jakarta and the Beslan tragedy have also impacted on Western audiences/readers, as did the attack on the US consulate in Jeddah by Islamic militants on 6 December 2004 (Kabir 2005; 2006).

Since the 9/11 Twin Towers attacks in New York, British people have focused even more on the impending 'Islamic threat', especially since some events have involved British Muslims. For example, in 2001 the Islamist group al-Muhajiroun claimed that nearly 1,000 Britons had travelled to fight the coalition forces in Afghanistan. Although many British Muslim leaders disputed this claim, Geoff Hoon, the British Defence Secretary, warned that those who left the country to fight for the Taliban could face charges of treason on their return ('The Editor – Britons claim to be Taliban fighters', *Guardian*, 3 November 2001: 6; see also Thorne 2004). However, in 2001 three young Muslims from the UK were killed in Afghanistan. Then a British Muslim in Pakistan claimed to have helped recruit more than 200 British volunteers to fight for the Taliban (*Daily Telegraph*, 8 January 2002, cited in Modood 2005: 200). In fact, three of the first fifty captives from Afghanistan, brought to the US prison in Guantanamo Bay, Cuba, were British, and eventually they were joined by six others (by mid-2004 none had been charged, and five were released in February 2004) (see Modood 2005: 200).

In 2001, Richard Reid, a British convert to Islam, boarded an American Airlines flight with shoes packed full of explosives. Crew members restrained him before he could set them off. In July 2002 a British national of Pakistani background, Ahmed Omar Saeed Sheikh, was convicted in Pakistan for the murder of the American journalist Daniel Pearl. In 2003, two British Muslims blew themselves up in a Tel Aviv bar, killing three and wounding 55 (Thorne 2004). In 2003, British police foiled a massive Muslim bombing plot targeted inside Britain, and three British Muslims were alleged to have joined the radical insurgency of Al-Qaeda affiliate Abu Musab al-Zarqawi in Iraq (Thorne 2004). Under new anti-terrorism legislation in the UK, 664 persons, mainly Muslims, had been detained by September 2004, though over half had been released without charge. Nevertheless, while some Muslims from a variety of Western countries have been drawn into *jihadi* activities, British Muslims seemed to be quite prominent (Modood 2005: 200). Finally, the London bombing on 7 July 2005 confirmed the possibilities of home-grown terrorism. Later, on 30 June

2007, a burning jeep Cherokee, packed with explosive material, slammed into the airport terminal building in Glasgow, Scotland. Two men – a British-born doctor of Iraqi descent, Bilal Abdullah, and an Indian engineer, Kafeel Ahmed, were engulfed in flames. Kafeel Ahmed received burns to 90 per cent of his body. He was taken to a hospital and was treated in intensive care but later died in August 2007. Therefore, Muslim acts of terrorism have been impacting on both mainstream Muslims and non-Muslims.

Bhikhu Parekh (2007: 133) observes that some British Muslims define their moral identity in religious terms and some in secular terms:

> Many of them do not just want to be *Muslims in Britain*, treating Britain as a morally neutral territorial space where they happen to live. Rather, they take their British citizenship seriously and want to be good Britons. However, they want to be *Muslim Britons* not *British Muslims*, that is, British in a Muslim way rather than Muslims in a British way.

It appears that Parekh meant that by being 'British Muslims' one could retain both their national (British) identity and religious (Muslim) identity. But 'Muslim Britons' would mean the opposite, that is, one would use Islam to justify their British citizenship. For example, 'Muslim Britons' would accept the British values that suit their Islamic beliefs, such as accept the right of free speech but disregard the 'equality or mixing of sexes'. In an extreme case, 'Muslim Britons' may find their *Ummah* more important over Britain, as Parekh (2007: 133) notes that they might consider:

> . . . [it is] a moral duty, to go and fight against the British forces in Afghanistan and Iraq . . . A Muslim Briton who bases his entire life on a particular reading of his religion might also reject the country's secular and 'permissive' ethos and withdraw into an inner world of rage and revolt.

This multifaceted identity debate brings to the fore the complexity of British identity. As stated above, it can be defined in terms of English language, communication, integration and multiculturalism; it can also be connected to one's place of birth, ancestry, place of residence, length of residence, upbringing and education, name, accent, physical appearance, dress and commitment to place (Keily et al. 2001). Some scholars, such as Hussain (2007), Modood (2007) and Parekh (2007), believe that British Muslim identity has been affected by British foreign policy in Iraq, Palestine and Afghanistan. We have seen that many mainstream British people (Channel 4 2006 'What Muslims Want') believe Muslims can only have British identities if they conform to or believe in one law, British law, whereas some Muslims (e.g. Faiza's interview) invoke the spirit of multiculturalism as being integral to their identity.

Against the backdrop of social identity theory, contested definitions of Britishness, the *shariah* law debate and radical Islam, I began my research with the aim of understanding the identity of Muslim youths and young adults in contemporary Great Britain. In subsequent chapters I examine the cultural surroundings and wider society environment and analyse the factors that influence the identities of young British Muslims. In the remainder of this chapter I outline my research methodology, beginning with the reasons for a qualitative approach. Next I briefly describe my data-gathering sources and challenges, and finally acknowledge the shortcomings of my study.

The research methodology

The rationale in choosing the five cities for my study are as follows. London was the target of the 7/7 bombings. It is predicted that by 2012 the immigrant population will become a majority in Leicester. Bradford drew the world's attention when some Muslims burned a copy of Salman Rushdie's book *The Satanic Verses*. Three of the four 7/7 London bombers lived in Leeds. The early Muslim settlers (Yemeni and Somali Muslims) lived in Cardiff.

The major part of my data gathering in the UK comprised in-depth, semi-structured interviews with young Muslims. And it is the responses of the young people to the interview questions that constitute the main part of the empirical material discussed in this book. By eliciting the respondents' life histories, I ascertained the complexities of their identities. I asked the participants about their early school memories, family members, parents' work status, part-time work, family and community life, sporting activities, music, entertainment and cultural interests, opinions on the media and current affairs (such as the debate on *shariah* law), national identity (sense of belonging), impact of the 7/7 London bombings, together with their hopes, ambitions and dreams. Another important question was: How would you (as a young British Muslim) advocate establishing harmony within the wider community?

Because of the age of the participants (15–18 years), and the sensitivity of the topics of investigation, I decided that the best way to elicit the views of these British Muslims was to interview them face-to-face. The alternative survey approach would have ensured a larger sample, but it was deemed inappropriate because of difficulties in gaining access and sufficient trust. I have employed a qualitative approach to my study, which aims to explore the meaningfulness of participants' lives, rather than measure causal relations according to preconceived variables. The goal of this research was to gain a better understanding of the participants' life stories, their hopes and aspirations.

The main data-gathering method was via semi-structured interview questions and a form of narrative analysis (Charmaz 2006), whereby interview responses were regarded as a story about each interviewee's life. Of course, each narrative contains unique elements, but some patterns could be detected in the participants' lives that enabled the identification of themes and low-order generalisations.

Table 1.1 Total interviews 216: youths and young adults, age group 15–30; Muslim leaders, age group 30 years and over

Cities	Male	Female	Leaders: 11 males and 2 females
London = 108	44	57	7
Leicester = 12	9	2	1
Bradford = 31	12	17	2
Leeds = 35	16	17	2
Cardiff = 30	13	16	1
Total = 216	94	109	13

The religious affiliations of the interviewees were as follows: Sunni 206 (1 Sufi, 1 Brelvi, 1 Salafi, 10 Deobandi); Shia 6; and Ahmediya (offshoot of Islam) 4. These groups are defined in Chapter 3. The ethnic compositions of the interviewees are shown in Table 1.2.

I realise that my interpretation of the data can be biased. By reporting on patterns and frequencies and by displaying my analysis of samples of interview responses, I endeavour to demonstrate to the reader that I have dealt with the data in a fair and reasonable manner.

The interviews with the Muslim leaders were also in-depth and semi-structured. A brief migration history was drawn from each one. Their perspectives on the changes or development in the Muslim community were noted. Finally, they were asked to reflect on the government policies and recommend if further policies were needed, or if there was a need for reform or harmony within the Muslim community.

Total number of interviews

I conducted 216 interviews in the five cities, comprising 94 young males, 109 young females and 13 leaders (11 male and 2 female) (Table 1.1). The interviews (digital recording) were face-to-face and in-depth, lasting 30 to 60 minutes. The interviewees (except some Muslim leaders) were given fictitious names.

To recruit people for my sample I used the snowballing and representative sampling techniques. The snowballing technique involves referrals from initial participants to generate additional participants. Whereas this technique can be effective in building up the number of willing participants, it comes at the risk of the sample being unrepresentative. To counteract this, I used the representative sample technique of commencing with a diverse set of groups of participants from an entire population of possible participants. For example, I deliberately selected different schools, colleges and youth centres from a wide range of educational institutions in Britain. Similarly, Muslim leaders and community workers from different cities were chosen because they formed different personalities and had views more relevant to their locality or city.

Young British Muslims

Table 1.2 Ethnic groups of 216 respondents in different cities of Britain

London (108)	Leicester (12)	Bradford (31)	Leeds (35)	Cardiff (30)
Bangladeshi (48)	Bangladeshi (1)	Bangladeshi (4)	Bangladeshi (10)	Bangladeshi (1)
Pakistani (30)	Pakistani (9)	Pakistani (25)	Pakistani (22)	Pakistani (19)
Others (30):	Others (2):	Others (2):	Others (3):	Others (10):
Algerian	Indian	Algerian	Malawian	Iraqi
Danish	Malawian	Singaporean-	Somali	Iraqi-Belgian
Egyptian		Indian	Sudan	Somali
English				Syrian
Indian				Yemeni
Iranian				
Iraqi				
Kenyan				
Lebanese				
Libyan				
Mauritian				
Moroccan				
Nigerian				
Palestinian				
Scottish				
Somali				
Sudanese				
Syrian				
Ugandan				
Yemeni				

All 216 interviewees participated voluntarily, knowing that the study was about Muslim identity. I respected their identity as 'Muslims' and did not delve into their degree of religious practice. However, many respondents (particularly women) were visibly Muslim insofar as they wore the *hijab* (even in state schools and colleges).

Other data sources

Among other primary sources, I have drawn on newspaper reports (hardcopy and from factiva database) and internet blogs; the latter enabled me to glean mainstream British perceptions of Muslims, such as commentary from the wider society after the documentary on Muslims in Britain in the Channel 4 television programme *Dispatches*, which gave me insights into the fears and concerns of mainstream British society members. I have also sourced research reports from youth organisations and Muslim associations.

Fieldwork challenges

As stated above, I interviewed Muslims from five cities in the UK – London, Leicester, Bradford, Leeds and Cardiff. Since I live in Australia, networking with the people of the UK was not an easy venture. In October 2007, I started contacting schools, local councillors, youth organisations, education departments, Muslim organisations, a couple of young Muslim adults and some young people involved in Islamic affairs who were referred to me by acquaintances in Australia. I also contacted a few British academics who had published on Muslims in the UK, and asked them for some relevant contacts.

The method of contact was first through emails, but in most instances there was no response. Then I called prospective sources over the phone, explained my research background, including that I was the author of the book *Muslims in Australia,* and that I had conducted many youth interviews for the Australian Muslim identity project, and published the results in academic journals. I assured the prospective UK participants that the interviewees' confidentiality would be maintained. I also told them that I was a family person with a husband and three children, and informed them of my ethnic background – that I was born into a Muslim family in Bangladesh (then East Pakistan), lived in Pakistan (then West Pakistan), and in the Middle East for 10 years.

Building trust with my prospective collaborators was both demanding and challenging. Some concerns were registered by my known acquaintances (young male adults) about my approach to the study, how the data would be used, and who was funding this project. I contacted the known participants' (young adults) families (parents and relatives) over the telephone, and later visited them overseas to assure them that the research would be used with good intentions. Fortunately, trust became established gradually, most fears and concerns dissipated, and participants contributed willingly to the 'snowball' and sampling process.

Schools, colleges, youth centres

In London I approached eight educational institutions (seven schools and one college). The college prepared students for undergraduate degrees (age 18 years and over). I picked out four educational institutions randomly, and the other four were suggested by a British-Pakistani academic who had worked on British Muslim school students for her PhD project. Five of the eight institutions agreed to participate: four schools and one college.

In Leicester, I contacted two Islamic schools. One school agreed to participate when I contacted them from Perth but later declined. Another school was concerned about the information going out to the media, so they did not participate in the study. In Bradford and Leeds I approached the Education Boards. They approved my research proposal and helped me find schools for the study. Finally, in Cardiff, I contacted three state schools. The two schools predominantly attended by Muslim students said they would not participate in this study. The third school, with fewer Muslim students, would have participated in the study if the research information had been passed on to them by one of their new administrative recruits. Though I was not successful in recruiting young Muslim participants through schools in Cardiff and Leicester, various youth centres in both cities supported my study and organised the participants' parents' consents. The young Muslims at the youth centres enthusiastically participated in the study.

Young adults

'Young adults' were people aged 18–30 years, comprising high-school students, college and university students, shopkeepers, employed and unemployed people, youth workers, teachers and councillors. I received access to some young adults through high schools and colleges, but to obtain access to other young adults I employed four strategies: first, I sought help from my acquaintances in Perth and young Muslim adults who lived in the UK, and they introduced me to their contacts in Britain; second, I made contact with the Federation of Student Islamic Societies in the UK; third, I contacted academics who had worked on young British Muslims; and finally, I randomly approached people on the streets and in shops, asking if they would like to participate in the survey. In some cases they did not wish to do so but directed me to the relevant youth centres.

Muslim leaders

Muslim leaders (aged 30 years and over) comprise a sample of people who were leaders in Muslim organisations, or prominent members of the wider community – for example, community workers. I interviewed the Member of Parliament for Tooting, London, Sadiq Khan, who was a successful man of Islamic faith, and councillors in London's East End. The councillors then introduced me to other people involved in the Muslim community. I also interviewed spiritual leaders (imams), Muslim community workers, and academics involved in Muslim affairs.

Location of interviews

Most of the interview sessions were held in the respective schools and colleges. Other venues were youth centres, shops, mosques, hotels where I stayed (some respondents made it easier by coming to me for the interviews), respondents' houses, offices, a café, and a car (one interview was taken in a car as the interviewee had to reach somewhere on time). I tried to make it as convenient as possible for the interviewees. However, being a woman travelling on my own, I had to be careful about propriety and my own safety. In the hotels, I conducted male adults' interviews in the lounge rooms, or I asked them to come with their partners.

Insider status

Overall, I was in a relatively advantaged position. Being a Bangladeshi-born Muslim woman, I enjoyed insider status with the interviewees. Perhaps the most influential factor in gaining support for my study was my authorship of the book *Muslims in Australia* (based on my PhD thesis), and that I had interviewed 225 Muslim youths in Australia for my research on Australian Muslim youth identity, and also that I had a family (my husband and three sons) in Australia. But I needed a rationale for studying the identity of young British Muslims, which I constructed in terms of the 7/7 London bombings, and the need for the general public to know more about the realities of young British Muslims. Before the interviews, generally the participants asked me a few questions, as they wanted to know more about me, where I was staying, when the book would be published, and whether they thought my study was worthwhile. A few school students initially appeared very nervous, but they became relaxed enough to want to continue with the interview. In some cases, though, I had to work hard throughout to gain their trust.

The Bangladeshi respondents were mostly from the district of Sylhet (see Chapter 3). Typically Sylhetis speak their local dialect rather than the standard Bangla (Bengali language). Though my village is in the Noakhali district, I was actually raised in Dhaka, the capital of Bangladesh. I had a very middle-class or professional upbringing because both my parents were educated, my father was the Deputy Governor of the Bangladesh Bank (the reserve bank), and I attended a private English-medium school in Bangladesh. However, in my childhood I had Sylheti friends in Dhaka who spoke the Sylheti dialect at home. I also visited Sylhet twice. So I was quite familiar with their culture. Sylhetis in the UK normally cling to their own village circle. But when I introduced myself as a Bangladeshi person from Australia, they included me in their broader Bangladeshi community. When I spoke with them in standard Bangla, they shyly said in their Sylheti accent, '*Ami shodhu Bangla jani na*' (I don't know standard Bangla). Anyway, I could see they were very happy as they said, '*amader ak jon amader golpo shunte ashechen*' (one of us has come to listen to our (life) story). The interviews were conducted in English, as most of the respondents were born in the UK.

With the Pakistani participants, it was easier. In my childhood I lived in Karachi, Pakistan (then West Pakistan) for six years with my parents. In my school I studied two Urdu subjects and I am well versed in reading, writing and speaking Urdu (the official language of Pakistan). I still cherish my childhood memories of Pakistan. There had been political issues between East and West Pakistan, but it did not affect my friendship with the Pakistani girls. Even though East Pakistan separated from West Pakistan in 1971 and they became Bangladesh and Pakistan respectively, when I meet a Pakistani I feel I am meeting my people. In the same context, the Pakistani interviewees in Britain felt that '*ye to apna hai*' (she is our own). My sample shows the highest number of the participants were Pakistanis, which is indicative of the fact that I mingled with them very well.

The Pakistani respondents' places of origin were Mirpur, Jhelum, Lahore, Faisalabad, Rawalpindi and Peshawar, whereas I lived in the city of Karachi.

They had their own dialects – Punjabi, Pashto, Hindko and Mirpuri – whereas I spoke Urdu. But these people also knew Urdu, which is the standard/official Pakistani language. However, all the interviews were conducted in English, as most respondents were British-born or had lived in Britain for a very long time.

Other respondents (Muslim youths and leaders) were from Algeria, Iraq, Iran, Mauritius, Syria, Somalia, Sudan and Yemen. I connected with them as a Muslim. I told them that I had lived in the Middle East (Dhahran in Saudi Arabia and Muscat in the Sultanate of Oman) for ten years (five years in each country), and that I had performed the *Umrah Hajj* (a pilgrimage that is done throughout the year, rather than the main *hajj* which is done in the Islamic month of *Zil Hajj*). They felt connected with my Islamic identity, and that made the interview process much easier.

Informal informants

The modes of transport I used in London were Underground trains, and taxis. In Leicester, Bradford, Leeds and Cardiff, I depended solely on the taxi service. As my period of stay in all these places was short, I wanted to make the best use of my time. The taxi venture was quite expensive, but with hindsight I was able to communicate with the grass-roots level people, and obtained a feel of the place. In London, the drivers of the traditional black taxis were mostly Anglo-English, but the private mini taxis, which were relatively cheaper, were run by immigrants.

In Leicester, I met Indian taxi drivers from Gujarat, mostly Muslims. In Bradford, all taxi drivers were originally from Pakistan. I felt 'at home' in Bradford as I communicated with these people in Urdu. Leeds is a bigger city, and the taxi drivers were immigrants from Asia and Africa, both Muslims and non-Muslims, while some were mainstream British. I found the taxi drivers in Beeston, Leeds, particularly important. Talking to them informally, I became aware of the tensions existing in that part of Leeds. Finally, in Cardiff, the taxi drivers were both mainstream Welsh and immigrants (including Muslims).

As an outsider

After my marriage to a Bangladeshi-born man who was doing a PhD in the University of Texas at Austin, I joined him in Austin. When I socialised with my husband's American friends, I observed the culture of a free society, such as *de facto* relations with their partners (sex before marriage and living together before marriage), alcohol consumption, fewer family bonds, and children moving away from home at the age of 18. However, by communicating and socialising with them (within my Islamic boundaries), I was able to learn about the positive aspects of their culture, exchange views on our respective cultures and beliefs, and develop respect for each other.

My husband and I are now Australian citizens and have lived in that country for sixteen years. We have integrated with the wider society, and I now understand the wider community's cultural celebrations, fears and concerns, such as their fear of the unknown people, 'Muslims', especially after the 9/11 tragedy and Bali bombings. For my PhD thesis, I interviewed some mainstream Australians (before 9/11); some of them were concerned with the atrocities of the Taliban in Afghanistan, Saddam Hussein's dictatorial regime in Iraq, and the influx of refugees/asylum seekers into Australia. Some were concerned about Islamic attire (*hijab*) and many others placed an emphasis on integration. They would say, 'We want Muslims like you.' I kept wondering: do they want to see more non-visible Muslims (who do not wear the *hijab*), or visible Muslims (with Islamic attire) who communicate well and socialise with them to a certain extent? I was conscious that my integration into the wider community was always facilitated by living in Anglo-Australian professional suburbs, and having our sons attend expensive private schools in Brisbane and Perth where they socialised with the wider community (as well as with the Muslim community, our family friends).

So when I started this study on young British Muslims' identity, I was mindful of the importance of integration. By integration, I follow Kettani (1986) in assuming that this does not entail immigrants abandoning their own identities. Ideally they should retain their ethnic and religious identity while adopting aspects of the host society's culture. My role as researcher was another form of biculturalism: on the one hand, as a Muslim studying Muslims I was somewhat an insider; on the other hand, my theoretical and critical interest as a researcher put me in the realm of being an outsider.

Limitations of the study

As outlined above, all of the interviews were in-depth and semi-structured, and all the 216 interviewees responded to the topic of national identity and media. But some subtopics, such as the *niqab* and the *shariah* law debate, were not discussed with all respondents. In some cases there was limited time available at the outset, and in some cases domestic and Muslim community issues were discussed with such passion that I did not have the time to address these issues. And in a few interviews that did not flow easily I deliberately chose not to push the interviewees to more questions. Overall, there was a rich set of responses on all topics and this enabled me to present themes that I believe are characteristic and informative. Ultimately, of course, the reader will judge the credibility of my work.

As indicated above, qualitative research involves fieldwork, in this case organising and conducting face-to-face interviews, which in turn generate a lot of data to be analysed. Hence the work is very labour intensive and by necessity entails a smaller sample of subjects. Furthermore, this raises the question of whether the sample is representative in terms of sociocultural dimensions, geographic location and other factors. For example, not all the regions of the UK could be included in this study. Since my research topic was on young British Muslims, it would have been a more complete study if I had interviewed Muslims in Scotland and asked them about their national identity. Here I have had to resort to references to other scholars' work, for example Hopkins (2004, 2007) and Mir (2007), who found that many young Muslims in Scotland felt very connected to Scotland, and proudly identified themselves as Scottish Muslims.

MUSLIMS IN BRITAIN: AN OVERVIEW

Britain has had contact with the Muslim world since the seventh century through trade contacts with Egypt and Palestine, which had come under Muslim control. It is likely that Britain also conducted trade with Muslims residing in Andalusia (Muslim Spain and Portugal). Later records indicate the presence of Arab Muslims in London from the twelfth or thirteenth centuries, presumably for trade purposes. From the sixteenth century to the end of the eighteenth century, British relations with the Muslims were cordial. In the late sixteenth century, following on from the steps taken by her father King Henry VIII, Queen Elizabeth I arranged a defence treaty with the Ottomans in 1587, and later Britain formed political links with Muslim territories as far away as India and Persia (Hellyer 2007: 226–7). A few centuries later, Muslims began to migrate to Britain.

In this chapter I examine the migration of Muslims to Britain, their settlement patterns and transition to becoming citizens of Britain. The material produced here is a precursor to my discussion on the national identity of Muslims in Chapter 4.

I begin with a brief migration history of British Muslims, including an account of resistance and support from the wider society in the course of their settlement and of the contribution Muslims have made to their new 'home'. Second, I discuss Muslim settlement in five cities of Britain – London, Leicester, Bradford, Leeds and Cardiff – based on research I have conducted in these cities consecutively. Finally, I consider the socioeconomic status of the respondents of this study.

Migration history

From the nineteenth century to the early twentieth century, when Britain colonised many predominantly Muslim territories, some Muslims from Bengal

(India), Yemen and Somalia began to arrive in Cardiff and London. Some Yemeni and Somali people have settled in Cardiff since the late nineteenth century. Yemeni sailors settling in Cardiff's Tiger Bay registered a house for use as a mosque as early as 1860. In Liverpool the Muslim community was indigenous in character, led by a Muslim convert, the Manx solicitor Abdullah Henry William Quilliam. In the 1880s Quilliam converted to Islam in Morocco, where he was educated to become an *alim* (Islamic scholar). In the 1890s, Quilliam established the Liverpool Mosque and the Muslim Institute. In the early 1940s, some South Asian Muslims purchased three houses in London's East End and converted them into the East London Mosque and the Islamic Cultural Centre (Ansari 2002: 6; Sheddon et al. 2004: 2–18). Some Muslims also petitioned the British government to build a mosque in London. Thus, during a war cabinet meeting in 1940, Churchill allocated funds to build the Regent's Park Central Mosque in London, which was opened in 1944 in the presence of King George VI (Hellyer 2007: 230).

However, after World War II the influx of 'coloured' (both Muslim and non-Muslim) immigrants met resistance from a section of the wider British society. In particular, the working-class people living in the poorer areas to which the new immigrants gravitated were sensitive to the disruptions that immigration caused to their everyday life and attitudes. Attitudes to the newcomers were often hostile. In the 1960s, a right-wing Conservative Member of Parliament, Enoch Powell, was critical of the influx of 'coloured' migrants to England as they were 'incapable of ordinary and decent family life' (Ward 2004: 134). In a 1962 speech in Birmingham, Powell envisaged an extraordinary growth in the non-white population in Britain: 'Like the Romans I seem to see "the River Tiber flowing with much blood"'. A Gallup poll showed that 75 per cent of the population was broadly sympathetic to Powell's views (Giddens and Griffiths 2006: 503–4). To Powell, English national identity was exclusive to the English race. In 1968, he declared, 'the Indian and the Asian do not become English by being born in England' (Cesari 2004: 32). Powell feared that, 'In this country in 15 or 20 years' time the black man will have the whip hand over the white man' (Ward 2004: 134). A survey in the late 1960s suggested that two-thirds of white Britons considered the British superior to Africans and Asians. As the historian Paul Ward (2004: 136) noted, 'There was a clear sense of British superiority, linked in many ways to imperialism'. In 1977, *Time* magazine noted:

> 'A tide of colour threatens to engulf Britain'. So warns the National Front, a neofascist party whose main goal is to expel the estimated 2 million 'coloured' – Jamaicans, Indians, Pakistanis and other nonwhite former colonials – who have migrated to Britain since 1945. ('The coloreds must go', *Time* 1977: 23)

The National Front (later the British National Party, BNP) exhibited overt racism against the 'coloured' immigrants in the 1970s and 1980s. There were records of 'Paki bashing', graffiti writings of 'White rule' on walls, and smashed windows in areas in Bradford where one-fifth of the city's people were non-white immigrants ('The coloreds must go', *Time* 1977: 23–4). However, these attacks were not confined to Bradford. Some respondents recalled BNP racist incidents that they had experienced personally.

The post-war migration of 'coloured' immigrants to Britain was encouraged by the British Nationality Act 1948, which provided the legal framework within which multicultural Britain emerged (Julios 2008: 85–6). But due to strong resistance from mainstream British people, the Commonwealth Immigrants Act 1962 passed measures to restrict the entry and settlement of non-white people. It was later amended as the Commonwealth Immigrants Act 1968. Julios (2008: 96) observed, 'While the government denied that the 1968 Act was racist, it was clearly designed to restrict the entry of British citizens without close ties to the UK, the vast majority of which were not white.' Subsequently, the Immigration Act 1971 brought about some new clauses on immigration. Julios (2008: 98) pointed out the difference between the 1968 and 1971 Acts: 'Before the [1971] Act came into force, Commonwealth citizens arriving under the voucher system could settle in Britain; whereas afterwards they entered on the basis of work-permits', which meant that immigrants would be subjected to annual work-permit controls and face the possibility of non-renewal of their work permits. However, Britain's transition towards a multicultural ideology was greatly enhanced with the enactment of the Race Relations Act 1976, which meant that direct discrimination on racial grounds (colour, race, nationality or national origin) was illegal (Julios 2008: 98–9).

Hansen (2000, cited in Julios 2008: 140) observes that the United Kingdom began the post-war years with a non-white population of some 300,000 people and towards the end of the twentieth century it had reached over 3 million people 'whose origins extend from Africa, the Pacific Rim, the Caribbean and the Indian Subcontinent'. The increase of migrants also brought about a debate on 'ethnicity', 'race', 'identity' and 'diaspora' in the academic realm (Julios 2008: 141). However, Modood (1997: 329) found that nearly two-thirds of visible ethnic groups in Britain agreed with the statement: 'In many ways I think of myself as British', which was obviously a step forward.

The 1960s and 1970s saw a rise in the number of Muslims in Britain, particularly immigrants from British colonies and Commonwealth countries. In 2001 there were 1.6 million Muslims in the United Kingdom (which was 2.7 per cent of the total population of the UK). British Muslims were predominantly South Asian (43 per cent Pakistani, 16 per cent Bangladeshi, 8 per cent Indian, and 6 per cent from other Asian backgrounds), approximating 75 per cent of the total British Muslim population. Approximately 12 per cent of Muslims were white (5 per cent with UK heritage) and approximately 8 per cent had an African black origin (Office for National Statistics 2001, see also Rehman 2007: 845).[1]

In England, the largest Pakistani settlements were in West Yorkshire and the West Midlands. Bradford, for instance, in 2001 had a Pakistani population of 67,295. Birmingham, Leeds, Sheffield, Preston and Glasgow (in Scotland) all have a substantial Pakistani presence, and there are smaller Pakistani settlements in Bristol, Oxford, Reading, Slough and parts of London. The largest Bangladeshi Muslim population was in East London (Office for National Statistics 2001).

Some British Muslims have been actively involved in politics for several decades. For example, there have been several Muslim mayors and mayoresses in London: Karamat Hussain (1981, Brent); Saleem Siddiqui (1995 and 2001, Hackney) and Lal Hussain (2000, Sutton). In the 2005 General Election four new Muslim Labour Members were elected: Sadiq Khan for Tooting, Shahid Malik for Dewsbury, Mohammad Sarwar for Glasgow Central and Khalid Mahmood for Birmingham Perry Barr. There are two Conservative Muslim Members of the European Parliament: Syed Kamall (London) and Sajjad Karim (North-west England). There are a small number of Muslim peers in the House of Lords: Lord Nazir Ahmed and Baroness Pola Uddin were raised to the peerage in 1998, Lord Adam Patel of Blackburn in 2000, Lord Amirali Alibhai Bhatia in 2001 and Lord Mohamed Sheikh in 2006. There is one Muslim member of the London Assembly (of twenty-five members elected in 2004) and Muslim representation on the boards of the London Development Agency, the Metropolitan Police Authority and Transport for London (Mayor of London report 2006: 76–7). Muslim celebrities include the boxers Amir Khan, Prince Naseem Hamed and Danny Williams; footballer Omer Freddy Kanoute and cricketer Bilal Mustafa Shafayet (Salam 2009). Whereas some Muslims in Britain have achieved success in British society, many have remained disadvantaged in terms of education, employment, health and housing (discussed later in this chapter).

Muslim settlement in five cities of Britain

In this section I discuss the settlement history of Muslims in London, Leicester, Bradford, Leeds and Cardiff, drawing on the oral testimonies of the participants of this study. In 2001, the total Muslim populations of the five cities were: London: 607,083; Leicester: 30,885; Bradford: 75,188; Leeds: 21,394 and Cardiff: 11,261 (Office for National Statistics 2001).

London

In 2001, of the total Muslims resident in London (607,083) 22 per cent (130,653) were of Pakistani origin and nearly half of them lived in Redbridge and Waltham Forest. A further 24 per cent were of Bangladeshi origin and half of these people lived in Tower Hamlets (Mayor of London report 2006:

22); thus the Borough of Tower Hamlets had the largest Muslim population (71,389). In this section I discuss the settlement patterns of Bangladeshi Muslims in Tower Hamlets. The settlement patterns of Pakistani Muslims in Britain are discussed under the Bradford and Leeds sections of this chapter. However, the socioeconomic condition of all Muslims in London is examined later in this section.

Since the nineteenth century there has been migration from rural Sylhet, a place in Bangladesh, to Britain. Many Sylheti men have been employed by British shipping companies, and travelled the world as crew members (Gardner 1993: 218). This trend is partly attributable to the fact that a number of Sylheti *sarengs* (foremen who controlled employment) understandably favoured their kinsmen and fellow countrymen and recruited them to similar jobs (Gardner 1993: 218). Although work on the ships was exhausting, by Sylheti village standards the wages were considerable: a year's work in a ship's engine room might enable a man to buy land or build a new house back in Sylhet. Many seamen did not confine themselves to the sea. By the early 1950s, a small number of Sylhetis had settled in the London Borough of Tower Hamlets, which included the areas of Bethnal Green, Poplar, Stepney, Bow, Bromley by Bow, Mile End, Shadwell, Spitalfields, Brick Lane (Banglatown) and Whitechapel. Since then their numbers have increased dramatically (Gardner 1993). A resident of Tower Hamlets, Naveed (British-born male of Sylheti background, aged 28) recalled:

My father worked in different parts of London as a machinist. His education was limited back in Sylhet. In those days the families were content with their own kind of land so they didn't pursue an education. (Interview, London, 31 March 2008)

The rural Sylheti extended family and kinship structure have been transplanted to London's East End. One local person from Brick Lane commented, 'Sylhetis have enormous extended families. Traditionally they have always lived close to one another. Banglatown is like a village. Everyone is either related or they know one another' (cited in Hall 2005: 157).[2] Dench et al. (2006: 33) observed that from Bethnal Green to Whitechapel, almost everyone knew their county of origin, Sylhet, because either they were born there or their parents were born there. Despite the preponderance of rural Sylheti people, the secular urban character of Bangladesh is also noticeable in Tower Hamlets. Neela, a local Bangladeshi woman remarked (cited in Lichtenstein 2007: 215):

There are so many Bengali-owned businesses there now and the Brick Lane has the largest Bengali population outside of Bangladesh. The *melas* [fairs] are the best [times] to see Brick Lane, because the smells of good food cooking are everywhere and the street is filled with women in yellow and red saris, the colours of spring. The *Baishaki mela* [Bengali New Year fair] is the primary Bengali celebration outside of Bangladesh, and thousands of people all over the world celebrate with us. It is a great way to show others about our culture and this is something that I am really keen to do.

In Tower Hamlets, Bangladeshi secular community leaders (both Sylheti and non-Sylheti) refer to a set of values (secularism, nationalism, socialism and democracy) linked to the 1971 Liberation War (*Muktojudho*) against Pakistan; these values also define Bangladeshi cultural and political aspirations in Britain. Initiatives reflecting their commitment to transmit a secular Bengali heritage are regularly undertaken: festivals (such as *Nobo borsho* or the Bengali New Year), youth cultural-awareness programmes, celebrations of independence movements, etc. (Garbin 2005). The availability of Bengali newspapers (written in standard Bangla) in the shops of Tower Hamlets reflects the urban character of Bangladesh.

The secular Bangladeshi leaders have also been keen to shape the local urban community space through symbols of Bengali nationalism. One of these symbolic markers is the *Shaheed Minar*, a monument which commemorates the martyrs (*shaheed*) of the Bengali Language Movement (*Bhasha Andolon*) in 1952.[3] In Tower Hamlets, the *Shaheed Minar* was erected in Altab Ali Park, Whitechapel, after funds were collected from a large number of secular Bangladeshi community groups (Garbin 2005). On the other hand, Islamist activists (both Sylheti and non-Sylheti) in Tower Hamlets stress their moral commitment to an 'authentic' religious identity and oppose the Bangladeshi nationalist initiatives of the secular leaders. These Islamist activists describe the *Shaheed Minar* as a 'waste of money' because it encourages Muslim youth to stop thinking 'Islamically'. They describe the Bengali New Year as a syncretic (*shirk*) event, which was influenced by Hindu traditions and promotes unrespectable behaviour and practices (Garbin 2005; see also Glynn 2002).

It is widely believed that when the Bangladeshi people settled in the East End, the white residents moved out. Regarding the 'white flight', local white teacher Guy Portman said (cited in Dench et al. 2006: 67):

I don't think there are that many racist incidents around here now, and I would imagine that things have got better over the last ten years. Over that period more of the people who would have had racist attitudes have actually moved away – as an expression of their racism, if you like. They have been replaced by more Bangladeshis, and that leads to a very nice atmosphere in the area.

Some of the Muslim respondents of this study also commented that harassment by the right-wing British National Party in East London had declined. The British-born Ejaz of Bangladeshi background (male, 27 years) recalled:

There were racial tensions in London during the '70s and the early '80s. I can remember them myself; the BNP marched through, there were thousands of BNP, skinheads marched through outside my house, through East London. In the early '80s, I saw them with my own eyes; it was terrifying! (Interview, London, 27 March 2008)

Ghalibah, another interviewee in London (British-born of Bangladeshi background, female, 22 years), recalled:

When we lived in East London . . . it was late '80s, early '90s, the BNP they used to set fire in our letterbox. They used to break into our balcony and steal stuff from our balcony, yeah. Just swear, break windows everything. And yeah chased my brother with dogs and after school they used to wait there with knives and my brother used to have to run home from school, so it was quite bad back then. (Interview, London, 9 April 2008)

Although the BNP faction has seemingly disappeared from East London, it has been very active in other parts of Britain. For example, when the Danish press published Prophet Muhammad's [PBUH] cartoon, about 500 Muslim protestors gathered outside the Danish Embassy in West London after a two-hour march. Amid chants of 'Denmark go to hell' and 'Bomb, bomb Denmark', protesters called for a *jihad*, or holy war (*Mirror*, 4 February 2006: 27). The BNP printed half a million copies of a cartoon of Prophet Muhammad [PBUH] with a bomb in his turban in a leaflet for distribution nationwide. It was set alongside a photo of a rally in London in which protestors carried placards reading: 'Slay those who insult Islam.' The far-right party was thought to have handed out about 5,000 of the documents outside London, in north Staffordshire. But the Bishop of Stafford, the Right Reverend Gordon Mursell, criticised this action by saying, 'It is wrong and irresponsible that this cartoon has been produced by the BNP with the intention of causing hurt to our Muslim brothers and sisters . . . An attack on any religion is an attack on all religions' (*Daily Star*, 3 March 2006: 35).

After the 7/7 London bombings, many Muslims of Bangladeshi background felt they were being treated as the 'Other', particularly through media representation. The feeling of being the 'Other' was also discussed by the participants of this study who had diverse backgrounds, such as Pakistani, Arab and Somali (see further discussion in Chapters 4 and 5). In the month after the 7 July 2005 bombings, there were reportedly 269 faith-hate attacks (compared to forty in the same period in 2004) against Asian and Muslim people (Smit 2006). However, some positive initiatives have been taken by Muslims and wider British society since the 7/7 incident. For example, the East London mosque has an 'Open Day' when it invites the wider community into the mosque, and throughout the year the mosque receives organised visits. Furthermore, some Islamic schools in London have interfaith discussions with other schools.

Overall, Muslims in London are economically marginalised people. In 2006, the Mayor of London published 'Muslims in London', a report based on data from the 2001 census and other sources, where he acknowledged that there is a 'systematic pattern of discrimination against Muslims', and that of all the faiths in London, Muslims are the most disadvantaged people. The report found that London's 600,000 Muslims were less educated, less healthy and less likely to have a job or to own a home (Mayor of London report 2006: 41–75; also see Smit 2006). The report highlighted that 43 per cent of working-age Muslims in London had no qualifications, compared to 27 per cent of average workers. At this time one in twelve Londoners was Muslim, but only 42 per cent aged 16 to 24 were economically active, compared with 60 per cent of the general population. Economically active people are defined as being in employment or unemployed and looking for a job. Just 15 per cent of Muslim women over 25 worked full-time, compared with 37 per cent of women in the general population. Seventy per cent of Bangladeshi and Pakistani children in London were living in poverty. Thirteen per cent of Muslim men and 16 per cent of Muslim women reported their health as 'not good', compared with 8 per cent of the general population. Only 38 per cent of Muslims owned their home, compared with 56 per cent of the general population. A third of Muslims across Britain lived in households that were overcrowded. This figure jumped to over 40 per cent in London.

The 'Muslims in London' document called on the government to do better research, to investigate discrimination and to increase Muslim representation on public bodies. Mayor Livingstone said he hoped that the report would combat some of the ignorance, prejudice and Islamophobia stirred up by some sections of the media. As cited in the *Morning Star Online* ('Livingstone publishes report', 24 October 2006), the secretary-general of the Muslim Council of Britain, Dr Muhammad Abdul Bari, noted that the ground-breaking report documented the needs of the community and identified policy initiatives. Dr Bari said, 'The report is a role model for other major cities in Britain and even for mainland Europe.'

Leicester

In the 1960s and early 1970s, under the 'Africanisation' programme, many people of Gujarati Indian background (both Hindus and Muslims) were expelled from East African countries like Uganda and Malawi. Most of these people moved to the UK and settled in Leicester, perhaps because they were already urbanised entrepreneurs used to British administration. However, some of them faced resistance in their initial settlement. One of the 80,000 native Asians expelled from Uganda by Idi Amin in 1972, Pravin Dattani (non-Muslim) recalled:

I have lived through a changing history in Leicester. We are more multicultural than anything else now. When I first arrived with my family, we weren't welcomed by Leicester City Council – even though we had British passports, so we had a right to be here. They told us they didn't want Ugandan Asians taking white jobs and they didn't give us housing. So we set up our own business selling textiles. We ended up thriving and there are millions of us here now . . . (*Observer*, 28 October 2007: 24)

Leicester also had its share of skinheads and right-wing National Front march-ers; an immigrant remembered being called a 'wog' and seeing 'Paki Go Home' graffiti when he came here in 1975. But racial antagonism lessened when it became apparent that instead of taking away the jobs of working-class whites, Leicester's new arrivals were creating employment through the services, retail, wholesale and real estate they generated (*New York Times*, 8 February 2001: 1). The early immigrants (including some people from the Indian subconti-nent) have settled in, but since 2001 Leicester has witnessed another wave of arrivals: Somalis, Bosnians, Kosovars – a smaller and more diverse group from the Hindus and Muslims who had arrived en masse from East Africa. Many of the recent immigrants came from the Netherlands because they could not find work there and faced dispersal under the strict housing policy. Some of the Somalis were highly skilled professionals who integrated well into the Asian business community. But others, especially those who moved into the poorest inner-city districts, had more trouble (*International Herald Tribune*, 7 November 2005: 1, 3). A social analyst, also a resident of Leicester, Arifin (male, aged 40), gave an overview of Leicester:

Leicester is one of the more mixed of the British cities, English cities. In fact it is projected that by 2012 the white population of Leicester might become a minority, and that obviously will create a lot of debate and discussion and maybe even anxiety amongst white people here, but at the moment from the last Census the overall population of Leicester I think is about 270,000. According to the Census in terms of religious affiliation, it has about 40,000 Hindus, about 30,000 Muslims and about 15,000 Sikhs. There is also a significant African and Caribbean community who are mostly Christian. We have also had an inflow of people who are Somali, mostly Muslim. The city council estimates about 10,000, so that would bring the Muslim number up to almost 40,000. (Interview, Leicester, 12 April 2008)

Arifin further spoke of Leicester as a distinctly diverse city:

It has a very strong vibrant Indian culture. Belgrave Road, which is worth visiting in fact, we can go there if you wish, has a very strong Indian spirit and gold shops, sari shops, music, Indian video shops and things like that, and Leicester is well known for that part of the shopping environment. (Interview, Leicester, 12 April 2008)

As advised by Arifin, I ventured into the Belgrave Road, and noticed the presence of a large Indian community. In one of the shops I heard *Hindi* (Indian) songs played through the radio, and when I asked the shopkeeper where the music was coming from, he smiled and replied, 'Ye, *Bombay hai, Bombay'!* [This is Bombay] (The old name of Mumbai). Later, as I walked through the streets of Leicester where there were Asian concentrations, I noticed mosques in almost every other street. When I remarked on the number of mosques, Arifin said, 'The number of mosques are growing gradually. I think at the moment it stands at about 30 mosques. That's quite a large number for a community. I mean of 40,000, that's nearly 1,000 people per mosque.' However, Leicester appeared to be a very divided city. I could not see mainstream British people in the residential areas or Asian shops and restaurants. I only spotted them in the city centre. Later, I took a taxi to see where the mainstream British people lived. Regarding the division, the local resident Nabihah (female, aged 25) said:

> You'll find that a large Muslim community live in Evington and Highfields. There's not many white people there, so they have very little interaction. They [the Muslims] go to the local schools; again there is no interaction with white people. (Interview, Leicester, 10 April 2008)

There have been several reports of ethnic tensions in Leicester. For example, in the poorest inner-city districts such as the tatty streets behind the city railway station, which is the usual destination for the poorest new arrivals, some Somalis have clashed violently with West Indians (*International Herald Tribune*, 7 November 2005: 1, 3). The Muslims of Leicester were not immune to the backlash of the 9/11 and 7/7 incidents. After 9/11, Nabihah reported:

> We didn't have that many problems. My cousin was telling, 'Oh don't go out after 10 o'clock because Muslims are getting harassed'. So I was prevented from going out at a certain time. (Interview, Leicester, 10 April 2008)

About the repercussions from the 7/7 London bombings, Hisham (male, aged 18) said:

> I think it did affect Leicester a tiny bit because in the newspapers and everywhere, it's just that Muslims have done this [bombing], and the mosque window got smashed straight after the 7/7. But the thing is around here no-one would come up to you face to face, and say something. They'd cower away, so that when you're asleep, they'll come and smash your windows, things like that. We're not saying that it's based on Christian white people; it could be Hindu people; it could be anyone really. (Interview, Leicester 10 April 2008)

So there have been tensions within the ethnic communities on majority–minority relations, but some members of the wider community have taken initiatives to promote peace and harmony. The interviewee Arifin said that after the 7/7 London bombings the Bishop of Leicester played a mediating role between the different communities. The Bishop made a statement after 7/7 saying that the communities of Leicester would pull together, they would behave as one community, and if there was a backlash on the Muslim community, if buildings or people were attacked, then this would be considered as an attack on all communities (Interview, Leicester 12 April 2008). Similarly, after Prophet Muhammad's [PBUH] cartoon controversy, the Bishop of Leicester, the Right Reverend Tim Stevens, and Professor Richard Bonney, director of the University of Leicester's Centre for the History of Religious and Political Pluralism, criticised the publication of the cartoons by the Danish media (*Leicester Mercury*, 4 February 2006: 6).

Bradford

In contrast to Leicester, Bradford took in thousands of Muslims directly from Pakistan's rural hinterlands to work in the textile mills. Bradford also attracted smaller communities of Bangladeshis with roots in rural Sylhet. Like some northern cities in Britain, Bradford has been dependent on one major industry, textiles. When this collapsed, 60,000 textile jobs, or 80 per cent of the total, were lost between 1960 and 1990, and the majority of the first-generation Muslim migrants were affected (Lewis 2007: 25). A 28-year-old British-born Muslim woman of Pakistani-Mirpuri background, Munira recalled her parents' migration story in Bradford:

I think it was probably late 60s. My father came here first and then through chain migration my mother came afterwards and then settled. And again like most people, they didn't necessarily think that they would be staying here, but they became rooted here. Father worked in the factories, which is a common story. Worked practically seven days a week it was; you know it was very hard. Both my mother and father were illiterate and came here really for survival.

Munira recalled that her father always feared that he would lose his job:

My father still tells me to this day how when he first came here he had to make *roti* [bread] for about 20–30 men. And how when they came here all of them had to live in very cramped conditions and there was racism, open to the point that he retired. He says that you always referred to your managers as 'Yes Boss', 'No Boss', and because . . . it was almost like a colonial mentality. They'd always, in a sense, been controlled by you know, from the British Raj, the white man was boss. And he put, yeah, that you had to be nice because otherwise they could, you know, throw you out of the country, you just don't know. (Interview, Bradford, 24 August 2008)

Regarding her mother's settlement story in Bradford, Munira said:

My mother when she came here she always believed in the fact that she would maintain her identity at all costs . . . wearing *shalwar-kameez* [trousers and shirt] to this
day even she doesn't speak much English. Sometimes people in Pakistan would say
things like 'Pakistan has moved on, yet you're still almost stuck in this time warp [of
the 1960s]'. (Interview, Bradford, 24 August 2008)

Similar stories were heard from other participants of this study. For
example, Akram, a 26-year-old British-born man of Pakistani background
from Faisalabad said that his father migrated first and stayed with a lot of
different relatives. Later, mother came and stayed with the same relatives. So
'There was a lot of what we call in Urdu *kitchatani* [pull along]' (Interview,
Bradford, 25 August 2008). In other words, after Akram's parents' arrival
there was a chain of migration from his extended family and they supported
each other. The pattern of Pakistani settlement in Bradford was more like
the pattern of Bangladeshi (Sylheti) settlement in East London. Just as East
London has a vibrant Bengali culture, Bradford has a vibrant Pakistani culture.
Speaking of her Pakistani connection, the British-born girl, Saamiya, aged 17,
spoke of the *Chand Raat* (Moon night) Eid festival in Bradford:

That's basically just before the day before *Eid* [Muslim religious celebration] and it's
the night where the women go . . . Yeah *Chand Raat*. And it's the girls get together,
they get all dressed up and then like you pay £5 to go in and you sit there and obviously the money goes to world charity and stuff. And then there's like *mendi* [henna]
going and there might be a fashion show going on, so you can buy clothes and jewellery, get your *mendi* done, so basically you get an outing that women do over here.
(Interview, Bradford, 7 October 2008)

Some young male participants of Pakistani background aged 17–18 spoke
of *Bhangra*, a form of music and dance that originated in the Punjab region
of Pakistan and India, which they performed on special occasions such as
weddings.

Bradford received a negative national and international image in connection
with the 'Rushdie Affair' in 1989, when the city became 'the epicenter of protests' against the novel *The Satanic Verses*, which was publicly burned (Lewis
2002: 156; 2007: 25). There were two major riots: one in 1995 that involved
conflict between young Pakistani men and police (Burlet and Reid 1996: 144–
57), and the other in 2001, which involved Pakistani and Bangladeshi men
against the right-wing BNP. A group of participants, Muffakir, Najeed and

Matiur (British-born of Bangladeshi background, male, aged 21–5), recalled the riots on 7 July 2001:

> Basically what's happened is Bangladeshi lads from . . . raped a white woman apparently. They've [BNP] got this image out, so they've got a recruit of all these people saying all these Pakis come to our country, living off our benefits, you know, our costs, you know, just the system and stuff. So they got these people together, they've gone and held them, insulted women with *hijabs*, brothers with beards, anything black, whatever race it were, yeah. They've gone [to] Oldham, and Barnsley, and they've got away with it. What they didn't know when they come to Bradford, which is *Bradistan* and now fortunately enough we've got a lot of insiders.
>
> Every Asian community got together. We've seen them in the city centre and they've run around, they've turned around about 30 or 40 of them, they've turned around thinking all the Pakis are here, or how many Asians are here? They [the Asians] were that many that they [BNP] backed themselves into a pub, so obviously we started smashing the pub, right. The police have turned up, police have guarded the pub off, we've turned around and said, 'Hang on, when these lots have insulted our mothers and sisters in Rochdale, in Oldham, and in Barnsley there were no police presence there, there was no one to protect their [Asian] women . . . Well it was in Manningham, it was just up the road so obviously there were people from this area involved against BNP white basically. (Interview, Bradford, 27 August 2008)

I assume that there were grievances from both sides (BNP and the Asians) that led to the riot. But the participants thought that the law was heavy-handed only against the Asians:

> Yeah, speaking of sentencing, during the riots people were getting five years just for chucking a stone. You get less for manslaughter, you know, it's really bad. First time down the history of British history that someone has been sentenced for riots, for Bradford riots. (Interview, Bradford, 27 August 2008)

In 2004, a BBC documentary filmed undercover Nick Griffin, the BNP chairman, at a party meeting, condemning Islam as a 'wicked vicious faith' that preaches that 'any woman that they can take by force or guile is theirs'. In addition, a BNP member also confessed to a racial attack in the 2001 Bradford riot in which he kicked the victim until he was 'floppy'. Another member, a council candidate, was secretly filmed boasting of putting dog excrement through the letter-box of an Asian takeaway over a three-week period. The makers of the documentary said they would give police and prosecutors their material (*Financial Times*, 15 July 2004: 6). On the other hand, in 2007 Kabir Hussain, aged 26, of Heaton, Bradford admitted taking part in the riot on 7 July 2001. On 9 February 2007, the Bradford Crown Court gave Hussain a 27-month sentence for his behaviour during the riots (Crown Prosecution Service 2007).

The interviewees Muffakir, Najeed and Matiur, aged 21–5, said if they go to hard-core white estates, such as Eccleshill, Ravenscliffe, Holmewood, Odsal or Keighley, they would be called a 'Paki' or 'black' (Interview, Bradford, 27 August 2008). The 'hard-core white estates' may not have been exposed to diversity. So when some people from those places see unfamiliar people they may view them as the 'Other'. For example, Keighley is about 10 miles from Bradford, a town of about 60,000 people (though in the City of Bradford Metropolitan Council area) and it may not have been exposed to diversity as much as Manningham.

In spite of racial tensions in a section of the Bradford community, there was also solidarity among people of different faiths. For example, after the 7/7 London bombings, a joint statement on behalf of the Christian, Hindu, Jewish, Muslim and Sikh faiths by the Right Reverend David James (Bishop of Bradford), Mr R. Pal Johar (Hindu), Mr Ken Fabian (Jewish), Mr Sher Azam (Muslim) and Mr Mohinder Singh Chana (Sikh) said: 'As religious leaders in Bradford, we pray for the victims and the grieving families of those caught up in this unspeakable horror.' They also added, 'Such an atrocity impacts indiscriminately on people of diverse faiths, adults and children alike. We salute the courage, compassion and selfless labours of the emergency services, whose humanity shines out amidst such a dark, pitiless and unforgiving cruelty . . .' (*Yorkshire Post*, 8 July 2005, online). In 2007, Muslims and Christians in Britain joined in prayers for Benazir Bhutto as the assassinated former Prime Minister of Pakistan was laid to rest. Ms Bhutto had close links to Bradford and had visited the city on a number of occasions. A Pakistani flag flew at half-mast over the Town Hall and the Bishop of Bradford, David James, also paid tribute (*Yorkshire Post*, 28 December 2007, online). In 2008, a Keighley-based Islamic scholar, Sheikh Sa'ad Al-Attas, spoke at the Anglican Church of All Saints, Keighley, on the need for Christians and Muslims to respect and honour each other. His speech was warmly received by a large Christian audience. Reverend Dr Jonathan Pritchard, Vice-Chair of the Faiths Forum, also emphasised the need for such discussions (Fiaz 2008: 5).

Leeds

In the 1950s and 1960s, many Muslims came to Leeds from rural parts of Pakistan, particularly from Pakistani-controlled Kashmir. Most of them were illiterate and had poor English-language skills. They primarily came to work in the textile industries. In the 1980s, when the textile mills gradually started to decline, these people lost their jobs, and because they were mostly non-skilled it was not easy for them to get other work (Brown 2005). In Beeston Hill, the dilapidated part of Beeston, Pakistanis make up 20 per cent of the population. They are a minority, but a large enough one to form their own partially ghettoised and cohesive community. Almost every family is ultimately from a rural part of Pakistani Kashmir called Mirpur, where the rules of tradition are strict. Malik (2007) observed that in Mirpur the basic structures of life – justice, security and social support – were organised by the local tribe and not by a central state. One consequence was that people could not just marry whoever they wanted to. If they did, then over time tribal lands would be broken up by the rules of inheritance, and the economic base of the tribe, or *biraderi* (brotherhood), would be destroyed. This was one reason why children in rural Pakistan were often treated as the property of their elders and encouraged, or forced, to marry within the *biraderi* (Malik 2007).

However, there are some Mirpuri people in Leeds who have settled in other parts of Leeds, such as Harehills, Chapeltown and Hyde Park. Omema, a 40-year-old British-born and university-educated Muslim woman of Mirpuri-Pakistani background, recalled that her father came to Leeds in the 1950s:

> When he first came he began working on the buses. Yeah, I can't remember which order. But he worked in the factories. And he worked on the buses. And then he decided to set up his own business, so he had a market stall for many years and then a shop on the Headrow, which is like the main street in the city centre. And then he sort of decided to take a council job and became an interpreter . . . I mean in Pakistan he kind of got a scholarship for studies, so he was very bright. But the opportunities there were limited so his achievements were major considering what background he came from and the kind of opportunities that were open to him. When he came here, because he didn't have a degree-level qualification, he had to start sort of you know the manual-type labour, and then he moved from that into office-type labour and then he became a manager really at the end. So considering how he started off, he moved to a high position. (Interview, Leeds, 28 August 2008)

Omema's family (parents) never lived in South Leeds (Beeston); they settled in North Leeds, which is a white area. Perhaps being integrated into the wider community residentially helped Omema's father to move upwards in occupational status. 'Ghettoised' living can sometimes hamper job prospects in the wider community (Peach 2006, also discussed later in this chapter). Another British-born and university-educated Muslim male of Pakistani-Mirpuri background, Ehsan, aged 30, said that his parents came to Leeds in the 1960s, and his father worked as a labourer. Ehsan spoke highly of his mother, who forbade him to attend a 'mixed' school in an economically deprived area that did not have a high standard:

> My mother sent me off to a Middle School in a leafy suburb of Leeds, whereas where we lived was like classed as an inner-city deprived area. So she sent me off to a leafy suburb and it was quite a culture shock for me cos I was used to living, working, studying with young people that looked like me, same skin colour, same kind of background, family background you know, father was a labourer, mother was a

housewife. So when I was sent off to school, it was quite an upper- class kind of you know Middle School, and I think I was one of maybe four or five Pakistani students there really. So I found it a real culture shock. I also found it difficult really conforming to kind of standards that those kind of white young people had. They were quite rich, you know parents were professionals and so forth, so it was quite a challenge for me to fit in there really . . . I mean at that time I probably hated my mum for sending me to that school. But now I think I've benefited. I am able to communicate and appreciate different cultures. (Interview, Leeds, 1 September 2008)

Ehsan is engaged in a profession where he has to communicate with both the Muslim and the wider community. He believed that the integration process through school benefited him in his career. Ehsan also departed from the stereotype attached to the British people of Mirpuri background (see Malik 2007). He was married to a Pakistani woman of non-Mirpuri background.

As in other UK cities, Muslims in Leeds also felt the impact of the 9/11 Twin Towers tragedy. Kamran Siddiqi of the Leeds Muslim Forum said that anti-Muslim feeling rose to a level where Muslims were being targeted, with attacks ranging from verbal abuse in the street to physical assaults. In 2004, Dr Siddiqi said, 'There has been a rise in Islamophobia. Racially motivated attacks are increasing across the country and Leeds is no different.' Crown Prosecution Service figures show that more than 400 people were charged with racially motivated offences between April 2002 and March 2003 (*Yorkshire Evening Post*, 8 June 2004, online). After the 7/7 London bombings, Beeston in South Leeds came under media and police scrutiny as three of the four London bombers lived in this shabby, rundown suburb of Leeds. Racial harassment against the Muslims in Beeston was intensified (Murtaza 2006). One anonymous person from the Beeston area reported, 'I got attacked by two white lads. They got me in there with a knife and they got me in the head with a crowbar. I was in the hospital for a week' (Brown 2005). The unnamed person also observed that with racism, poverty and high unemployment, the beleaguered community felt cut off from the white population. He said the predominantly English area next to Beeston feels like another country. He further said regarding the next white working-class suburb, 'And you feel like you're crossing a borderline because you won't see no Asians around there. They're all whites who live down there. It is very segregated here, and, well, that's a big problem, not part of it; it's the biggest problem' (Brown 2005). Similar sentiments were expressed by Ehsan:

The gangs and so forth actually stems from people affiliating themselves to the far-right groups and so forth. So in here, there are BNP candidates that stand in the majority of the wards and so forth, but the ones that are kind of, probably I would say that stick out like a sore thumb in terms of being, you know highly populated with white and quite racist are Middleton and Belle Aisle which is just across the road from Beeston really . . . Belle Aisle and Middleton, they're predominantly white working-class areas so forth . . . (Interview, Leeds, 1 September 2008)

Racial tensions also occurred in other parts of Leeds. After the 7/7 incident, a Muslim-owned store in Harehills was set ablaze in what witnesses called a racially motivated crime. Iqbal Khan, the store owner, said four white youths who were inside lit a fire, then ran out. He said he had escaped before the store went up in flames (*New York Times*, 23 July 2005: 7). Muslim leaders were especially concerned that anti-immigrant groups such as the BNP would try to rile young Muslims. Eight white people were arrested on disorderly conduct charges at the Broadway Pub in Beeston, not far from a heavily Muslim neighbourhood, in what is believed to have been an attempt at agitation. Muslim leaders said that the far-right BNP was looking for opportunities to take advantage of the 7/7 tragedy and they tried to organise meetings in town to call for new laws against immigrants. The leaders warned the Muslims to advise their children 'not to fall into the hands of the BNP' (*New York Times*, 23 July 2005: 7). However, there was a positive aspect: the 7/7 London bombing tragedy brought the Muslim and the wider communities together. Hanif Malik, a Muslim community spokesperson in Beeston, condemned the London bombings. Mr Malik was also supported by the Catholic Bishop of Leeds, Arthur Roach, and his Anglican counterpart John Packer (*Daily Mirror*, 14 July 2005: 8).

Cardiff

There has been a Muslim presence in Cardiff for over a century. Muslims arrived in Cardiff in three distinct periods of immigration: before World War I; between the two wars; and since 1945. The first relatively permanent Muslim community comprised merchants and sailors, known as 'lascars', mostly from countries connected with the British Empire, such as Yemen, Somalia and the Indian subcontinent (Ansari 2004: 36). By 1860, there was a small settled Muslim community in Cardiff, and the first mosque (South Wales Islamic Centre) in the UK was registered in the city that year. It probably doubled as a temporary boarding house for Arab seafarers, but the fact it provided a place for collective Muslim identity was significant (Gilliat-Ray 2005/6: 4). By 1881 there were enough seamen to warrant the establishment of a so-called Home for Coloured Seamen. In the 1911 Census it was estimated that there were around 700 seamen (perhaps with a majority of Muslims) living in Cardiff (Ansari 2004: 36). Marzia, a 27-year-old British-born third-generation Muslim woman of Yemini background recalled:

My grandfather came here as a seaman by ship obviously. They did not come here to live. They were here just to work and then go back home. Well my grandmother she didn't come up here anyway so my grandfather didn't bring her here but my father came like a couple of years . . . I think my father used to do two years here and then go back two years so . . . he would gather all his money for two years and then go back to Yemen and just spend it all on something . . . and then he brought my mother and then so on . . . Yeah, and some [Yemeni men] used to marry Welsh women. (Interview, Cardiff, 23 October 2008)

Regarding the nature of her grandfather's and father's work, Marzia recalled:

I think it was transportation of coal. I think . . . to pick up coal from Cardiff [and take it to other countries] . . . Yemen was very important, yeah it was a station. Yeah but it wasn't just like coal and all that cos they used to have, you know, India was spices and so on, and there was cloth and silk so they used to go to different countries to get the stuff and then they would come back here. Yeah, then my father he got into steel. (Interview, Cardiff, 23 October 2008)

Yemen is located in the southwestern corner of the Arabian Peninsula, commanding the junction of the Red Sea and the Gulf of Aden. To help secure this crucial passage for trade, Britain colonised the port of Aden in 1839 and gradually expanded its rule to include the southern region of the country. The northern part became independent on the collapse of the Ottoman Empire in World War I, while South Yemen achieved independence from Britain in 1967. The two halves of Yemen were merged into a single nation in 1990.

The Gulf of Aden was of strategic value to the British Empire, being 'a vast bunkering station, piled high with British coal, refuelling passenger liners and cargo ships alike' (Smith 2008, cited in *Guardian*, 12 November 2008: 3). Locally recruited men from poor villages in Yemen worked below decks in conditions that the British assumed they would be well suited to. Most Yemeni wives stayed in their villages, bringing up children who were fathered before the men left for the UK or on their infrequent visits home. Social conventions and the Yemeni government discouraged the migration of women because it was feared that this would lead to a decline in the flow of remittances home (Smith 2008, cited in *Guardian*, 12 November 2008: 3).

Cardiff remained a focal point for the Yemeni seamen as they shipped Welsh coal to some of the big importers such as Spain (Richards 2005: 52). The Arab Muslim families made their presence felt in Cardiff as early as the 1950s, when they celebrated their religious festivals (Lee 2007: 71). However, in the 1980s, just before the end of the coal age, the spiralling decline of heavy industry persuaded many Yemenis to leave Cardiff and return home for good. Some men stayed in Wales because their wives had arrived and the family had settled. These men either set up or joined small businesses (Smith 2008, cited in *Guardian*, 12 November 2008: 3).

Other Muslim immigrants in Cardiff were from Somalia and the Indian subcontinent. The Somali seamen worked alongside the Yemenis (Ansari 2004). The people from the Indian subcontinent came later, settling in Cardiff in the 1960s and 1970s. Some of the Cardiff participants in this study were British-born Muslims of Pakistani and Bangladeshi backgrounds. Their fathers worked in factories in other British places, such as Sheffield and Manchester, and later moved to Cardiff, while others chose to settle in Cardiff from the beginning and set up their own small businesses. While responding to interview questions, some respondents of this investigation shared their life stories as they recalled some unpleasant incidents. For example, one of the female respondents, British-born of Pakistani background Sarah, aged 30, was horrified by her experience with the British National Party:

When I was younger, when I was about 5 or 6, I was attacked by BNP skinheads. Physically attacked me, they kicked me on the streets and said, 'Paki go home' . . . In that time, skinheads were common. Now they are a lot more clever . . . they could be a random person walking down the street. In those days a lot more [skinheads] could be seen with Dr Martens boots on? . . . it shocks me even to this day that, you know, a five-year-old walking through the street . . . and an adult would kick her, and say, 'Paki, go home'. (Interview, Cardiff, 18 October 2008)

It appears that as the number of Asian immigrants was increasing, the right-wing British National Party became more aggressive and started attacking immigrants. Some participants spoke of the impact of the 9/11 Twin Towers tragedy and the 7/7 London bombings on the Muslim community. An overseas-born male respondent of Syrian background, Habib, aged 30, noted after the 9/11 Twin Towers tragedy:

Ah, in Cardiff not that much difference – a little bit – you know, one brother, he gave me a gift *shalwar-kurta*, the Pakistani-style men's dress. I wore that, I put it on and went outside, and they [mainstream Welsh] called me, 'Bin Laden'! I know [there was] an attack on a woman one day because she was wearing *hijab*. They just tried to take it off her. (Interview, Cardiff, 23 October 2008)

A Welsh-born male student of Bangladeshi background, Imran, aged 20, however, said that after the 7/7 London bombings Cardiff was not affected badly:

I don't think it was that bad honestly. There was a bit of tension but that was I think natural. I remember that old mosque, the Bangladeshi Shah Jalal mosque square . . . a pig's head was left outside it, but apart from that we didn't hear any hate crime. (Interview, Cardiff, 18 October 2008)

Nevertheless, some of Cardiff's older settlers noted a great change in the perceptions of the wider Welsh community on the Muslim community. Mehr, a 24-year-old third-generation female respondent of Yemeni background, commented:

> I don't know with 7/7, the 7/7 bombers straight away Muslims, they had to be Muslims. How can you call someone [Muslim] who kills innocent people and children and women? It's *haram* [forbidden in Islam] to kill innocent women [people]. [After the 7/7 incident] sometimes, you feel like you don't belong here . . . You don't have a choice you have to forget it, I mean this is your life now. (Interview, Cardiff, 23 October 2008)

Another third-generation male respondent of Yemeni background, Khurram, aged 26, said he felt different because of Islamic visibility:

> It's actually not the same. When I went to Yemen for a couple of months I came back and cos I'd been, you know, not here for some time, I could actually see what was going on in the bus, people's expressions on their face, how they actually look at you and I never, ever noticed that before . . . Especially if you have a beard . . . This is our own country, it's just bizarre . . . Even our [Welsh] friends these days they don't, you know, feel comfortable to take us to their houses cos their parents might dislike us. (Interview, Cardiff, 23 October 2008)

It appears there is a great deal of apprehension between the Muslims and the wider Welsh community since the 7/7 London bombings. But there are also initiatives taken by both the leaders of the Muslim community and the wider Welsh community to address some of the misconceptions about Islam. Mr Saleem Kidwai, General Secretary of the Muslim Council of Wales, said:

> One thing which we have got in Wales is a good inter-faith relationship understanding . . . and it is very personal that, you know that you have got that contact with the Archbishop or the Hindus, or the Sikhs, and the Bahais and everybody, you can talk to them and get them involved. (Interview, Cardiff, 23 October 2008)

Nowhere in Britain were the Danish cartoons of Prophet Muhammad [PBUH] published, except in the University of Wales magazine and later in a Church magazine. Both the magazines were recalled before extensive circulation and the Vice-Chancellor of the University of Wales and the Archbishop of Wales (and Bishop of Llandaff), the Most Reverend Dr Barry Morgan, apologised to the Muslim Council of Wales (Interview, Cardiff, 23 October 2008). Also, the BBC News (2006b) reported that the Church in Wales had recalled 500 copies of its magazine featuring a cartoon caricaturing the Prophet Muhammad [PBUH]. The editor resigned after the image was published in the Church's Welsh-language magazine *Y Llan*. And the Archbishop of Wales apologised to the Muslim Council of Wales, which accepted the 'unfortunate mistake'.

Socioeconomic characteristics of British Muslims

Based on the oral testimonies of the participants of this study and other literature, this section evaluates the overall socioeconomic condition of Muslims in Britain. As discussed, the Mayor of London's report, 'Muslims in London' (2006), revealed the disadvantaged position of Muslims in that city. The Annual Population Survey revealed that in 2004, Muslims in Great Britain had the highest male unemployment rate, at 13 per cent (ONS). This was about three times the rate for Christian men (4 per cent). The unemployment rate for Muslim women at 18 per cent was about four times the rate for Christian and Jewish women (4 per cent in each case). Among working-age men, Muslims had the highest overall levels of economic inactivity in 2004 – 31 per cent compared with 16 per cent of Christians (ONS 2004).[4] Muslim women were more likely than other women to be economically inactive. About seven in ten (69 per cent) Muslim women of working age were economically inactive, whereas Christian women were least likely to be economically inactive (25 per cent). Furthermore, Muslims aged 16 to 24 years had the highest unemployment rates. This is partly explained by the youthful age profile of Muslims and the correspondingly high proportion of students (ONS 2004). Table 2.1 (below) shows the socioeconomic status of the parents of 216 participants of this study. This is a very small sample, but it is an indication that a large number of Muslim women have not been employed in the labour market.

In Table 2.1, 'employee' means a person with a job. But out of 91 fathers who were employees, only 18 held professional jobs, such as banker, accountant, solicitor, doctor, manager, engineer, geologist, lecturer and pharmacist. Thus, 73 fathers held other jobs, such as chef, tailor, vegetable supplier, casual jobs, odd jobs, tube train driver, taxi driver, imams, day centre carer, factory workers, postman, salesman, shopkeeper and security guard. The 12 mothers who had paid jobs worked as a nurse, primary state school teacher or teacher

Table 2.1 Socioeconomic status of the 216 participants' parents

Employment status	Father	Mother
Employee	91	12
Self-employed	39	3
Unemployed	22	190
Retired	26	not applicable
Ill-health or permanently sick	6	1
Other	32	10

in a faith school, pharmacy technician, artist, saleswoman, occupational therapist, youth worker, child carer and solicitor. In the 'self-employed' section, 39
fathers and three mothers owned shops and restaurants. Twenty-two fathers
had no work, and 26 were retired, while the vast majority of women (190)
were unemployed. In the ill-health section, two male parents had been in the
workforce but retired early because of ill-health, whereas four men were sick
permanently and one mother was permanently disabled. The 'other' section
included 32 fathers who had passed away, divorced parents and father left,
or father working overseas, while 10 mothers were living overseas with their
husbands. Three fathers had two jobs (paid job and self-employed, office work
and owned restaurants) and one mother had two jobs (for example, saleswoman and teacher).

Lewis (2007: 27) observed that the Pakistanis and the Bangladeshis were
the largest Muslim groups in the UK, and they were only one generation
removed from rural peasantry (see also Dench et al.). Therefore, one might
expect that it would take a longer time for these communities to develop their
English-language skills and qualifications in order to obtain equal opportunities in the British labour market. However, focusing on British-Pakistani
people in Birmingham, Cressey (2006: 131) has observed significant changes
occurring among some young people in Britain: several of the young men, as
well as young women, who were interviewed expressed real commitment to
changing the pattern. For example, some young men and women were keen to
pursue education and obtain professional careers, and young women learned
to drive to become self-reliant (Cressey 2006: 131). My research findings,
though a very small sample (Table 2.2 and Table 2.3), show the significant
changing pattern of skills and qualifications among the second-generation
Muslim immigrants in the British labour market. In Table 2.2, I have only
included the data of 22 second-generation male respondents plus their fathers'
qualifications and work status (Muslim adult immigrants, aged 19 and over).[5]

In Table 2.2, out of 22 first-generation fathers, only one was highly qualified (with a doctoral degree in engineering), and four had overseas qualifications that were not recognised in the UK. The rest of the seventeen fathers
did not have any qualifications. Though all fathers (except one) belonged to
the working class, it is quite obvious that there is upward mobility among the
second-generation Muslims, corresponding to the trend observed by Cressey
(2006: 131). There are also debates about whether British Muslim women are
beginning to achieve higher levels of education. Dwyer and Shah (2009: 56–7)
observed that some scholars see the pursuit of higher education by young
Muslim women as evidence of the renouncement of 'traditional' Islamic values
and practices, whereas others have argued that aspirations to higher education do not necessarily represent a challenge or resistance to parental values.
Some scholars argue that educational aspirations are sometimes encouraged by
the parents if their daughters pursue a career which holds a good reputation

Table 2.2 Twenty-two fathers' and sons' educational and employment status

First generation, fathers' occupational status	Second generation, sons' work status and qualification (19 years and over)
Engineer, PhD	Corporate job (Engineer)
Imam, Arabic degree from back home	Solicitor (Law)
Tailor, no qualification	Educationalist (National Vocational Qualification, NVQ)
Local councillor (overseas qualification)	Youth worker (BA)
Bus driver (overseas qualification)	Corporate executive (Law)
Bus driver (overseas qualification)	Manager (BCom)
Self-employed (overseas qualification)	Youth worker (BA student)
Tailor, no qualification	IT consultant (BSc)
Labourer, no qualification	Manager (BCom)
Unemployed, no qualification	High school dropout
Factory worker, no qualification	Community support worker (NVQ)
Factory worker, no qualification	Community worker (BCom)
Factory worker, no qualification	Director (MA)
Self-employed, no qualification	Real estate agent (Engineer)
Self-employed, no qualification	Social worker (Engineer)
Self-employed, no qualification	Imam (BA student)
Self-employed, no qualification	Bank employee (BA student)
Self-employed, no qualification	Community worker (BA)
Self-employed, no qualification	Medical student
Taxi driver, no qualification	Medical student
Machinist, no qualification	Administration officer (A-level)
Grandfather, labourer; father, factory worker, no qualification	Youth worker (A-level) [third generation]

(Dwyer and Shah 2009: 56–7). Mohammad (2005: 197, cited in Dwyer and Shah 2009: 57) noted an increase in aspirations for higher education among young Muslim women, but that those who go to universities were likely to have educated parents. Shaw (2000: 166) observed in her study of Pakistani Muslim families that parents generally show more leniency towards their sons than their daughters, but may adopt different strategies for different same-sex children. For example, one daughter may be encouraged to leave school at sixteen and accept an arranged marriage to a relative from Pakistan, while her sister enters further education or a profession, thereby postponing the question of her marriage. Parental attitudes can also change over time; parents may relax their notion of honour or *izzat* and become more or less ready to accommodate change in the light of their own or others' experiences. Table 2.3 shows the changing pattern among some second-generation Muslim women in Britain. In Table 2.3, I have only included the data of 35 second-generation female respondents plus their fathers' qualifications and work status (Muslim adult immigrants, aged 19 and over).

Table 2.3 Thirty-five fathers' and daughters' educational and employment status

First generation, fathers' occupational status	Second generation, daughters' work status and qualification (19 years and over)
Geologist	Councillor (BA)
2 professionals	2 Medical students
Doctor	Medical student
Pharmacist	Medical student
Engineer, PhD	BA student
Physicist	Medical student
Bus driver (overseas qualification)	Academic (PhD)
4 labourers (one had overseas qualifications)	4 daughters, Medical students
Shopkeeper (overseas qualification)	Community worker (BA)
Supervisor (overseas qualification)	BA student
Travel agent (overseas qualification)	BA student
Postman (overseas qualification)	Unemployed (BA Law)
3 self-employed, no qualification	3 school teachers (BA)
2 factory workers, no qualification	2 social workers (MA)
Factory worker, no qualification	Educationalist (MA)
Tailor, no qualification	Teaching aide (A-levels)
4 self-employed, no qualification	4 BA students
Ill-health, no qualification	BA student
Building contractor, no qualification	Medical student
Builder (retd), no qualification	Private company (A-levels)
Builder (retd), no qualification	Single mother (A-level)
Seaman (retd), no qualification	BA student
Seaman (retd), no qualification	School teacher (BA)
Factory worker, no qualification	Housewife (Chartered Accountant)
Grandfather: labourer; father: factory worker, no qualification	Social worker (MA) [third generation]

Table 2.3 shows the qualifications and employment status of 35 female respondents (20–30 years) compared with that of their fathers: 19 of the female participants were university students; 11 were tertiary-educated working women; 1 was a tertiary-educated housewife; 1 was tertiary-educated but unemployed; 2 were employed with A-level qualifications, and 1 with an A-level pass was an unemployed single mother. Only 7 female respondents' fathers had recognised professional jobs (engineers, doctors) in Britain, and 3 respondents' mothers worked as a therapist, technician and teacher in Britain. One mother had a college degree from back home but had never worked in Britain. All the rest of the 28 fathers belonged to the working class or were self-employed, and all 32 mothers were housewives. Out of 28 working-class fathers, 6 had university degrees (including one

engineering degree) from Bangladesh and Pakistan, but they were not recognised in the UK, so they ended up doing menial jobs. Among 35 females,
four who were of Pakistani heritage were married and three were divorced.
Of the four married women, one participant had a husband who permitted
her to pursue higher education, one was working as an academic, one was
working as a social worker, and another was a professional but quit her job
to look after her children. Of the three divorced women, one was a successful professional woman, one was in the workforce and one was unemployed.
So out of 35 fathers only 13 had university degrees either from back home
or in Britain. This suggests a changing pattern of education among Muslim
women; in most cases, uneducated parents were encouraging their daughters
to pursue higher education, and some daughters were refusing to get married
(further discussion in Chapter 3).

Reasons for high Muslim unemployment

Tables 2.2 and 2.3 reflect the changing pattern of socioeconomic status in
some Muslim families but they are not representative of the overall demographic of Muslim placement in the British labour market. In the context of
Britain, Bowlby and Lloyd-Evans (2009: 38) point out that some researchers
have found differences in employment outcomes between the mainstream
population and the ethnic minorities, where the latter remained disadvantaged.
This difference is sometimes called an 'ethnic penalty'. Several factors lead
to the 'ethnic penalty' or ethnic disadvantage: lack of educational qualifications, age, English-language ability and cultural attributes. Cheng and Heath's
(1993, cited in Bowlby and Lloyd-Evans 2009: 38) survey suggested that in
the 1980s members of the first generation of immigrants were discriminated
against in the labour market because of their skin colour. The Commission for
Racial Equality (CRE 1996) also found evidence of direct discrimination on
the grounds of race and ethnicity.

Between 1995 and 1996, and 1998 and 2001, Bowlby and Lloyd-Evans
(2009: 37–52) conducted research on working-class Pakistani people in the
Borough of Reading and the town of Slough. Both towns are in the M4
corridor west of London, with very low levels of recorded unemployment.
However, Muslims were disadvantaged compared with the mainstream
population (Bowlby and Lloyd-Evans 2009: 39–42). Bowlby and Lloyd-Evans
(2009: 37–52) noted that Muslim disadvantage could be regarded as 'some
form of "Islamic penalty"', and after the 9/11 Twin Towers tragedy it may
have been aggravated.

Peach (2006: 641–2) argued that in 2001, in England and Wales, nearly
40 per cent of the Muslim population had no qualifications. And one-third
of the population was long-term unemployed or in the 'never worked' category. Of those employed, a much lower proportion was in the white-collar

category (higher managerial and professional class). The main reason for this low Muslim participation rate in the formal labour force was the absence of Muslim women in the workforce. The Muslims' poor educational qualifications, lower percentage of those economically active and low-paying jobs led to an unfavourable tenure pattern in housing among the Muslims. Muslims had the lowest proportion of owner occupation and the highest dependence on social housing of all other faith groups. Peach (2006: 652) observed that though the Muslims in Britain (particularly the Pakistanis and Bangladeshis) have a depressed socioeconomic position, socially they are strong. Their social organisations are conservative and family-centred. In their enclave-style living they tend to protect their women and children from Western culture. They emphasise the importance of family honour and *purdah* in the protection of Muslim women. Fear of contamination by the lax morals of British society, such as drunkenness, sexual promiscuity and lack of respect for elders, was strongly felt by the ghettoised Muslim community (Peach 2006: 641–2). Thus for cultural reasons some Muslims (particularly women) preferred to live in isolation, which of course affected the labour market.

Bowlby and Lloyd-Evans (2009: 46) observed that some employers were unhappy with the Pakistanis, who were generalised as Muslims because they took large amounts of leave and returned to Pakistan at short notice or left often to attend religious celebrations, such as Eid. Muslim women were constructed as passive subjects, controlled by men. Some employers were not happy with Muslim women who tended to prioritise their family commitments over their employment. Some employers also perceived Muslims as 'not fitting in' with corporate identities in terms of dress, appearance and styles of communication (Bowlby and Lloyd-Evans 2009: 46).

Young people in general are sometimes perceived by employers to be unreliable workers (Bowlby and Lloyd-Evans 2009: 46; Dench et al. 2006: 130). In the context of employing young people in East London, a restaurant manager said:

> Young people who grow up here are quite reluctant to take those jobs because the conditions are not good money-wise, and the work hours long. And people have a sort of taboo about the boys of Brick Lane, and Tower Hamlet boys. Boys who are growing up here: the restaurant owners are quite reluctant to take them because they would fight; they would end up fighting. And they argue with the customers, and so forth. (Cited in Dench et al. 2006: 130)

On the other hand, there were arguments that the young Muslim people were educated (compared to no qualifications of their first generations), so they considered the restaurant jobs to be a servile occupation with bad hours and low, unreliable pay. The second generation often struggle with the fact that their parents expect them to find white-collar jobs and be 'officers'.

They found such employment hard to get, whereas for the restaurants they appeared over-qualified (Dench et al. 2006: 130). Rehman (2007: 847) observed that among young people aged 16 to 24, Muslims had the highest unemployment rate of all faith groups – 17.7 per cent, as compared to 7.9 per cent Christians and 7.4 per cent Hindus. The overall Muslim unemployment rate was three times higher than the national average. About 50 per cent of these children lived in overcrowded accommodation with a 'home environment of low morale, poor educational achievements, narrow social circles, and generally depressive attitudes'. Rehman (2007: 847) further noted that young Muslims may not be radicalised for living in social deprivation and discrimination, but both repressive parental attitude and alienation from the mainstream society could provide them with a recipe of rebellion or radicalisation.

In my survey, I found that some highly qualified Muslim men were under-employed. For example, an overseas-born scientist with a doctoral degree from the UK was a high school teacher, and a British-born and educated engineer was a social worker. I also found that part-time work was not popular among students (16–24 years). Only eight school students (16–18 years) had part-time employment. Most students appeared to be focused on their studies, though a few were looking for work. Peach (2006) argues that ghettoisation has led to isolation and that has contributed to high Muslim unemployment. However, in my study I found that Muslim people in some economically deprived areas, such as Beeston in Leeds, and Butetown and Grangetown in Cardiff, were marked as the 'Other'. The interviewees (18 years) from these areas said that they could not find jobs outside their 'ghettos', perhaps because they lived in the 'ghettos'.

Regarding Muslim women's high unemployment, in the patriarchal family women have to abide by men's rules, though in some cases women preferred to stay at home and do home duties. A second-generation British-born Muslim girl (age 18) of Pakistani background, Mussaret said she could not convince her mother to go to the gymnasium because she (the mother) prioritised her home duties and did not find time for other things. A second-generation Muslim woman of Pakistani heritage, Monowara, aged 26 (married to a Welshman), worked in a multinational company, but after the birth of her children she left the job. She then embraced an Islamic identity and wore the *hijab*, which she said was her choice, and stayed at home to look after her children. Monowara said:

> I've set up a mother and toddler group in Cardiff. I set it up to encourage Muslim mothers to take their children out to do other things, and I also encourage non-Muslims to come there too. There's a play scheme that's running in Cardiff over the summer for school children to go to every day and I do the tax and the payroll and everything for that. (Interview, Cardiff, 22 October 2008)

However, some 16–18-year-old girls noted that wearing the *hijab* was a barrier in the workplace. They did not wear it because they feared that they would lose their jobs. On the other hand, and here was a dilemma: at school a few *non-hijabi* girls found it difficult to socialise with their Muslim friends who wore the *hijab* because they considered them as the 'Other'. A Somali girl, aged 18, said that if she submitted her CV in the shops while wearing her *hijab* she was told that there was no work, and later if she submitted her CV in the same shop without wearing her *hijab*, they offered her work (further discussions in Chapter 4).

Conclusion

Britain has had contact with the Muslim world for centuries. However, Muslims only began to settle in Britain (in small numbers) from the late nineteenth century; their arrival in large numbers has taken place since the 1960s. Some Muslims have been regarded as 'coloured' immigrants and have faced resistance from some mainstream working-class British people for racial, cultural and economic reasons. The BNP anti-immigration propaganda and 'bullying' has been at the forefront of this resistance. Since the 7/7 London bombings, some Muslims became the 'Other' because the home-grown terrorists (three of them British-born) were of the Islamic faith. However, some mainstream British people have been sympathetic to the Muslim community, distinguishing the terrorists (minority Muslim militants) from the majority peaceful Muslims.

The Mayor of London's report (2006) acknowledged that Muslims in London were relatively disadvantaged compared to other faith groups, and arguably this sector needs attention both from the Muslim community and the wider society. The small samples (Tables 2.2 and 2.3) of this study show that many first-generation Muslim males had poor qualifications and English skills, which impacted on their employment status. The second-generation Muslim males were better educated but some were underemployed. In the case of female employment status, many first-generation Muslim women had no qualifications, and their family structure did not encourage them to pursue education. As for the second-generation Muslim women, many were university-educated or striving to pursue a career. But in some cases, highly educated Muslim women had prioritised their children's upbringing and remained unemployed by choice. The young participants of this study (147 school students, 15–18 years) were more focused on education and only a handful of them had part-time jobs. Sadly, Muslim females faced rejection in the workplace because they wore the *hijab*. For a better future, the Muslim community has to prioritise their children's education and integration with the wider community (in terms of engaging them in charity work, debates and sporting activities). On the other hand, the wider society needs to recognise and encourage the minority's achievements.

Notes

1. The 2001 Census data has been accumulated from several sources: Office for National Statistics 2001 and 2004; Forsyth and Gardener (2006), 'Geographic diversity'; Mayor of London (2006) *Muslims in London*; and City of Bradford Metropolitan District Council (2001), 'The Ethnic Mix'.
2. Banglatown (synonymous with Chinatown) was coined in recognition of the large Bangladeshi community living in and around Brick Lane (London, E1).
3. The Bengali Language Movement, also known as the Language Movement (*Bhasha Andolon*), was a political effort in Bangladesh (then known as East Pakistan) advocating the recognition of the Bengali language as an official language of Pakistan. Such recognition would allow Bengali to be taught in schools and used in government affairs.

   On 21 February 1952, the students of the University of Dhaka, Bangladesh and other political activists organised a protest. The movement reached its climax when police killed student demonstrators on that day. The Language Movement catalysed the assertion of Bengali national identity in Pakistan, and became a forerunner to Bengali nationalist movements, including the later 6-point movement and subsequently the Bangladesh Liberation War in 1971. In Bangladesh, 21 February is observed as Language Movement Day, a national holiday. The *Shaheed Minar* monument was constructed in Dhaka, Bangladesh in memory of the movement and its victims. A similar *Shaheed Minar* monument was erected by the Bangladeshis in East London for the commemoration of the martyrs.
4. The 2001 Unemployment rate: based on the ILO definition as a percentage of all those economically active. Economic inactivity rates are expressed as a proportion of the working-age population (men aged 16 to 64, women aged 16 to 59). Source: Office for National Statistics, 2004.
5. In Tables 2.2 and 2.3, 147 school students (including one dropout) aged 15 to 18 were not included. Though most of their parents belonged to the working class, the students expressed their desire to go to university, so a changing pattern was revealed through that data. I have also left out nine overseas-born first-generation Muslim leaders and three British converts because they don't fit in the comparative analysis.

THE RELIGIOUS AND CULTURAL DILEMMA

Identity is always 'in process', always 'being formed' (Hall 1994: 122), and I argue that it is influenced by the surroundings in which people live. The surroundings are influenced by internal and external factors. The internal factors are family and ethnic and religious community settings. External factors are schools, workplaces and institutions, including government, in the wider community. The focus in this chapter is on how young British Muslims' identity shapes up through internal factors: family, ethnic and religious community. A Muslim male scholar in Britain, Shaykh Mogra, identified two issues that have generally confronted Muslim women in Britain. First, women have not been encouraged to pursue higher education; and second, women have faced restrictions in some mosques. Shaykh Mogra gave examples of his family members:

> If I look back at many of my female cousins in Britain of my generation, none of them actually have any proper GCSEs which, you know, is the basic educational achievement in our country. At the age of 16 you should have English, maths, science at least; they don't have any of that and when I look back and think why this was the case, they were not encouraged to be in the state school and there was preaching that suggested that if they go to state schools they would be corrupted, etc. (Interview, Leicester, 14 April 2008)

Regarding women's treatment by some mosques, the Muslim scholar pointed out:

> Women are not allowed to come to some mosques because they might be a *fitna* or some misbehaviour which I find very difficult to accept . . . There are two projects that are going in our city which, I could say multi-million pound projects to build,

renovate mosques. And I'm sorry to say that both these premises will not allow women to attend the prayers. (Interview, Leicester, 14 April 2008)

No doubt Muslim women face more cultural restrictions than just these two, but some young Muslim men also remarked that they are constrained by the boundaries of their ethnic culture. Sometimes, cultural limits are endorsed willingly by young Muslims and sometimes they are met with resistance. In some cases, young people confront 'enforced religiosity'. In this chapter I examine the placement of young British Muslims, both men and women, within the framework of their religion and culture. First, I discuss the broader context of Islam. Second, I discuss Muslim women's issues in two sections: mosque restrictions and how they impact on Muslim women; and Muslim women's marriage dilemma. Third, I discuss youth issues in three categories: literacy and numeracy issues; cultural issues and drugs; and music in Islam.

Islam in Britain

The religious affiliations of my interviewees in this study were as follows: Sunni 206 (including 10 Deobandi, 1 Barelvi, 1 Salafi, 1 Sufi); Shia 6; and Ahmadiyya (offshoot of Islam) 4. Of the 206 Sunni Muslims, most respondents said that they belonged to the Hanafi school of thought (which is explained below), though one said that he was from the Maliki school of thought. Some did not know the concept 'school of thought'. They just said that they were Sunni.

The word *Sunni* in Arabic comes from the term *ahl al-sunnah wa'l-jama'ah*, that is, people who followed the *sunnah* of Prophet Muhammad [PBUH] and worldwide they are in the majority. Shi'ism comes from the Arabic term *shi'at 'Ali*, meaning partisans of Prophet Ali, ibn Abi Talib, son-in-law and cousin of Prophet Muhammad [PBUH].

The major point of contention between Sunnism and Shi'ism is who should succeed the Prophet Muhammad [PBUH] as the 'rightly guided' caliph of Islam (Nasr 2002: 65–6). After the death of Prophet Muhammad [PBUH], while Ali and other family members were burying him, the rest of the Muslim community gathered in Medina and chose Abu Bakr as the Prophet's successor, not in his prophetic function but as ruler of the newly established Islamic community. He was thereby given the title of *khalifah rasul Allah*, or the vice-regent or the Messenger of God, from which comes the title caliph. A number of people thought that Ali should become Prophet Muhammad's [PBUH] successor and rallied around him, forming the first nucleus of Shi'ism (or Shi'ites). Ali himself refused to oppose Abu Bakr and in fact worked closely with Abu Bakr and his two successors, Umar and Uthman, until he himself became the fourth of the 'rightly guided' caliphs of Sunni Islam (Nasr 2002: 65–6).

The followers of Sunnism are divided into four schools of law (*fiqh*, or jurisprudence): Hanafi, Maliki, Shafi'i and Hanbali. Today the Hanafi school has the largest number of followers in the Sunni world. Malikism is based mostly on the practice of Medina and is very conservative in its approach to the *fiqh* (Nasr 2002: 68). The Shafi'i school is followed by some Arabs, particularly the Egyptians (Nasr 2002: 69). The Hanbali school provides a very strict interpretation of the *shariah*. Wahhabism, which is dominant in Saudi Arabia and is really an offshoot of Hanbalism, is very much opposed by the vast majority of Sunnis and also Shi'ites (Nasr 2002: 70).

The Shi'ites follow all the four Sunni schools of law and they have one additional school of law called the Ja'fari (al-Qazwini 2000: 4–9). The difference between the Sunni school of law and the Ja'fari is minor, especially when it comes to the practise of rites (five pillars of Islam). In certain fields, such as the laws of inheritance or the legality of temporary marriage, there are, however, notable differences (Nasr 2002: 70–2).

There are three separate theological schools of thought among the Sunni Muslims in the Indian subcontinent: Deobandis, Barelvis and Tablighi Jamaat, and they are mostly Hanafi-Sunnis. The other two theological schools of thought within Sunni Islam are the Wahhabis and Salafis, which are most prevalent in the Middle East.

The Deobandi movement is named after the city of Deoband in India, where founder *Hajji* Mohammad Abid established his *Darul Uloom* (knowledge centre) in 1866. It is primarily concerned with the teaching and transmission of Islam through the creation of its Quranic schools. Whereas the Deobandis insist on an extensive knowledge of *hadith*, they reject Sufi practices and saints as an innovation (*bida'ah*). The Taliban in Afghanistan took the Deobandi as their inspiration (Cesari 2004: 93). The Barelvis, founded in India by Ahmed Raza (1856–1921), also emphasise the figure of the Prophet and believe that the souls of the Prophet and saints act as mediators between believers and God (Cesari 2004: 93). Commenting on the difference between the Deobandi and Barelvi, a Muslim scholar in Britain, Sharfaraz (male, British-born of Bangladeshi background, aged 40) noted:

> Mostly it will be the Barelvis who will be very supportive of celebrating *Eid-e-Milad-un Nabi* [the birthday of Prophet Muhammad, PBUH]. The Deobandis are a little bit hesitant of that because some of them see this as a *bida'ah* [un-Islamic] to perform such action; they see it as an innovation, that something; they say that the Prophet didn't do this in his own lifetime and we have to very strictly adhere to what the Prophet did and not bring new things into the religion. (Interview, Leicester, 12 April 2008)

Another group that takes a traditionalist and legalistic approach to Islam is the Tablighi Jammat, a subsect within the larger Deobandi movement. The

Tabligh movement was founded in 1927 by Maulana Illyas in India. It is usually described as a pietist and apolitical movement, whose primary aim is to strengthen Muslim orthodoxy. The Tablighis generally approach Muslims in their door-to-door mission and advise them to practise Islam. Tablighi Jamaat has millions of followers worldwide; it claims to be a peaceful, apolitical revivalist movement that promotes Islamic consciousness among individual Muslims. The adherents of this group run more than 600 of Britain's 1,350 mosques (*The Times*, 10 September 2007: 32).

In contrast to the traditionalist branches of Islam, the Wahhabis and Salafis reject the importance of juridical schools and advocate a direct relation to the revealed Text of the Quran. The Salafi puritanical line of thought prevails in the Arabian peninsula, and also in Syria, Jordan and Egypt. The main difference between Salafi Islam and Wahhabi Islam is the difference in audience (Cesari 2004: 95). Also, the Salafis hold certain opinions on the issue of visiting graves. They believe that Prophet Muhammad [PBUH] encouraged his companions to visit graveyards, because it is something that can remind Muslims of death and make them think about preparing for it by doing good deeds. However, the Salafis believe that Prophet Muhammad [PBUH] gave stern warnings about not falling into excess in this regard, because the end result of this is to associate dead persons with Allah and that is what negates one's Islam (Oliver 2004: 62). The Wahhabis and Salafis also denounce the celebration of *Eid-e-Milad-un Nabi*, and Sufism.

Sufism is a mystical movement that preaches tolerance and incorporates the commonality between all religions through poetry, lyrics, music, songs and chanting of many different kinds and in many different dialects. The Sufi sect have a group and also a method which allows an individual to join or leave a group at will, sometimes even without the requirement to be Muslim (Cesari 2004: 51; Kabbani 2007: 24–5). Of course, Sufism differs from the conservative Wahhabi and Salafi ideologies. Sufi Muslims believe that by nature Islam is a religion open to people of every race. The Sufi saint Bayazid al-Bistami said, 'Sufis, in general, seek God's mercy for everyone, not solely Muslims' (cited in Kabbani 2007: 23).

In this study, four interviewees identified themselves as Ahmadiyya Muslims. However, mainstream Muslim leaders do not consider the Ahmadiyyas to be Muslims. The Ahmadiyyas believe in the five pillars of Islam, but their central belief is that their founder, Mirza Ghulam Ahmad, is the Promised Messiah and *Mahdi* (Guided One) (Chaudhry 1996), which is deeply refuted by mainstream Muslims. As a researcher, I have incorporated their views into my study. However, I consider them to be an offshoot of Islam. In this study, some mainstream Muslim interviewees have expressed their views on the mosque culture in Britain. I have noted their views as they impacted on Muslim women, as discussed next.

Focus on Muslim women

Mosque restrictions and women

The majority of the mosque imams across Britain have no public or civic role (Lewis 2007: 103). The mosque committee members bring imams from back home and pay them with the understanding that they will perform the basic duties, such as give *Azan* (call for prayers), pray, give sermons, whisper the *Azan* into a child's ear after birth, perform *nikah* (solemnise marriage contracts), prepare the dead for burial, and deal with issues put before them by the committee members. It is expected that the imams will not say anything that would hamper the interests of the committee members (Lewis 2007: 104). Regarding the authority of the mosque committee members, a male youth worker in Leeds, Sobhan (British-born of Indian background, aged 27), commented:

> If you try and question the mosque committee, they say, 'We're doing this for the community.' But you're saying, 'Have you asked the community what they want?' They'll be saying, 'We don't need to ask them, we are the community.' It's a very negative backward sort of habit. (Interview, Leeds, 6 October 2008)

Sobhan commented further that there were two mosques in his neighbourhood: one allowed women, and the other did not. Sobhan comments, 'I'm not sure how the women themselves feel like going to a mosque or not. Because of the way they're brought up . . . so I'm not sure if it's a big issue' (Interview, Leeds, 6 October 2008).

Sobhan noted that back home (in the Indian subcontinent) Muslim women were brought up to pray at home and the mosques' prayers were reserved for men. This was the case when I (the author) was brought up in Bangladesh and Pakistan (then West Pakistan): I never saw my mother or my grandmothers or other female members of my extended family attend the mosques for prayers. Even when I lived in the Middle East, I observed that Muslim women prayed at home and the male members of the family attended mosques. Only in the Muslim holy places of Mecca and Medina, I saw both male and female Muslims gathered from all over the world praying in the mosques, for example *Masjid-i-Haram* in Mecca where the Holy *Ka'bah* is situated, or *Masjid Nabawi,* the Prophet's mosque in Medina. Although, it should be noted that in *Masjid Nabawi* women prayed in a separate section. I assume some Muslim women residing in the West like to attend mosques because a mosque congregation reinforces their Islamic identity, which they might feel is threatened in the Western world. Some Muslim women also live in a diaspora and have very lonely lives. In that case a mosque could be a focal point for Muslim women to socialise and discuss certain issues and seek advice from other women. In Cardiff, a female respondent of this study commented:

> Some mothers are very depressed because they live in a closed environment, you know, do same sort of work, they don't have exposure and, at the end of the day, they are tired. Yeah, they have many children to look after. I think the major problem is language. That's a barrier because you find a lot of them come from their native countries and they can't speak English as well. Say, for example, the Iraqi or Syrian women group; they can get together in a mosque. (Interview, Cardiff, 22 October 2008)

The respondent spoke from her first-hand experience because her mother suffered from solitude and depression. She thought women with English-language barriers needed some sort of social gathering within their ethnic community and a mosque could be a place where, after prayers, women have a chance to socialise with their ethnic female counterparts. Another interviewee noted that it could also be a place where after prayers young Muslim girls would discuss their teenage or cultural issues with other women – the issues they may be afraid to discuss with their parents (Interview, Leicester, 14 April 2008). In Leicester, a British-born woman of Pakistani background, Mariyam, aged 24, said that she belonged to the Deobandi group, but she was not allowed to attend the Deobandi mosque, so she attended the Barelvi mosque:

> I actually go to a Barelvi mosque even though I'm not Barelvi and the reason for that is that [it] is like a Sufi-type mosque. Even though I don't follow the Barelvi prac-tice; I don't do *milads* [chanting religious songs in praise of Prophet Muhammad, PBUH] . . . But the Pakistani Barelvi mosques all allow women to attend. (Interview, Leicester, 12 April 2008)

Mashroof, a male respondent in Leicester, who defined himself as a Deobandi, was critical of the traditional Deobandi attitudes towards Muslim women. Mashroof observed that the Deobandi school generally was very con-servative and had 'chauvinistic attitudes' towards women that needed to be challenged and addressed by the Muslim community. The Deobandis did not see that women had a public role to play in the community. Women were per-ceived to be private people whose role was that of motherhood, which was to be played inside the house. Mashroof said that though the Deobandis believed in education for women, as they have set up primary schools for girls in Britain, they think that the education to be achieved should be limited. The real role for women is at home nurturing children and not in the public domain. So when it came to giving space to women in the mosques, the Deobandis argued, 'We don't have enough space for women', which Mashroof thought 'a bit of a nonsensical argument' (Interview, Leicester, 11 April 2008).

Mashroof noted that women sometimes donated their jewellery and savings, just as much as men did. But ultimately, when it came to benefiting from these services, women did not get any direct benefit. Mashroof noted that the mosque committee in Leicester has introduced a system of broadcasting services in most of the mosques, so that in their homes women are able to buy radio receivers, and listen to the *Azan*, sermons and the speeches. Mashroof said:

> Personally I have mixed feelings about this because on the one hand, this is spreading education and it is making education available. But my concern is that it is really supporting the status quo and it is in a way keeping women in the home rather than changing their position, which I think is what we need to really try to do. (Interview, Leicester, 11 April 2008)

Though a Deobandi himself, Mashroof was a minority voice within the Deobandi group. Mashroof did not hold a position in the mosque committee, so his views remained unheard. Mashroof was self-critical and justified the media's intervention:

> Yeah people are picking up on it, even the media is learning about it now slowly. My position is that we cannot afford to hide these things. If we think these things are problems in the Muslim community, we have to talk about them and we have to address them. You know there is no point in us pretending that everything is perfect. (Interview, Leicester, 11 April 2008)

Grievances against the mosques were not only confined to Leicester, Leeds and Cardiff. In London, the British-born male Muslim student Shiraj, aged 18, was involved with his family in mosque affairs. Shiraj noted:

> Maybe 90 per cent of Mosques in Britain don't allow women. So whereas if you look in Tooting, you know, one or two of the mosques allow women. The thing is, in the Quran it says to have, you know, equality. Now there are a few lobby groups who have got them to make some space. Then one mosque will make a little room with about ten people and say, 'This is for women.' [Then I thought] 'There is like half the population in Tooting is Muslim women, so how can you have ten people?' Basically you need to change the mosque leaders . . . because you get people from villages running the mosque and they have no idea how to run a mosque. (Interview, London, 18 April 2008)

Muslim women's marriage dilemma

Some scholars (Jacobson 1998; Hall 2005; Shaw 2000; Cressey 2006; Dwyer and Shah 2009) have noted that Muslim women in Britain are confined by the shackles of patriarchy. Pakistan and Kashmir are explicitly gendered societies, and Pakistani and Kashmiri cultures are a particular form of the patriarchal system. Society in that context is clearly divided along gender lines regarding roles and expectations (Jacobson 1998; Cressey 2006; Shaw 2000). In the context of young British Pakistani Muslim women, some authors (Jacobson 1998: 90–1; Shaw 2000: 166; Cressey 2006) have found that for the first generation of Pakistanis in Britain, the tradition of marrying within the caste group or, more precisely, within the kinship group or *biraderi* group, has acted to preserve their community feeling. However, the younger second and third generations have been critical of such marriage arrangements. Many younger people disapproved of marriage between cousins because they considered them to be like their brother or sister (Jacobson 1998: 93). However, some girls did not object to arranged marriage and considered it to be their traditional norm (Cressey 2006: 153). Similarly, in the context of the Bangladeshis in Britain, arranged marriages (with kin or outside kinship) are considered a matter of pride by the first generation. For example, Mr Mukim, of Bangladeshi background (cited in Dench et al. 2006: 95), stated:

In Bangladesh, as well as in Britain, girls and boys are refusing to allow parents to select their marriage partners. According to our religion this is OK. But it is affecting us as a community, as a society. Traditionally we hold high respect for our elders. And that is the way of showing respect, by trusting their choice . . .

Five girls of Bangladeshi background said that they would be happy with an arranged marriage because it successfully worked out with their family members. Sheba, a 16-year-old British-born girl of Bangladeshi background, commented:

It's one of the most successful marriages you can get. Love marriages don't work. Because it's in our culture and religion . . . Tell the media that we are not oppressed. (Interview, London, 27 March 2008)

With regard to arranged marriage, some families in this study have embraced changes for at least one of their daughters. For example, British-born woman Alizah of Pakistani heritage, aged 28, said that all her brothers and sisters were married, but she wanted to pursue higher education and a career, and her working-class parents gave way to her wishes:

All of them [my sisters] yeah, all of them got married in Pakistan and I'm the only one that is left! I am the first highly educated one as well in my family. To be honest I think from a very young age when you're exposed to British culture, whether that's the television or teachers at school, or other people, you just learn to live with what's around you. It's not something that you question in a big way, you just get on with it, you negotiate those identities. Because my father was used to see me wearing *shalwar-kameez* [trouser-shirt], and all of sudden I wanted to wear skirts. And it was interesting because for the first time my father was almost learning to listen and thinking, 'Wait a second, if my daughter is asserting this identity which means that it's made her a better person, then actually this isn't a major issue. Then why am I feeling so threatened?' My father was compromising with me though all my sisters were taken to Pakistan for marriage. (Interview, Bradford, 24 August 2008)

In the following section I describe the marriages of two women and note the changing patterns in families.

Changing patterns: Case One

The British-born woman of Pakistani heritage Noori, aged 28, provided a fascinating story of her childhood, marriage and education. At the time of interview, she had a postgraduate degree from a prestigious university in Britain, and had a professional career. Noori's parents were from Pakistan, and her father came to Britain at an early age to work in the factories in the 1960s. Both her parents were uneducated. Noori was brought up at a time when Pakistani girls in Britain got married at the age of 14 and by the age of 16 they became mothers. Noori was caught up in that trend – girls would marry early. Noori said:

I dropped out of school at the age of, was it 10 or 11? And I disappeared sort of, yeah. Well, my parents said, 'Now your time's coming', which is what everybody else in the community used to do: their daughters just used to disappear, so either they said they'd gone to Pakistan or they actually sent them to Pakistan for a number of years. Until they could come back as adults then they weren't forced to have an education. They have done it with my older sister . . . who is now a professional woman [who pursued her career later].

Noori recalled that some members of the wider society, such as her teachers and youth workers, were aware of this cultural trend in the Pakistani families:

My teacher noticed this in our community and she kept saying to my parents, 'Look, whatever you do, your daughter's too clever. You can't allow her to miss.' And she kept saying it to them and emphasising it and then my parents started having this moral conflict, that if we allow her to have an education, what's the older one done wrong that she can't have an education? And they ended up, it . . . the straw that broke the camel's back was actually one of my brothers got ill or something and the liaison officer came to our house to find out why he wasn't at school. I opened the door unbeknown to me and she said, 'What are you doing here?', and I said, 'Oh I wasn't well or something', and made up an excuse. But she realised that something wasn't quite right so she went and did the checks and I was kind of an unknown for a number of years. And that's how I got forced back into going into education. (Interview, Bradford, 30 August 2008)

Noori said that her parents felt relieved because deep down inside they wanted to offer education to their daughters, but under community pressure they had to lock their daughters at home and prepare them to get married at an early age. Noori said that there was not much restriction on the boys as:

Young boys are not the same because remember in our societies or communities the shame is carried by the girl. So if the guys create problems he doesn't disrespect the name in the same way as the girl does. It is the *izzat* or honour the girls carry in the community [so she has to abide by the family/community's rule regarding marriage, etc.]. (Interview, Bradford, 30 August 2008)

Later, according to the family's custom, Noori was taken to Pakistan and was married at the age of 20. Noori and her husband both returned to Britain; however, the marriage ended in a divorce. Later, Noori finished her higher education and was happy with her successful career.

Changing patterns: Case Two

The British-born woman of Pakistani heritage Monowara, aged 26, was married to a Welshman. She discussed her family history and the objections she received from her father regarding her marriage. She recalled that her parents were from a remote village in Pakistan. Her father came from Pakistan at a young age as a labourer and he worked in the factories in London. Neither of her parents has been educated. Her father wanted her to marry his brother's sons, his nephews, who lived in Pakistan. Monowara said:

If I hadn't have met my husband I would have been happy to meet people by an arranged marriage and see, but it just so happened that I met my husband and I was happy to marry him. But my father was originally upset because how would he face his brother, how could he say, 'No' to his brother? (Interview, Cardiff, 22 October 2008)

Monowara continued:

It gave my father a big shock and he wasn't happy. He said he was happy that I would marry a Muslim but everyone would talk and it was more for other people, the community. What would the community think that I was marrying a white man? So then it took my father a year of people persuading him, and then after a year my dad allowed us to get married. We didn't have a big wedding. We had a *nikah* [solemnised marriage contract] at the house. My mother was very happy. But my mother was very happy that he was a practising Muslim, which is all she wanted for her daughter. (Interview, Cardiff, 22 October 2008)

Regarding rejection from the community, Monowara recalled:

We had a lot of difficulties with family because when an Asian girl gets married, after she gets married, everyone invites the bride and the groom over for dinner. Nobody invited us over, nobody wanted us to come to their house because what would I encourage their children to do? (Interview, Cardiff, 22 October 2008)

Monowara said that after the birth of her children her father was back to normal and loved her children. Later, Monowara quit her job, wore the *hijab* by choice, and became a devout Muslim. Monowara wanted her children to be the same:

I was brought up culturally Muslim as opposed to Islamically Muslim. I want my children to grow up strong in their belief that they know why they believe in Allah; they know what they are. My parents would tell us to go and pray upstairs; we would go and pray but we wouldn't really pray. We didn't quite understand Islam. I want my kids to question everything, to know that everything that they do is impor- tant to *sunnah* [Prophet Muhammad's, PBUH, deed]. I just want them to be happy Muslims, you know, good happy Muslims and, you know, go to *jannat* [heaven], *Inshallah* [God willing]. (Interview, Cardiff, 22 October 2008)

In Monowara's case, changes had not only occurred with her father over time; she herself chose to embrace an Islamic identity and be a home-maker.

Uncertain future

There were two trends among the young Bangladeshi and Pakistani Muslim girls in this study. One trend was arranged marriage at an early age (and in some cases the marriage ended in divorce), and the second trend was that the young woman stayed single until later in life. Three female respondents of Pakistani heritage in Britain were of the opinion that one of the reasons why Pakistani women in Britain remained single until later was that they were highly educated compared to their male counterparts, so they were reluctant to marry the less-educated males (see also Dwyer and Shah 2009: 67). For example, the tertiary student Mehnaz (British-born of Pakistani heritage, aged 23) said, 'There's loads of Pakistani girls at 30 or 31 or 32 . . . still unmarried.' But generally marriage by choice was not preferred by the elders. As Mehnaz said:

To be honest, there are lots of Pakistanis here, they haven't gone out their house, and they are very stuck in their old ways. For example, my cousin she had a love marriage to another Pakistani boy. There was no problem because he was Pakistani, but still his parents disagreed because they were from, you know, back home . . . same caste, the problem was his parents, both his parents were uneducated. (Interview, Cardiff, 17 October 2008)

On the other hand, through arranged marriages, the woman could foresee an uncertain future. When I asked Saleema, a British-born girl of Bangladeshi origin, aged 16, about her hopes, she replied:

Obviously, study, do my A-Levels and mum she's arranging for me to get married. I have to do it, take a gap year and go to university and get, I'm hoping for a law degree. After that, study more, get a job and hopefully I want to become a lawyer. (Interview, London, 4 April 2008)

Nadeen, a 17-year-old British-born girl of Pakistani origin, also expressed her concern that once she gets married she may not be able to achieve a career:

Well if I wasn't going to be getting married I would want to study, you know be something big like, I don't know, get my degree in journalism – I was quite interested in that. But now, because I'm getting married, that just seems like the main thing for me. So I just want to get some kind of degree; it doesn't have to be something big and then just get married and yes. (Interview, London, 19 April 2008)

Nadeen also mentioned that her fiancé had less education. Her in-laws were self-employed and had a good business in Britain, so they may not encourage her to obtain higher education. Nadeen's father was retired. Her mother was in favour of Nadeen's higher education, but she was also concerned (as Nadeen said) that she (the mother) may not get a better son-in-law, so she wanted Nadeen to get married and later pursue her career.

A British-born woman of Pakistani heritage, Nazarat, 27 years, said that she got married to her uncle's son at the age of 18 (after her A-levels). Nazarat found her husband to be abusive and the marriage ended in a divorce. Nazarat said:

I'd always, you know, thought, 'Oh I could be a lawyer, I'll do this or something.' But it's just once I got married then, I don't think I was mature enough to realise that I'd need to build a future for myself and to look forward to that life of . . . you do need that piece of independence, to be a strong woman, you know, or just an individual woman or man. But at that point it had just happened; it was easy to go with the flow. (Interview, Cardiff, 26 October 2008)

Nazarat continued:

> Once I got married my aim was just to keep my husband happy, you know? But the
> thing is he was in like a religion of his own, that his Islam was different; he was like
> abusive, had a lot of problems towards me and the children as well, so in a way that's
> what turned me so against him. Because to me he was a Pakistani . . . I don't identify
> myself as Pakistani. Even to the extent, I was saying to my family a few days ago, for
> the past two years I didn't speak Urdu to my children and now they've lost speaking
> Urdu. (Interview, Cardiff, 26 October 2008)

Nazarat also spoke of her contribution towards her husband's visa:

> I used to work in the shop across the road for work experience and then the only
> other time I worked was when I had to apply for my husband's visa . . . and because
> I was still studying [in high school] I had to fit work around there. So I used to go
> at 5 o'clock in the morning to University for cleaning and then I'd finish by then,
> come home, get ready for school, go to school and then on separate evenings I would
> work at a take-away bar on Fridays and Saturdays until 3 o'clock in the morning,
> just work enough to get the payslips . . . You know for the visa of my husband.
> (Interview, Cardiff, 26 October 2008)

At the time of her interview Nazarat defined her identity as a Welsh Muslim;
she was still recovering from her divorce and was uncertain of her future. On
the other hand, the British-born woman of Pakistani origin Mussaret, 18 years,
working in Leeds, said that she had married her cousin in Pakistan which was
'a love marriage'. Her husband did not have a proper education but was self-
employed in Pakistan. Mussaret defined her identity as, 'I'd classify myself
as British Muslim, cos if you're Pakistani, that means you're from Pakistan.'
Mussaret also liked fish and chips and other 'fast foods', and she could not live
only on *roti salan* (Pakistani bread and curry) all the time. However, she was
concerned that she may have to live in Pakistan because her husband may not
be allowed into Britain as he may not pass the new citizenship test (Interview,
Leeds, 15 October 2008).

There is often a stigma attached to the Mirpuri people as rural and back-
ward (see also Jacobson 1998; Shaw 2006). As Mariyam, a female respondent
of this study, said:

> I think, generally there is prejudice from the Pakistani community about the Mirpuri
> community. My family would prefer me not to marry a Mirpuri. They're very rural
> in terms of education . . . I mean most of the Mirpuri people that we know . . . they've
> either been forced to marry their cousins or majority of them have been forced to
> marry people from Pakistan which has ended up in divorce. We come from the
> Punjab. Like Lahore is very quite you know progressive, you know my parents aren't

educated to university level, but they have basic education. (Interview, Leicester, 10 April 2008)

Like most interviewees' fathers, Mariyam's father migrated to Britain at the age of 15 to work in the factories. Her mother, however, has a college degree from Pakistan. Among the interviewees discussed in this section, only one woman had a Mirpuri background and the rest were from other parts of Pakistan, such as Liaqatabad, Jhelum, Lahore and so on. Shaw (2000: 137) noted that marriage with kin was not exclusively a Pakistani practice. Parts of the Middle East and North Africa also have this practice. Shaw (2006: 137) noted that marrying kinsfolk meant that the living standards and personalities of the groom's immediate family were known beforehand. Presumably, it would minimise their daughter's trauma of separation from her parents and the transition would be smoother (Shaw 2000: 137). However, some of these marriages ended in divorce.

Though most of the arranged marriages of British-Pakistani women (living in Britain) with Pakistani-born men (living in Pakistan) have been successful, there is a general fear among some British-Pakistani women that their marriages won't last long. Charsley (2009: 141) noted some marriages in Bristol ended in divorce once the husbands who came from Pakistan gained their 'permanent right to remain in Britain' or got 'their British passport'. In some cases, the women feared that once their husband's position in Britain was secured, he would contract a second marriage in Pakistan. So then there is a possibility that the wives and children would be deserted when the husband imports another wife. As discussed earlier, Nazarat's case appears to be similar to Charsley's (2009: 141) observation. Though Charsley's (2009) research findings were on Muslim women in Bristol, the plight of some women has been similar elsewhere in Britain, for example Nazarat's case in Cardiff.

Focus on Muslim youth

Literacy and numeracy issues

Some Muslims were not happy with particular mosques because they failed to perform a civic role within the Muslim community. For example, in Leeds the youth worker Moustafa (British-born of Pakistani background, aged 27) believed that a mosque needed to play an active role for its young members:

And it's [Mosque activities] not just for teaching Quran and Urdu, it should be, you know, for other activities. Why can't they teach English and Maths . . . who are not doing very well at school and so forth? Their parents might not have the income or the capacity to be able to send them, you know, to private tutorial or whatever really. For example, my workers and I have offered the mosque that we will go there and

provide free study support sessions for the young people and they've refused it . . .
So there is a real problem of leadership amongst the Muslim community. (Interview,
Leeds, 10 September 2008)

Moustafa observed that mosques could be an appropriate venue to teach
Muslim youths who had low literacy and numeracy skills. Werbner (2002:
178) observed that mosques in Britain were supported by Pakistani factory
workers, small shopkeepers, market traders, petty manufacturers, artisans,
professionals and businessmen. The supporters were all men 'with a sense of
individual pride, a measure of personal autonomy who hold strong ideas about
the rights due to them as citizens and productive workers. They are not to be
pushed around' (Werbner 2002: 178). In other words, the mosque committee
and the majority of men who influenced the committee were holding on to
their traditional guidelines, and were unwilling to move with the contemporary needs and stretch them out to the needs of Muslim youths.

A study titled 'Thwarted Dreams: Young Views for Bradford', based on
the interviews of 300 young people (both boys and girls) from 14 to 18 years,
a large majority of whom were from the South Asian Muslim communities,
revealed the vulnerability of Muslim youths within the Muslim community.
Most of these young people's parents were from rural Pakistan (Lewis 2007:
40). In comparison with the national data, which focused on young people
of similar socioeconomic backgrounds, only 11 per cent of the local sample
(compared to 34 per cent nationally) showed a high level of 'life skills'. These
are skills deemed essential to make the transition to adult life, such as handling money, eating well, dealing with stress, applying for work, making good
relationships and knowing how to find services for young people. Thirty-eight
per cent (three times the national figure) said that their families needed them
at home, which influenced their decision either to drop out of education or
to choose to study near home (Lewis 2007: 40). Furthermore, many young
Muslims did not have sufficient communication skills. One of the reasons was
that after school they did not have time to play, or socialise with their friends.
They were sent to *madrasah* – mosque school – for a couple of hours to receive
Islamic teachings, and then they returned home, did their homework and went
to bed (Lewis 2007: 41).

Cultural issues and drugs

Certain societal issues also confronted young Muslim men. For example,
some parents took their children out of school and sent them back home
to Bangladesh or Pakistan to give their children a cultural education. In the
process, their children fell behind in the British educational system. One
British-born male respondent of this study, Hakem aged 27, who identified
himself as a British-Pakistani Muslim, said:

My brother wasn't attending to his studies, was going off the rails as it were, keeping bad company and it was seen if I wasn't sent to Pakistan, that I may follow my brother's path as a role model. Whilst I was at my high school I went to Pakistan for two years. I learned Urdu there, I did the usual subjects, and the standard of English wasn't very good. I'd missed a substantial amount of my education. So after my return to Britain I had to work very hard in a short period of time to scrape together two Bs and three Cs, I didn't pass English language the first time. I had to retake that afterwards. And when I took a test when I came back from Pakistan they told me, 'Your level of English is exactly where you left it.' (Interview, Bradford, 26 August 2008)

Hakem continued:

I used to have a lot of complaints about them sending me to Pakistan. With what I'm looking at now, I will consider whether I need to send my son in a number of years. Whenever it is, we'll see when the time comes, if he should live with his grandparents to get some sort of understanding of his culture. (Interview, Bradford, 26 August 2008)

Hakem appeared to be constantly negotiating with his identity. His British identity revealed his concern about his English-language skills, whereas the cultural factor justified his stay in Pakistan. Hakem was not happy about going back home to learn Pakistani culture while missing school in Britain and falling behind in English. Hakem now appreciated his parents and thought of sending his son back home at some stage because he was concerned about the 'social ills' persisting in Britain:

Now when you look at our youngsters in this country, drink, alcohol, drugs, what do they call it, sexual promiscu-ation or something [promiscuity] whatever the word is, I don't know what the word is right – sleeping around essentially right. Sexual education in this country starts at a very young age, they are now talking about introducing it at primary age. (Interview, Bradford, 26 August 2008)

In her book *Kinship and Continuity: Pakistani Families in Britain,* Shaw (2006: 167) notes that for many Pakistanis across the generations the experience of living in Britain has reinforced aspects of the traditional view of relationships between men and women. This is because images of women in the West provide constant reminders of the contrasting Islamic ideals. Some Muslims hold the stereotypical notion that Western women 'break all rules of *purdah* and are regarded as sexually promiscuous, moving freely from one man to another, behaving and dressing in order to provoke men' (Shaw 2006: 167). Hakem's interview also revealed the opinion that certain practices, such as alcohol and drug taking, were associated with Western behaviour, so he was thinking of moving his child back home for a few years. However, my observation is that alcohol and drugs should not be exclusively regarded as Western practices, because there are a lot of drug issues in Bangladesh (my country of origin) and Pakistan (see Lewis 2007: 49–50). In the Middle East I have seen some Arab Muslim men who wore the traditional *jilbab* (long dress) but who also drank alcohol.

The British youth worker of Pakistani heritage Akhtar, noted that some Pakistani Muslim parents send their drug-addicted children back home to their 'so-called village rehab'. Parents believed that their village offered a secure environment away from the influence of drugs, but, according to Akhtar, in most cases the village rehabilitation seldom works (Lewis 2007: 49–50). The village rehabs do not have enough money for medical treatment, and therefore fail to provide proper treatment to their patients. The youth worker Akhtar observed that the Pakistani community in Britain is divided into *biradaris* – a system of ancient clans, which give families their identity, code of behaviour and support network. Akhtar points out that using *biradari* as a resource is for many people an obligation to respect '*biradari*-ism', but that this holds the communities back. '*Biradari*-ism' promotes 'honour', emphasising that 'our clan is better than the other clan'. So when there is a drug issue in one's clan, they need to send their drug-addicted sons back home to hide the issue from other clans in Britain (see Lewis 2007: 47–8).

It appears that the issue of drug use among young people (irrespective of their culture, religion and nationality) is a global phenomenon. Aashir, a 21-year-old British-born male youth worker from a Bangladeshi background, said that he became involved in drugs when he was at school:

And school's a lot of truanting and stuff like that. And, you know, I was starting to hang around with the wrong crowds obviously. With that you tend to lose your grades and stuff – because I was one of the very good students but . . . But within the GCSE years I tended to slack away from that. (Interview, Bradford, 27 August 2008)

At the time of interview, Aashir was involved with several youth projects to help young Muslims of Bangladeshi background with drug issues. Aashir observed:

There's a big issue of drugs which is going around, a lot of drug usage. Well, to be honest nowadays it's becoming more open in this day. Before I recall, you know, when people used to be taking these drugs, even cannabis, well they used to go around different places, or go to some parks somewhere, or some derelict place. But now you'll see them strolling around the park and stuff.

Well it's all kinds of background from white to black to Somali to Chinese, every single kid on the street nowadays. I'm telling you, drugs are so easy to get, it is easier than getting soft drinks such as Coca-Cola . . . It starts at home, yeah, *Haffiz* [one who has memorised the Quran] are becoming drug dealers! (Interview, Bradford, August 2008)

Another British-born male interviewee of Afghan background, Maymun, aged 27, observed that there were two kinds of parents in the Muslim families: one who punishes his son for his drug involvement, and the other who tacitly supports him:

> You've got two [kinds of] parents, like a pal of mine, he's doing very well in powder, not so long ago he had $1 million on the table and he goes I don't know what to do with it, yeah. His father won't let him in the house. His dad's a *Tablighi Jamaati*, he would not let him inside the house.
>
> But then I know another friend of mine that's a drug dealer. His son says, when he goes home, his dad goes, 'Give me some money.' He gives his dad money. He's getting paid . . . and the father's enjoying the money as well. (Interview, Bradford, 27 August 2008)

I assume in the dynamics of high unemployment, home restrictions, segregated living, high levels of deprivation and lack of communication with community leaders, some young Muslim men have resorted to truancy and drugs.

Radicalisation of Muslim youth

Since the 7/7 London bombings, one question has been raised: why home-grown terrorism? In his book *The Islamist* (2007), Ed Husain comes very close to answering that question. Husain analyses the root causes of Islamic extremism in the UK, drawing much of the analysis from his life story. He focuses on the diasporic life in which migrants keep memories of their original homeland alive through cultural practices; but, he surmises, their children may be a casualty of the clash of cultures and conspiracy theories that can impact on confused Muslim youth. He notes that through transnationalism and globalisation various ideologies of political Islam are imported into the non-Muslim world (that is, countries like Britain), inducing ethnic and religious conflict within the Muslim community.

Born of an Indian father and Bangladeshi mother, Husain is a second-generation migrant who was raised in a lower socioeconomic working-class suburb in London. Husain's father made a living in a blue-collar job and maintained a strict patriarchal structured family. As a consequence, Husain faced these imperatives: abide by strict family rules, maintain cultural and religious practices, attend a single-sex school, and deal with racism at the societal level (Husain 2007).

In his childhood, Husain attended a local primary school where some caring British teachers made him aware of the challenges faced by ethnic minorities in the wider society. One of his teachers used to take him to the after-school martial arts class so that he learned to defend himself from the racist attacks of the skin-headed National Front group in his neighbourhood. However, he also heard racist comments about 'Allah' (the Muslim God) from one of his teachers. In spite of advice from Husain's primary school principal about the poor standards of single-sex schools, his uncompromising father saw the single-sex secondary school as a place that would protect cultural values, such as abstinence from pre-marital sex. However, his father was unaware that the school was attended by 'at risk' students, mostly of Bangladeshi background, who were involved in gang warfare and truancy. Husain had two choices: go along with the gang culture of his school mates, or become an Islamic fundamentalist. Husain believed that socialising with the wider community was not possible because of the British National Party's derogatory taunts: 'Pakis! Pakis! F – off back home' (Husain 2007: 2).

To his father's displeasure (himself a moderate Muslim), Husain gradually drifted towards radical Islam and soon became a member of the Young Muslim Organisation UK, where he came in contact with the ideas of Jamat-e-Islami, Hizb ut-Tahrir and Wahhabi Islam and attended regular meetings in the East London Mosque (Husain 2007: 41). Husain was exposed through telecommunications, emails and websites to the ideology of establishing an Islamic state, a Muslim *Ummah*, which transcends all nation-states. Whereas some groups were more aggressive than others, they all believed that 'the world was divided into two: Islam and *Jahiliyyah* (the ignorant) or *dar-al-Harb* (territory of war or chaos) and *dar-al-Islam* (territory of peace)'. By revealing the atrocities committed against the Bosnian Muslims and Palestinians (and later the non-Muslim occupations of Afghanistan and Iraq) through video clippings, these groups were able to manipulate Muslim young adults towards 'martyrdom'. Husain commented:

> In the multicultural Britain of the 1980s and 1990s we were free to you know practise our religion and develop our culture as we wanted . . . Britishness and the British values of democracy, tolerance, respect, compromise, and pluralism had no meaning for us. Like me, most of the students at college had no real bond with mainstream British . . . Cut off from Britain, isolated from the Eastern culture of our parents, Islamism provided us with a purpose and a place in life. More importantly, we felt as though we were the pioneers, at the cutting edge of this new global development of confronting the West in its own backyard. (Husain 2007: 73–4)

Husain (2007) observed that some Muslim youth came under the influence of political Islam because they were victims of cultural clashes, and that this victimisation was detrimental to both Muslims and the wider community. Though Husain (2007) did not specifically mention the 7/7 London bombers, I assume the factors that could lead to radicalisation mentioned in the book match the life story of one of the London bombers, Shehzad Tanweer. For example, Shehzad Tanweer had been involved 'in territorial battles on lines of race' a few years earlier. A British newspaper, *The Independent* (17 December 2005: 2), reported that Tanweer 'did receive a caution for a public order offence arising out of the gang battles', although he had no involvement in the murder of a white boy during clashes between white and Asian youths. Arguments put forward to explain the 7/7 bombings have ranged from young people's adverse reactions to being referred to as a 'Paki' (a term of disdain and insult), to structural causes such as long-term high unemployment.

However, the case of British-born Shehzad Tanweer, who belonged to an affluent Pakistani family, suggests that other forces may have been at work, including the growing importance of Islamic nationalistic identity as opposed to a secularised British identity. The terror attacks at Glasgow airport on 30 June 2007 by two Muslims, Kafeel Ahmed (PhD in Engineering, who later died) and Bilal Abdulla (a medical doctor), may be a further illustration of this phenomenon. Husain also observed that the emerging religious revivalism among some Muslim youth, particularly girls, had caused an increase in the use of *niqabs* (face veils) and *jilbabs* (long dresses) which was a barrier to integration in the wider community. In Husain's case, he departed from radicalisation through marriage: his Turkish wife influenced him to endorse Sufi Islam.

Youth issue: is music forbidden in Islam?

Certain Muslim schools of thought, such as the Deobandis, not only have conservative attitudes towards women but they also prohibit listening to music (Lewis 2007: 4–5, 114). Lewis (2007: 5) comments, 'Given the importance of music for young people, this prohibition renders its task of connecting with British Muslims that much more difficult.' The Deobandis are a mainstream South Asian Sunni tradition which has been most successful in creating large numbers of institutions in England for religious formations and the creation of *ulama* (body of Muslim legal scholars), but it shares the *ahl-i-Hadith* – the Salafi belief, which is the practise of the authentic tradition of Prophet Muhammad [PBUH] and the Quran, and Wahhabi view that music is prohibited (Lewis 2007: 5).

In the Australian context, I found that music played an important role in the formation of a bicultural identity for Australian Muslim youths (Kabir 2007a; Kabir 2008c). For this study as well, I found that some young Muslims did not like listening to music, particularly Western music, as it may contain 'immoral words'. In a few cases, I found young British Muslims did not want to discuss the fact that they listened to Western music because it was considered taboo in the Muslim community. They said, 'We must listen to *nasheeds*' (devotional Islamic songs). On one occasion, I conducted interviews with a group of male Muslim youths (16–18 years), and their mentor (a Muslim male adult) also sat in during the interview. When asked about music, the group of young Muslims resentfully said that they listened to *nasheeds,* and that they are supposed to listen only to *nasheeds.* These young men defined their identity as British and Pakistani, or British and Arab (Interviews, Cardiff, 20 October 2008). But later, their mentor told me in private they need to be 'Muslim first'. I was not sure to which group of Islam the mentor belonged. I consider the imposition of listening to *nasheeds* as 'an enforced religiosity'.

Conclusion

Muslims in Britain are diverse. The majority of Muslims are Sunnis and some are Shi'ites. But within the Sunnis, some groups are more traditional than others. Some of the respondents of this study gave particular reference to the Deobandis, and the restrictions they imposed on women. Other participants spoke of restrictions within Muslim families and the wider Muslim community generally.

It is generally believed that young Muslim women are under pressure to accept arranged marriages (Cressey 2006), and some young Muslim males in Britain, aged 16–18, remain under constant pressure to pursue an arranged marriage (Alam 2006: 43). An interviewee, a British-born male of Pakistani background in Leeds, said that he had to help his father in his restaurant from the age of 12 and left school early. At the age of 17 he was married and at the age of 18 he was the father of a child (Interview, Leeds, 9 September 2008). Early marriage of young Muslim men in Britain is not restricted to people of Pakistani heritage. One of the interviewees of this study, a British-born man of Bangladeshi background aged 23, said that he was married at the age of 21, which was 'very late' in his family, whereas his brothers all married at the age of 17–18 (Interview, London, 15 April 2008). In some cases, young Muslims protest against the custom of arranged marriages, and going back home to get married, and marrying a cousin. But apparently many young Muslims in Britain accept it graciously as a norm in the family. Research evidence indicates that many of the arranged marriages have worked out well (Alam 2006: 50–1).

Young Muslim men also face issues of numeracy and literacy. Some youth workers advocate that Muslim leaders give them as much help and support as possible, be it in mosques where the young people go for religious education or at youth centres. Drugs were also affecting some young Muslim men. Youth workers pointed out that the youth centres needed more funding and resources to deal with the crisis. But sending the troubled youths back home for reha-bilitation was not necessarily helpful. It appears that Muslim women's issues remain most complex. The Muslim women's dilemma is more of a family matter rather than a community issue.

TO BE OR NOT TO BE BRITISH

'Britishness'

British national identity or 'Britishness' has been variously defined (see Chapter 1) as possessing fluent English skills, loyalty to Britain, integration with the wider community, belief in democracy, tolerance, acceptance of equal treatment for all and respect for the country and its shared heritage. Smith (1991: 11) observes that it has taken several generations before new immigrants' descendants were admitted into the inner circle of the 'nation', and its historic culture through the national agencies of mass mobilisation. The Western model of national identity, for example in Western Europe, was seen as cultural communities, whose members were united, if not homogeneous, by common historical memories, myths, symbols and traditions. So, even if new immigrant communities were admitted into the Western states, they would not be absorbed as one of 'Us' by the wider community over a short period.

Academics Bhikhu Parekh (2000) and Modood (2007) advocate a civic notion of 'Britishness' that recognises and includes diversity. However, in 2000 the 'Parekh report' (after its author, Bhikhu Parekh) was published by the Runnymede Trust, an independent research organisation. It created a controversy by denouncing the 'insidious' racism of British society, and by recommending that, as much as possible, Englishness or Britishness should be detached from the notion of 'Whiteness' (Parekh report 2000: 38; Cesari 2004: 32; Ward 2004: 139). Modood (2007: 150) observes that immigrants' sense of belonging to their host country is necessary for a successful multicultural society. In my previous research, I (Kabir 2007a; 2008c) found that immigrants' sense of belonging to a host country develops with the length of stay, economic opportunities and social cohesion. Generally, the longer immigrants reside in a host country the better they understand the mainstream culture.

With economic opportunities new immigrants receive recognition from the wider society, which is conducive to social cohesion. I have also argued that exclusionary Muslim community practices (extreme cultural restrictions, living in enclaves, lack of integration, poor English skills) or the mainstream society's exclusionary behaviour (riots, racism, unemployment) definitely impact on the process of developing one's national identity.

I found that biculturalism is an important factor for building an immigrant's connection to their host country. By biculturalism I mean majority and minority ethnic/religious cultures. Biculturalism works at two levels: first, as a national policy (a variant of multiculturalism) of acceptance/expectation that migrants will retain much of their culture/heritage but will adhere to (new) national laws and gradually adopt the national language/culture; second, as a personal practice of blending the old and the new – retaining religion, ethnic culture and language and taking on new language and culture in order to have dual membership.

When the ethnic minorities adopt parts of majority culture such as speaking the English language, reading English novels, listening to music or watching English television programmes, engaging in contemporary politics, participating in mainstream sports, as well as retaining their ethnic and religious practices, this enables them to participate as citizens of their host society, with a hyphenated/dual identity or diverse/multiple identities. In this chapter, I first show the pattern of 216 participants' response to their national identity (summarised in Table 4.1). Second, I evaluate the factors that have determined their diverse identities. Third, I discuss why some respondents chose to have a distinct identity: national, ethnic or religious. Finally, I discuss whether British national sports have a positive impact on Muslims' national identity.

Table 4.1 shows that the majority of respondents (102) felt connected to their national, ethnic and religious identities (e.g. British, Bangladeshi and Muslim). Five respondents went beyond 'All three' identities and spoke of their multiple identities (e.g. 'I'm English, I'm British, I'm Yorkshire, I'm Pakistani'), 24 respondents proclaimed dual national and ethnic identity (e.g. British-Pakistani), 13 participants connected their identity with their country of origin (e.g. I'm Pakistani) and only one spoke specifically of his ethnic identity (e.g. I'm an Arab). Nineteen participants were proud to be exclusively British, and 9 respondents chose to speak of their Welsh identity. Fifteen interviewees identified themselves as British-Muslims and 15 respondents described themselves as Muslims. However, three respondents were confused or uncomfortable with the notion of identity; three participants said that they did not have a fixed identity; one participant said that he was of mixed race; three interviewees said that they were British but with reservations; two respondents defined themselves as English; and one declared that she was a 'Citizen of the world'. In the next section, I examine the variables (causal factors) through which the respondents justified their respective identities.

Table 4.1 Pattern of identity, 216 participants (203 young Muslims, 15–30 years; and 13 Muslim leaders, over 30 years) [105 male and 111 female]

Question asked: How would you define your sense of belonging? Would you consider yourself British? Or Pakistani/Bangladeshi/Iraqi/Somali, etc., or Muslim?

Number of participants	Responses	Key points
102 (56 males, 46 females)	All three: national, ethnic and religious	I live in Bradford, but when I go to London, I am told that I am a Bradfordian. Does that mean that I have three identities: Muslim, British and Bradfordian? I'm a British Bangladeshi Muslim. I live in Leeds. If I go back home they see me as a so-called 'Londoner' and then in this country they see me as a foreigner.
5 males	Multiple identities	I'm English, I'm British, I'm Yorkshire, I'm Pakistani. My mum's from Palestine. And my dad's from Sudan. To my black friends I'll say I'm black, to my mum's friends I'll say I'm Palestinian, and then to my white friends, well to somebody, if somebody was racist I'd say, 'Hey, listen I'm British you know'.
15 (4 males, 11 females)	Dual identity: national and religious	I want to get the best from both worlds: Britain and Islamic. I feel very proud to be Welsh and Muslim. I am learning the Welsh language. I'd like to translate the Quran into Welsh.
24 (10 males, 14 females)	Dual identity: national/ country of origin/religious	I am British Muslim. I wear *hijab, jilbab* and *niqab*. I am a British at school and a Pakistani at home. My dad has Pakistani ways of thinking. I wear T-shirt and jeans outside and *shalwar kameej* at home, and cover my arms.
19 (10 males, 9 females)	Single national identity: British	'Britishness' is multiculturalism; 'Britishness' is about citizenship. British 100 per cent, I was born here; I think differently from my parents; I speak English most of the time. British, mainly the way I dress and act as well.
3 (1 male, 2 females)	British but with reservations	I am slowly trying to be British. I live in a white area; they look at me because I'm different (Iraqi-born). I'm British but when people ask I say Somali (British-born, but colour issue). I'm British but when people ask I say Turkish.
2 (1 male, 1 female)	Single identity: national/ethnic English	I am English. I am 'white'. I don't want to be a Moroccan because there is a lot of corruption in Morocco. I consider myself English because I was born in England, I speak English at home, and I am not from Scotland.

Table 4.1 (continued)

Number of participants	Responses	Key points
9 (3 males, 6 females)	Single identity: national/ethnic Welsh	My great grandmother was a Welsh woman. [In sports] I'd support Welsh, Glamorgan; I don't support Pakistan, England I don't support at all, but Glamorgan I support.
13 (6 males, 7 females)	Single identity: country of origin	I'm British-born but I'm just straightforward 'Paki'. I am not a 'white' person. I have British passport but I lived most of my life in Iran. More Pakistani because of UK foreign policy. We go to Pakistan/Bangladesh every year.
1 male	Single identity: ethnic	I consider myself an Arab.
15 (5 males, 10 females)	Only religious identity: Muslim	I identify myself with the *Ummah*. I don't like English and Pakistani cultures. I like to call myself a Muslim girl.
1 male	Mixed race	I would say mixed race (my father is a Pakistani and my mother is English).
2 (1 male, 1 female)	Confused identity	Vague answer, and confused. Embraced Muslim identity after facing discrimination in workplace. I can't bring my Bengali culture, otherwise everybody will make fun of me. I just want to blend in the environment.
1 male	Apprehensive over identity	If 'Britishness' means pub culture, going to pub, then I am not British.
3 females	Identity changes	I don't have a fixed identity.
1 female	Transnational background	I am a 'Citizen of the world'.

Factors determining diverse identities

In this section I analyse the factors that may have determined respondents' identities.

A rich and complex historical connection

A third-generation British-born girl, Nawsheen, aged 17 years, spoke of her identity as:

> I was born in Britain, and Britain is my identity but I'm also Muslim and I also have culturally Pakistan as part of my identity, but predominantly I would say I'm British Muslim.

Nawsheen further explains what is meant by British identity:

> People always joke about fish and chips and going to the pub, that's British identity, but it isn't. I think British identity is being very open-minded, very democratic, being very diverse and very opinionated, having opinions but being subjective and open to other people's opinions and being respectful, enjoying life and respecting the laws. British identity is politically, economically and socially linked to the [British] culture. (Interview, Bradford, 7 October 2008)

Nawsheen attended a state school, wore a *hijab* and felt very connected to Britain. At the primary level, she attended a Christian faith-based school. Nawsheen said that her grandfather was a member of the British army during World War II, and he came to Britain on an invitation from the Queen. Nawsheen appeared to be bicultural. She enjoyed English movies, music, TV programmes and also liked Bollywood movies and music. In sports she supported Manchester United. Nawsheen acknowledged that there were distinct separations in some places of Britain, where white British people and Asian British people were separate, and didn't mix. But certain places mixed quite well and there was quite a lot of balance. For example, she said in her suburb in Bradford there was a white minority but they were perfectly happy. She said, 'My neighbour, he's very nice, he's British, he is really nice . . . They [white minority] seem to be getting along really well, like, you know, you smile at them and then you get a nice reaction'.

Mehjabeen, an overseas-born Somali girl (aged 18), had a transnational background. She had lived with her parents in the Middle East for eleven years, then moved to Wales:

> I wasn't born here, but I live in this country, this country accepted me and I go to a Welsh school, I have Welsh friends, I live in a Welsh house, which is built by Welsh people. I live in Wales. I should consider myself as Welsh.
>
> When I went overseas last year I stayed there for two months and I didn't feel at home. I was crying I was so homesick. What I call home is Cardiff. I came here young, obviously everything was new to me, especially the language. I used to get bullied because I didn't know English and I've learned it in less than six months. The English language made me stronger. Later, in school I learned the Welsh language, which was compulsory. (Interview, Cardiff, 22 October 2008)

Mehjabeen felt connected with the local Welsh people, their buildings and architecture. She learned to speak Welsh even though the Welsh language is hardly used in the public sphere. When I was conducting a survey in Cardiff, I asked some mainstream British such as the taxi drivers whether they spoke the Welsh language. They said, 'You don't need the language to be a Welshman.' However, when I visited the National Assembly for Wales at Cardiff, I noted an emphasis on the Welsh language. I was told by an informant that if Muslims knew the Welsh language they would be in a better position to compete with the 'White' people in the job market. With regard to the Welsh-language question, sociologist Graham Day (2003: 240) observed that Welsh identity had assumed a new dimension. It was reported that a broadcaster's job with a Welsh company was not renewed, allegedly because his voice sounded insufficiently Welsh (Day 2003: 240).

Mehjabeen's bond to Welshness could also have been because of an historical connection. She said that her great-grandfather came to Cardiff as a sailor, and married her great-grandmother who was a Welsh woman. Her grandfather was born in Cardiff but he went to Somalia to marry her grandmother. Mehjabeen's grandmother later came to Cardiff and her mother was born here. However, Mehjabeen's father is a Somali-born man. Though Mehjabeen felt strongly connected to Wales, she drew attention to the colour prejudice that existed in Wales, saying that she frequently heard the 'N' (Nigger) word. She also mentioned that the police hardly attended their telephone calls, citing an occasion when her brother was lost, and her mother called the police saying that her son was a white boy and was missing. Mehjabeen says:

> Well, they [police] found my brother and then they said, 'Oh he's not white, what's your point exactly', and then my mum goes, 'that's so you would get here as fast as you can'. (Interview, Cardiff, 22 October 2008)

Mehjabeen did not connect herself with her religious identity. She mentioned that if she wore the *hijab* and applied for a job, she would not get it, and if she did not wear the *hijab* on a regular basis she was condemned by the Muslim community:

> I'll tell you something about what happened last time when I came from the mosque. I had my CV in my bag and then I went to most of the shops. I had my *hijab* and my *abaya* and I was asking for a vacancy [part-time job] in most of the shops and they said, 'No, we are fully booked.'
>
> And when I went last week with no *hijab*, with trousers and stuff, obviously they can't tell if I'm Muslim or not, and most of the shops that I went last time and asked for vacancy, [where] they said it was fully booked up, they now told me, 'Yes, we need people.' (Interview, Cardiff, 22 October 2008)

Mehjabeen observed that Cardiff was multicultural, but some kids sold drugs and got into fights, or robbed places because they could not get a job. Mehjabeen said, 'In the job application, when the employers see that the applicant is from Grangetown, Riverside or Butetown Docks, they won't offer him/her a job.'

Historically, when Muslims were largely concentrated in Cardiff, for example in Tiger Bay and Butetown, these places were stigmatised by the rest of the city as 'unsavoury' and 'disreputable'; and the residents were seen as 'undesirable'. Sometimes, the residents of these areas were viewed as the source of venereal disease and tuberculosis. Muslims were portrayed in the media as 'turbulent' and 'excitable' (Arabs) and 'truculent' and 'vicious' (Somalis) by nature, 'who constituted a menace to peace at times of rioting' (Ansari 2004: 106).

After World War I, British society appeared particularly sensitive to the issue of who was and who was not 'an [enemy] alien', who had the right to be in Britain, and who ought to be compelled to leave (Ansari 2004: 42). This crystallised in 1919, in a series of riots mainly in Liverpool, South Shields and various ports in South Wales, in which the white protestors targeted those they perceived as unwelcome aliens. Thus the riots were ostensibly fuelled by the issue of race and the coloured people suffered the most (Ansari 2004: 96). Later, in 1936 when Cardiff City Council wanted to rehouse a few coloured residents from Butetown to the areas close to the city centre, petitions from the white population were immediately sent protesting to the move, as it would 'lower its tone' (Ansari 2004: 107). From the early twentieth century the main areas of Muslim settlement in Cardiff were Tiger Bay and Butetown. Because of their limited resources, Muslims were forced to live in deprived areas and then blamed for creating the miserable conditions (Ansari 2004: 105–7).

In 2006, Gilliat-Ray (2006: 5) noted that the areas of Muslim concentration in Cardiff still continue to be Butetown, Grangetown and Cathays. In interviews with the participants of this study, I was told by some respondents that Grangetown and Butetown remain disadvantaged areas. One female respondent, Tahseena (British-born of Pakistani heritage, 24 years), noted:

I think that's more like a media hype . . . bit of a stereotype. [As the media puts it] there are gangs in the Butetown area. You hear of violence, it is in fact Muslims fighting Muslims, like Somalis, Pakistanis and Indians. There's been I think a lot of conflict between Sikhs and Muslims. In that area I've heard recently it's not as bad. (Interview, Cardiff, 21 October 2008)

Williams (2003: 149) noted that statistics on the labour market participation of ethnic minorities in Wales showed that ethnic-minority men and women had lower economic activity rates, less likelihood of being employed, higher levels of self-employment, higher rates of unemployment and higher youth unemployment than the white population. Williams (2003: 149) also noted that there was a high correlation between areas of ethnic-minority settlement and high rates of unemployment and socioeconomic deprivation. Looking at unemployment alone, statistics showed huge disparities, with unemployment among black groups running at twice the national rate, and among Black Africans at least three times the national rate. An Equal Opportunities study in 1999 (Williams 2003: 152) identified some of the key barriers to labour market participation among minorities in Wales, and one of them was obstacles that are the result of institutionalised racial discrimination, direct or indirect. Racial harassment in South Wales during 1994–5 was recorded as the third-highest in Great Britain (Williams 2003: 152).

Though there are records of social exclusion in Wales (Ansari 2004) and Mehjabeen had experienced discrimination when she presented as a visible Muslim (wore the *hijab*), she was still optimistic for the future of black people in Britain. She regarded US black leader Martin Luther King Junior as her role model, and wished to be the first black woman Prime Minister! She expanded her Welsh identity when she supported Arsenal in sports, commenting: 'Yeah I'm an Arsenal supporter. Yeah, it's a London team. It's just the thing is there are more black players there.'

Cultural implications

Jawhara, a 17-year-old British-born girl of Sylheti-Bangladeshi origin, felt very British, even though she acknowledged that some of the cultural values of the Bangladeshi people were not aligned with British values:

> My [English] language, liking for English music, everything really makes me feel British. It's the way you think, if you're born here. The British thinking that you get, you can't get that from the Bangladeshi culture.
>
> With British thinking you have a right to think about what you want to do, who you want to be and you can go do that, and if you're Bangladeshi there's loads of barriers that stop you. With British thinking you should be mature, responsible, know right from wrong, have good morals, traditions and values and you should grow up knowing that you won't disrespect your freedom and you have independence. I think that's important and a lot of [Bangladeshi] parents don't understand that; maybe that's why I don't have that understanding with my parents. (Interview, Bradford, 7 October 2008)

Jawhara attended a state school, where she integrated with the wider society. She summed up 'Britishness' as having more freedom. She loved watching America's Next Top Model TV. She said, 'There's a new show called *Lipstick Jungle* and that's about three magazine editors and powerful business women in New York, so it relates a lot to me.' Jawhara hoped to become a journalist. In Jawhara's case, her British identity was linked with her protest about cultural restrictions. Jawhara equated Britishness with trust and responsibility, but apparently her parents did not appreciate Jawhara's Western way of thinking, and that is why there was conflict.

No doubt many first- and even second-generation parents were raised in strict cultural norms back home or in England. Their concern was more how they would be perceived by their ethnic or religious community if their children abandoned their ethnic values and endorsed British values which could be more open and unrestricted. Some parents viewed some of the British norms, such as drinking alcohol and clubbing (staying late at night clubs), as bad for their children, and were concerned that their children would abandon their Islamic cultural values (Alam 2006).

Feelings of cultural restriction were not exclusive to Jawhara. Monica Ali (2003) wrote about the cultural restrictions of Bangladeshi young Muslims in Brick Lane in London's East End, noting that some young people lied to their parents about their movements. In the American context, a Bangladeshi mother expected her daughter to live the lifestyle she had in Bangladesh (Haddad, Smith and Moore 2006). Such restrictions were again not exclusive to the Bangladeshi community in Britain. In an Australian study, a young Lebanese-Australian Muslim woman stated that she admired the Anglo-Australian culture of her teacher in High School who took them to the theatre in the city. The Lebanese girl wanted to travel, but she knew that her parents would not permit it, saying, 'In the Lebanese world there were no plays, no sport and no travelling' (Jamal and Chandab 2005: 47–52). Jamal and Chandab (2005: 52–4) wrote that most of the Lebanese parents in their study did not want to challenge the status quo. It appeared that they were living their lives for other people, worrying about gossip and what others might think of them (see also Abdel-Fattah 2005: 216–21).

Some respondents of this study related 'Britishness' to different food. Mussaret, an 18-year-old British-born woman of Pakistani origin (married to a man who lived in Pakistan), when asked how she would define her 'Britishness', said:

> Yeah, it's just that I was born here that's all. And it's probably the things I eat cos I can't eat *roti salan* (Pakistani bread or chapatti and curry) all the time. I don't know how my parents eat it. I'd maybe have it once in two weeks or something. They can't try a new food!
>
> When I got married in Pakistan, they [my in-laws] used to have the *roti* twice a day and because they're not really rich, they didn't buy [take-away] food. I didn't ask them, you know, 'Could I go out to this restaurant' and stuff like that. But you know I didn't always like the taste. I just ate it, without a fuss. I did have chips a couple of times. (Interview, Leeds, 15 October 2008)

Mussaret maintained her Islamic identity insofar as she wore the *hijab* and *jilbab* on a regular basis, but she felt British. She also associated 'Britishness' with dining out, different food and multiculturalism. She spoke very enthusiastically about her sports: 'In High School I did like doing PE. I have a bronze medal in the pentathlon challenge.' She was concerned that Asian women did not value going to the gym:

I've said to my mum, 'We could go to women-only gym, you know. If you go, then I'll go.' [But my mum says] 'I've got 100 things to do at home. I've got the house-work, the cooking' . . . that's why we are so heavy. (Interview, Leeds, 15 October 2008)

A 17-year-old British-born male of Mirpuri-Pakistani background, Sabur, was hurt that he was constantly reminded by his family that he was a Pakistani, although he felt British. Sabur attended a state school and culturally he identi-fied with India because he was fond of Bollywood movies and music, and he desired to visit India to meet his favourite Indian actress, Prianka Chopra (who was once Miss World). But emotionally he felt very connected to Britain. Sabur said:

I was born here, I'm bred here, I live here, I speak the language, I go to school here, I've got a British passport. Apart from that I've got a lot of white friends, and this is my home. Pakistan, I do class it as probably root, my mother and father's solid roots, but this is home. I'm not intending on moving over to Pakistan and living there for the rest of my life.

My dad sometimes says, 'You are lost between two cultures. You can't be proper British and you can't be proper Pakistani, you're in-between.' I tell my dad, 'I'm not lost in-between, we do get influenced by the Westernised culture because if you see a guy from Pakistan and a guy from England – huge differences.' I think,we're basically British, we're unique. I think if you mix black and white you don't get half-black, half-white, you get a mixture – you get like a grey – I think we're a mix between black and white. (Interview, Bradford, 7 October 2008)

In Sabur's case, Britishness became obvious from the cultural difference between the Pakistanis and British. Having lived in both Eastern and Western worlds: Bangladesh, Pakistan, the Middle East on one hand, and the United States and Australia on the other hand (and also being a mother of three chil-dren), I (the author) consider that there are big differences between a Pakistani from Pakistan and a British-Pakistani young man. First of all, there are some matters of etiquette among the people of the Indian subcontinent, which would not be easy to comprehend by the younger generations born and raised in the Western world. There could be a communication gap, lack of understanding of local (Pakistani) humour, local (Pakistani) politics, and so on. I speculate that being born and raised in a Pakistani family in Britain, Sabur would be able to relate to some of the social norms of a Pakistani person (who was born and lives in Pakistan), but he would not be able to relate to the level of thinking of the Pakistani because he was raised in a different country. For example, if the Pakistani man expected Sabur to understand about the Bhutto family politics or if Sabur expected the Pakistani guy to understand the British royal families' gossip or British politics or sports (Manchester United, Liverpool, etc.), they wouldn't be able to understand each other. Perhaps their only common topic of discussion could be cricket!

There could be other differences. For example, the school system in Pakistan or Bangladesh only focuses on studying (and memorising), but the school system in the Western world emphasises creative thinking, sports, debating, interfaith dialogues, work experience and voluntary community service. In that respect, Sabur would find the British education system, as well as the people, is unique. In the Indian subcontinent, people are less formal in some ways and more formal in others. For example, in Bangladesh people receive visitors without making an appointment. They just drop in to say hello or give *salaam* [Muslim greeting] to their friends and relatives without any prior notice, and spend time having a cup of tea at their friends' or relatives' place. But in the Western world such practice is uncommon even among the Bangladeshi community. Similarly, as Ali-Karamali (2008: 1) mentioned, in India when a visitor is offered a cup of tea s/he would say 'No', because at the first instance if they say 'Yes' that would mean that they were greedy. If the visitor was offered tea the second time, again the response would be 'No'. Only on the third offer would the visitor say 'Yes' because the third offer meant that the host was genuine. At the third instance, the guest's 'Yes' indicated that he was not greedy, but politely agreeing to the insistence of the host. So if a person (such as Sabur) was not raised in such an environment (in this case, Pakistan) it would be naive of their parents to imagine him wanting to fit in completely with their imaginary homeland (Pakistan). Sabur said that when black and white were mixed it becomes grey and his position was grey. In this context, I assume the grey meant being bicultural. Sabur aims to study dentistry. Rogler, Cortes and Malady (1991) suggest a bicultural position is best for the development of an individual's self-esteem. Biculturalism means a near native-like knowledge of two cultures, which includes the ability to respond effectively to the different demands of these two cultures. Rogler et al. (1991) contend that the combination of retaining traditional cultural elements, together with learning those of the host society, can enhance mental health and a hopeful outlook.

Identity and work experience

Two respondents, Hafsa and Manal, felt very British because of their positive experience at their workplace, whereas Shoma and Tahseena prioritised their Islamic identity over their British identity because they felt they were seen as the 'Other' at the workplace. The British-born girl of Pakistani heritage, Hafsa (aged 16), said:

Yeah I'm properly connected to British because I haven't been to Pakistan for many years. So I am connected to British; I do class myself as a British Muslim. (Interview, Bradford, 10 October 2008)

Manal, an overseas-born girl of Pakistani heritage who lived in the Philippines for many years (aged 16), said:

> Probably British Muslim because like I don't live in Philippines anymore so I've got to forget about that place! (Interview, Bradford, 10 October 2008)

Both the girls attended a state school and worked part-time at a British office at the customer service section, and felt positively about their British identity. Hafsa further emphasised that her 'Britishness' comes to the fore, 'When our school life comes in and my work life comes in; also [English] language and socialising with people of other ethnic origins.' Both Hafsa and Manal sat together for the interview, and when I asked them, 'What is expected from a British citizen?' Manal replied, 'Equal rights with everyone else', and Hafsa elaborated:

> What is expected is a good job, good pay. Yeah equal rights and then if you go towards Islamic way I think the [Muslim] community should be good with the British, it should be equal, and everything should be okay really. (Interview, Bradford, 10 October 2008)

Both Hafsa and Manal did not present as Muslims in that they did not wear headscarves. Their positive experience in the workplace helped them to think positively about British society. In my survey on young British Muslim identity I found that negative experiences at the workplace could impact on a person's identity. For example, Shoma (25 years), a Pakistani-born girl who came to the UK at the age of eight said that she faced prejudice at the workplace and that led her to become a practising Muslim:

> My university degree was four years and I took a year out. I worked in a consultancy as a knowledge management coordinator and it was really tough, and my manager, a British woman, she was a workaholic. I was really quite depressed actually, because I left home around 8 [am] and came back at 7.30 [pm]. Still she [my employer] thought I did not do enough work. It was very soul draining. And then I was able to reflect a lot because my train journey was two hours.
>   I left the job, and went back to university. I said to my friend, who's a non-Muslim, 'I'm not going to go clubbing anymore', and she's like okay. And then I started covering myself and started wearing long sleeves. (Interview, London, 20 April 2008)

Shoma said that her mother was a practising Muslim but did not wear a *hijab*. Shoma could not cope with the workload of the consultancy firm, and felt her employer treated her unfairly, so she decided to withdraw from the British culture of clubbing, etc. and embraced her Islamic identity. I wondered whether Shoma fully understood the culture of her workplace. Consultancy firms can sometimes be overloaded with work and are required to meet deadlines. Shoma's manager was a 'workaholic', and she apparently expected the same dedication from her employee. A few months later I interviewed Tahseena, a British-born woman of Pakistani background (aged 24) in Wales. Tahseena described herself as 'Muslim, Pakistani and British and Welsh':

> My *hijab* is the indicator of my Muslim identity (which I am proud of). Even though I can speak Urdu [Pakistan's official language], I can't express the same as I can in English. I think my 'Britishness' is more independence. My Welsh identity seems something unique. (Interview, Cardiff, 24 October 2008)

Though Tahseena felt very connected to Britain, her manager treated her as the 'Other' when she started wearing the *hijab* after a death in her family:

> I used to work for a British company at a call centre in the evenings because I was in university at the time. [The first day I wore the *hijab* at my workplace] people on my team, stopped speaking to me . . . I noticed a change in my manager. He [the manager] came up to me and asked, 'What's happened? Have your parents forced you to wear this?' And I said, 'No', and then he said, 'Why? You're very modern and very different, I didn't think you would do this', and I was just like, 'Do what?' I said, 'I'm a Muslim.' Then he was like, 'Oh okay . . . no, no I really respect that it's your choice and I respect it, I just wanted to be sure.' But then I noticed a change in him. (Interview, Cardiff, 24 October 2008)

Tahseena quit her job at the call centre and later worked for an ethnic-minorities organisation where wearing of the *hijab* was unreservedly accepted. The nature of her previous job at the call centre was customer service, but she had no face-to-face dealings with her customers. So her anecdote shows that her manager and team colleagues were not comfortable with the Islamic dress code (*hijab*). It could have been because they felt Tahseena was one of them and that by wearing the *hijab* she was setting herself apart from them.

Dynamics of changing identity

In this section I discuss the fluidity of one's identity. In April 2008, the British-born Yemeni student Ghaznafar (male, aged 15) said that he felt different identities in different environments:

> When I go to Yemen I do feel I'm a British, but when I'm in this country I feel that I'm a Yemeni, an Arab, and but I don't show that much, I show that I'm a Muslim more often. (Interview, London, 8 April 2008)

Ghaznafar said that the reason for feeling Yemeni was, 'It's probably because I don't see lots of Yemenis [in London] and I see myself as different.

Especially nowadays [there's] lots of cultures which are together.' In other words, with his ethnic identity Ghaznafar saw himself as a minority among the mainstream British, and also a minority within the Muslim community, and that made him feel different. According to the 2001 UK Census, there were 12,508 Yemeni-born people in the UK, and by recent estimates (including British-born people of Yemeni descent), the Yemeni-British community numbers around 70,000 to 80,000 people (BBC 2002). In 2001, the total Muslim population in the UK was 1,591,126. So in that context the Yemenis formed a minority of about 5 per cent in the Muslim community.

Ghaznafar played football once a week and his team members were Spanish, Portuguese, Asian and African-Caribbean. He also supported two Premier League football teams: 'My first [favourite] team is Arsenal, and my second team is Tottenham.' Surprisingly, his role model was Steven Gerrard, who didn't play for either of these teams. Ghaznafar said, 'Yeah he plays fair football and he's against racism. Yeah he's a British. He plays for Liverpool.' Ghaznafar attended an Islamic school and had performed *hajj*. I gathered that living in London, Ghaznafar spent more time in an Islamic environment, and that made him more connected with his religious (Islamic) identity. Also, with an *Ummah* identity it was easy for Ghaznafar to blend into the Muslim community. I assume that in Yemen, Ghaznafar felt British because he could not comprehend the social norms there (humour, language, accent, etc.), as mentioned by Subur in the Pakistani context earlier.

A few months later, the 25-year-old male respondent Dawood, of Pakistani background, said:

> I'm British on kind of a bigger scale, so if I was abroad and someone asked me where I was from I would be British, and if they wanted it broken down even further then I'm a Welsh citizen from the UK. So I've got a British passport, I'm a British citizen but I was born in Wales and I've lived here 99.9 per cent of my life. I'm Welsh with Pakistani heritage. (Interview, Cardiff, 20 October 2008)

Sociologist Graham Day (2003: 244) observes that a large number of people in Wales appear to operate with dual, overlapping, national identities; to varying degrees they are simultaneously Welsh and British (Day 2003: 244). In a plural society, there is nothing astonishing about this: 'Wales' and 'Britain' form different levels within the concentric rings of identifications which stretch from the local and parochial to the continental and global. In other words, identity is not fixed. Different identities appear in different contexts and for different purposes. Someone may see themselves as claiming to be from Pontypridd and the valleys, a South Walian, Welsh, British and European, while another is self-defined as from Anglesey, a Welsh-speaker (*Cymro-Cymraeg*), North Walian, Welsh, European – but not British (Day 2003: 244). To explain these identities, each individual would have to provide some direct definition; for instance, one individual might associate 'Britishness' with the monarchy, or a colonial power, as a celebration of Englishness; whereas for the other it means a shared history of fighting wars, discovering sports or establishing norms of mutual welfare. Day (2003: 244) observes, 'Such definitions are not idly constructed, but develop together, often in contradistinction, through an elaborate history of interaction and exchange.' So in this case, the 'Britishness' of Welsh-born Dawood comes from his citizenship and passport, and his Welsh identity comes from the place of his birth, where he was raised, and perhaps his workplace. His Pakistani identity comes from his heritage. However, Dawood's identity took a flexible position when it came to sports:

> I remember, a childhood memory, when Pakistan was playing England in the World Cup and it must have been over 15 years ago and someone asked me, 'Who are you going to support England versus Pakistan?' and naturally I said, 'Pakistan' and he was shaking his head in disappointment.
>
> I think maybe it's because at my age I was too young to understand what he was referring to. Since then I probably, if it was Wales versus Pakistan, I would support Wales, generally England versus Pakistan I would support Pakistan. (Interview, Cardiff, 20 October 2008)

Historian Gwyn A. Williams (cited in Johnes 2004: 52) notes, 'Wales is an artefact which the Welsh produce; the Welsh make and remake Wales day by day and year by year'. Johnes (2004: 52) argues that exactly what that artefact is and has been is a contentious question obscured by political debates about Wales' future, the absence of a nation-state and internal geographic, linguistic and ethnic divisions. Wales as a unified entity is thus an 'imagined community' and Welshness has different meanings for the people who possess and make it. I have argued in the context of Australia (Kabir 2007a; Kabir 2008c) that immigrants feel connected to their host country according to their length of stay. The longer an immigrant lives in their new 'home' and obtains equal opportunities and recognition from the wider society, the more they are likely to feel connected to their new place. Now, getting back to the respondent of this study, Dawood supported Wales against Pakistan in football because he felt more connected to Wales. But when it came to England versus Pakistan he supported Pakistan – the imaginary homeland of his ancestors. This shows that Dawood found England more distant (foreign) than Pakistan. Dawood felt quite connected to Wales, and he was concerned when other people refused to accept his Welsh identity:

> I remember when I was overseas [in another Western country] and someone asked me my name and they said, 'Where are you from?' I said 'Wales', and they said 'I've never heard that name, it's not a Welsh name.' Obviously it's not a Welsh name but I was born here. I can't see why someone who may be white Caucasian may be born here is more Welsh than say I am. I may be more patriotic than them; I may even

speak the language but they would probably be seen as being Welsh more than me.
(Interview, Cardiff, 20 October 2008)

Dawood's Welsh nationalism was mainly expressed during sports when Welsh people gathered and spoke their Welsh language, and his 'Welshness' was marked with the geographical demarcation with England. Otherwise, the means of communication in Wales was English.

> The Welsh seem to be losing an awful lot of the tradition, their language, and that's mainly due to the English . . . but you don't see it generally unless it is a rugby match, unless it is a football match, unless it's something to do with maybe language, but on the whole you won't generally feel it here. You may feel it in certain parts of England where it borders with Wales but generally everyone I would have thought gets along. (Interview, Cardiff, 20 October 2008)

Historically, after the Industrial Revolution in the nineteenth century, English became the dominant language of industrial Wales and was therefore identified with the forces of modernisation and progress (Day 2004: 216). The Welsh (Gaelic) language was affiliated more closely with the 'traditionalist' Wales of rurality, religion and the old-fashioned middle class of preachers, teachers and public servants. The Welsh language was associated with backwardness, even primitiveness, and barbarity. Attitudes have since changed, and the language is now accorded equal official recognition with English, and forms part of the nationally determined school curriculum for all pupils in state schools in Wales. The Welsh Language Board, set up in 1993 under the Welsh Language Act, is charged with ensuring that all private-sector organisations operate a language scheme stating what measures will be used to implement the equal treatment of the two languages (Day 2004: 216). It is said that in the Welsh case, 'all aspects of separateness having been lost', it might be thought that identity can rest only upon language (Aitchison and Carter 2000: 3). However, Dawood's experience of 'Welshness' was that Welsh identity was beyond place of birth and Welsh language, which was spoken by less than a fifth of the population (see Day 2004: 215–17). But in the context of overseas trips to a Western country, Dawood envisaged that the Caucasian people connected 'Welshness' with 'whiteness' and having a Welsh name.

Racial profiling

The 15-year-old British-born male student of Lebanese background Wahhab (a fan of the Liverpool football team) spoke of his identity as:

> If someone asked me where I'm from I would say, 'I'm from Lebanon because that's where my parents are from', and if they ask, 'What religion are you?' I'd say,

'Muslim', and of course, I'm British because I'm born here and learned here so, yeah all of, all three are together. (Interview, London, 7 April 2008)

However, Wahhab expressed his concern at how situations have changed for Muslims since the 7/7 London bombings:

Well, police are taking more actions against Muslims but it's mostly if you look like a terrorist and you've got a beard and you've got a big beard, it's more likely that then they would stop you. And mostly at airports and not really train stations anymore, but mostly airports they carry guns just in case and yeah . . . it's changed. (Interview, London, 7 April 2008)

Wahhab's comments were confirmed when later interviewees told of their experience of 'stop and search'. Muttaqui, a 22-year-old British-born imam of Bangladesh background, spoke of his national identity: 'If they ask me I'll say I'm British because I was born here . . . that's what I am, yeah British Muslim. If someone asked me what's my root then I'd say Bangladesh.' Muttaqui was a student of Islamic law. He loved playing tennis and was a fan of Manchester United. He also worked as a volunteer in a prison mentoring the Muslim prisoners. Muttaqui looked visibly Muslim and wore Islamic clothing (*topi* and *jilbab*). But inside he felt very British (and Muslim) and he was concerned that he was stopped and searched:

I mean I'll be honest with you, I've been stopped a few times at train stations. I was stopped, I had a bag with me, you know when you are off, when you go on holidays, you go home, you've got all the stuff to take home . . . clothes that need washing and stuff like that. I used to be stopped, they searched my bag, took me to the side and I've been questioned before as well. They took me to the police station. They've done that before, it happened twice now. I felt targeted because I know they've seen me before come and going but you get used to it after that I guess. (Interview, London, 5 April 2008)

A similar experience was resented by an overseas-born Muslim male student, Nawazish (aged 21), who came to Britain in 2005 and defined his national identity as Nigerian:

I got stopped and I don't know how to explain or to express that feeling that you feel, that now you are being profiled, that you are being targeted and you are the outcast and fingers are being pointed out at you. And so I was stopped and searched once and that is my personal experience. It didn't feel good.

It was in a tube station, coming out from a tube station with my bag which I had books of history and literature, I thought maybe they can concoct a story out of this, you know, you never know.

So you know, in the end they let me go. I don't have much hope in the state and the security, and the police. What hurts me more is ordinary citizens and ordinary human beings are targeted. (Interview, London, 23 April 2008)

The next two anecdotes are from two Muslim women who did not experience 'stop and search' but they felt the discomfort of their family members. The British-born Muslim teacher of Pakistani background Nazneen (aged 28), who also wore the *niqab*, said that her strongest identity was Muslim before anything else. She mentioned how her family members were targeted by the 'stop and search' process:

My sister who wore a *niqab*, that was last year and I think it was probably even around the time of the anniversary of London bombings, she got stopped for no other reason than the fact that she was Muslim and her bag was checked at one of the stations and she was on the way to university. She said they [the police] said explicitly to her, 'We're doing checks on Muslims.'
  Even my brother he was around, he was doing some course because he doesn't normally live in London and he had come down and he was travelling and he got stopped and searched – his entire body. Yeah, he has a beard, he just dresses normally . . . and a T-shirt, so yeah it was very humiliating for him. (Interview, London, 26 March 2008)

And finally, Mehr, a 24-year-old Yemeni-born Muslim woman (who has been living in Wales since the age of two together with her brother since the age of five), said:

A Welsh Yemeni that's how I see myself, this is my home, but . . . I mean my brother was actually stopped in Heathrow Airport. They [the police] asked why he went to Yemen, why did he stay two months, he [my brother] goes, 'I'm a student', [they said] 'Oh if you're a student why'd you, you missed two months from school', he's like [he said], 'It's summer holiday you know' . . . and he's just there, and I'm sure now he's on the records you know. And it's terrible because you know, we're far from it [terrorism], we're Welsh Yemenis. (Interview, Cardiff, 23 October 2008)

Mehr's family lived in Grangetown, which is a marginalised Cardiff suburb. As discussed earlier in Mahjabeen's case, Grangetown and Butetown are stereotyped as: Muslims, gangs, high unemployment. I assume young Muslims from these areas are often profiled as the 'Other'. Other anecdotes showed that racial profiling is not restricted to the Muslims of Grangetown and Butetown in Cardiff; it also happened in London. However, Muslims from particular areas could be more vulnerable than others. For example, when I visited places in Beeston, Leeds (where three of the four London bombers originated), I was informed by one source that young Muslims of Beeston were often targeted at the Manchester airport, and were sent back to Beeston instead of being allowed to board the aeroplane. I am not sure of the validity of such statements, though being a victim of 'stop and search' myself at the San Diego airport in the USA, I empathised with them being targeted as the 'Other'.

Poynting and Mason (2006: 374) state that Muslims in Britain faced disproportionate police 'stop and search' measures and targeting. From 2002 to 2003 the 'stop and search' of Asian people – a category which included Hindus and Sikhs and other non-Muslims – together comprised 45.3 per cent of the Asian or British population. From 2002/3 to 2003/4, counter-terrorism 'stop and search' incidents increased by approximately 40 per cent to almost 30,000. Similarly, Rehman (2007: 852) observes that discrimination can take a range of forms such as religious jokes, negative portrayal, disproportionate arrest, stop and search policies and targeted policing. Statistics showed that between 2001/2 and 2002/3 the number of white people stopped and searched under the Terrorism Act increased by 118 per cent, but for Asians the increase was 312 per cent.

After the 7/7 London bombings, obviously, Muslims were targeted more (as revealed by the above interviews). In 2008, Mr Aariz, a Muslim leader in London who was associated with a mosque, also said that the 'stop and search' method has proven to be disproportionate in connection with Muslims since the 7/7 London tragedy (Interview, London, 23 April 2008). The 17-year-old British-born student of Moroccan background Umair, who considered himself to be English-Muslim (also a fan of Manchester United), noted:

. . . they do get searched and stopped a lot and people say it's unfair . . . there is a lot of racists in police officers . . . but that is being stomped out. Personally myself I haven't had anything towards me because I am white, so I am considered an English person, and I speak good English, so . . . (Interview, London, 5 April 2008)

So how does this discussion relate to the issue of national identities? The respondents in this section described their identities variously as British-Lebanese Muslim, British Muslim of Bangladeshi background, Nigerian only, Muslim only, Welsh-Yemeni and English Muslim, and all were aware of how it felt to be the 'Other'. They all had different religious and ethnic backgrounds that were perceived to pose a threat to the wider community. But could these respondents actually pose a threat to the wider society? Turner (1984) and Turner et al. (1987) (cited in Jenkins 2008: 112–13) social identity theory held that each identity is shaped by membership of an in-group and opposition to an out-group (also discussed in Chapter 1). So when an individual who considers himself as an in-group member (British) but is treated as an out-group by the host society through 'stop and search' measures, the individual can become hostile. In the British context, Brah (2007: 143–4) observed:

Identity is not an already given thing but rather it is a process. It is not something fixed that we carry around with ourselves like a piece of luggage. Rather, it is constituted and changes with changing contexts. It is articulated and expressed through identifications within and across different discourses. To have a sense of being, say, Muslim is therefore different when confronted with non-Muslims than with friends and family. This sense of self will vary depending on whether the non-Muslims are friendly or hostile.

Brah also acknowledged that there could be cultural conflict within the Muslim community, but that conflict may not have an impact on one's identity in the same manner when the (majority) non-Muslims were antagonistic to the (minority) Muslims. That is, a Muslim's identity will shape up according to the friendly or hostile attitude of the non-Muslims towards them.

Identity and peer pressure

Aamanee, a British-born Muslim girl of Bangladeshi background (aged 16, national identity: British Bengali), said:

> Ever since I started year 7, I've got used to wearing the scarf because everyone I used to know, all my school friends and everyone they all wear scarfs. And when with them I didn't wear a scarf I felt uncomfortable, so I decided to wear the scarf and have kind of got used to it now. (Interview, London, 22 April 2008)

In Aamanee's case, she wanted to be in the in-group (*hijab*) so under peer pressure she started wearing the *hijab*. Ten young female Muslim participants (20–25 years) also embraced the visible Muslim identity when they entered the University. The young women said that they had two choices: either be with the Muslim students and wear the *hijab*, and attend their social gatherings, or socialise with the mainstream British students and go clubbing. They chose to brand themselves as Muslim students for the sake of everyday friendship and socialising. Hall (1992, cited in Douglas 2009: 15) observed that 'identity is not a free-for-all but must work within existing cultural representations'. So in some context, identity has to be constructed according to the prevailing environment. However, all these students showed flexibility in their identities (Interviews, London, 8 April 2004; Interviews, Cardiff, 20 October 2008). They liked rugby, football and cricket, which revealed their connection to both Britain and Asia.

Distinct identity: national, ethnic or religious

In this section, I examine the reasoning of some respondents who claimed an exclusive identity. First, I think it is necessary to mention that whereas participants spoke of their exclusive identity, sometimes other ethnic or national or religious affiliations were referred to. Perhaps the theorising of Stuart Hall (1994: 122) helps to explain this phenomenon:

> Identity is actually formed through unconscious processes over time, rather than being innate in consciousness at birth. There is always something 'imaginary' or fantasized about its unity. It always remains incomplete, is always 'in process', always 'being formed'.

Or, as in the Scottish context, Douglas (2009:19) observed that identity can go beyond nationality and place of birth. It can simply be 'a state of mind'.

Being only British

The respondents who said their identity was British had attended both Islamic and state schools. It seems the respondents have connected 'Britishness' with multiculturalism, freedom, free choice, free speech, being born in Britain, having a British passport, thinking differently from their parents and playing sports and typically supporting British football. However, the British-born male student of Bangladeshi background Badrul found football 'boring' but enjoyed boxing:

> I'm from Bangladesh and I'm British. I feel like it's my country because I was born here. I haven't been to Bangladesh for many years. I went when I was about six years old, I'm 15 now. I've been living here all my life, and I've got friends that are white as well . . . I want to be an engineer on planes. (Interview, Leeds, 13 October 2008)

Badrul lived in a marginalised suburb in Leeds and attended a state school. His suburb was predominantly inhabited by the people of the Indian subcontinent, which had tense race relations with the next suburb which was a working-class 'White' suburb. I gathered that Badrul has made good 'White' friends from school, and his integration has helped him to feel connected to Britain.

Zarin, a 17-year-old British-born girl of Pakistani heritage (fan of Manchester United), also expressed her identity as British. Zarin equated 'Britishness' with equality and citizenship rights:

> I think the main thing that Britain has so many different people from so many different countries and especially now so many immigrants are coming into our country, we really need to be less ignorant of other people's views and ethnicities and try and understand where they come from and what their beliefs are. And I think that will enable everybody in Britain to work together because even with say the new European immigrants [for example, the Polish] that are coming to the country, so many people, especially British individuals are saying, 'Oh they're taking all our

jobs', they're, all the hands-on labour kinds of jobs are being taken up by these individuals but at the end of the day they're coming here to earn a living just as other
people did, and as well as that they're enhancing our economy. People in our country
don't want to do those jobs, they want to get an education, they want to get high
status and high status jobs. (Interview, Bradford, 10 October 2008)

Though Zarin lived in Bradford, which is often called *Bradistan* or the
curry capital of Britain because it is hugely populated with people of Pakistani
origin, she felt very British. Zarin's mother (single parent) held a position in the
mainstream British workplace, and this probably influenced Zarin's identity.
I have also noted that in her interview she used the word 'our' twice, such as
they [the new European immigrants] are enhancing our [British] economy; and
'people in our country [Britain] don't want these [menial] jobs . . . '

Some respondents said that they identify themselves as 'British', but when
they spoke about their life stories they revealed a strong connection to their
country of origin, which suggests that their identity is not yet fixed. It is
situational and it overlaps according to passion, opportunity and recognition. For example, the Pakistani-born Muslim male student Rehmat (aged 15,
attended a state school) said he felt 'British' because 'I speak the language,
it's a nice country, but environment is not that good'. Rehmat mentioned
that the next-door suburb Belle Isle (White working-class suburb) had 'bad
streets' and 'wherever you go there's graffiti all over'. Though Rehmet was
born in Pakistan and lived in a predominantly Pakistani suburb in Leeds, he
felt very connected to Britain and said that his sad moment in life was when
Manchester United lost. Rehmet did not mention his Pakistani connection
when he described his identity as 'British', but as he discussed British cricket
players, such as Kevin Pietersen and Andrew Flintoff, he also spoke enthusiastically about the Pakistan cricket players Shahid Afridi and Shaoib Akhtar.
Rehmet said, 'I know Shahid Afridi sometimes makes only five, six runs but
when he gets going he made a 102 in 42 balls', and Shaoib Akhtar 'gets up to
100 miles per hour [in] his bowling'. Then the next moment Rehmet returned
to his beloved Manchester United, saying, 'The world's best player is Cristiano
Ronaldo and his mate Nani' (Interview, Leeds, 15 October 2008).

Muneer, an Algerian-born male Muslim student (aged 15), described his
identity as 'British'. Muneer attended an Islamic school, played football for
his local team, and was also a fan of Manchester United. His father was a
professional, and he lived in a suburb which he described as 'multicultural but
not like East London'. Muneer visited Algeria twice as his extended families
lived there, and his dream was to go back to Algeria and help people there
(Interview, London, 4 April 2008).

Based on this small sample, it appears that identity is not fixed. If someone
says that he is only British that does not mean he loses his ethnic connection
and vice versa. In the next section, I discuss why some participants chose to

disregard their national identity and frame themselves in terms of their ethnic identity.

My ethnic identity

In this section, I examine why some respondents chose a particular ethnic identity. The 18-year-old British-born male student Risay, whose mother was English and father Arab, stated:

> Though I speak English at home, I would consider myself more Arab because in my opinion, I don't know that this is just in the Arabic culture, but they take everything from the father. Like they take the surname from the father and they take the middle name from the father and so I would probably consider myself to be an Arab. Everything that we do at home is Arabic. We cook Arabic food, and also when I go to Libya I speak Arabic to our family [over there] because they can't speak English, so I would consider myself more Arab. (Interview, London, 16 April 2008)

Risay attended a state school in London. He said that because of his 'whiteness' he was not considered as the 'Other' in Britain. In Libya he was also not perceived as the 'Other' because he had a beard. However, Risay hoped to settle in a Muslim country, because he was unhappy with 'Britain's negativity towards Islam':

> My father [an Arab] was stopped and searched and they took his bag and searched in his bag and even a couple of my friends were searched as well, which in my opinion is wrong. They wouldn't go and search a white person, they would go and search a person for the colour of their skin and that is not right in my opinion. (Interview, London, 16 April 2008)

When I asked the 16-year-old Umair, whose father was Moroccan and mother English, 'What is your national identity, what do you consider yourself?', Umair replied:

> I consider myself to be English, and I consider myself to be Muslim. I don't want to consider myself Moroccan for one specific reason and that is due to corruption. Throughout the Arab world where all the Muslims are like jumping on each other for wealth, for oil, for money and there's no proper education . . .everybody's concerned about getting money for themselves and leaving their poor brothers to die, and they're making alliances [with rich countries] and everything like that. And it was especially so when the Egyptian President Anwar Sadat was assassinated because he accepted Israel, the first Arab to accept Israel as a state and then big problems. So, I don't want to associate myself with any Arab state until they get sorted. (Interview, London 18 April 2008)

In this context, it would seem that Umair's 'Englishness' refers to his sense of ethnicity rather than nationality. Umair asserted that he did not want to be identified with Morocco because it was associated with 'Arabness' and 'corruption', so he was more comfortable with his English ethnic identity. It is interesting to note that both Risay and Umair have English mothers.

The 25-year-old Nusaybah, who is British born and of Indian-Ugandan origin, considers herself English on the following ground:

> I would say I'm English because I'm not from Scotland; I was born in England. I have a couple of reserves regarding the term British and English anyway because I think British is more a term used for [or by] foreigners, whereas if I was born and brought up in this country, I've lived here, I've been to school, educated here I haven't got a country to go back to. (Interview, London, 24 April 2008)

In *The Idea of English Ethnicity*, Robert Young (2007) observes that 'Englishness' was never about pure Anglo-Saxon people, in other words about race. Since the nineteenth and early twentieth centuries, with the arrival of non-white immigrants, 'Englishness' has shifted to a more cultural essence. Young (2007) argues that there are non-Anglo-Saxon people who have acquired the right cultural capital to be English; they do not look Caucasian but they should be considered English. However, Nusaybah's argument was that she was born and raised in England, and this was 'home'. A corresponding argument of English ethnicity was provided by Shaykh Mogra (see Introduction). Similarly, nine respondents (four Yemeni, two Somali and three others) considered themselves to be Welsh (e.g. Mehjabeen's case discussed earlier in this chapter) because they argued that they were born in Wales, some of them had historical connections (see Chapter 3 for discussions on the Yemeni people) and they spoke the Welsh language. I note that 'Englishness' and 'Welshness' could also be considered as national identity. It is a somewhat nebulous descriptor that hovers between ethnic and national identity.

My identity: country of origin

In this section I discuss the Muslims who spoke of their exclusive connection to their parent's country of origin. However, in this study there were five overseas-born students: Danish, Iranian, Iraqi, Nigerian and Syrian, who were in Britain for a few years and said that they would go back home. Obviously, their national identity was their country of origin. About 14 participants (mostly British-born) specifically said that they felt that their sense of belonging was only to their parents' country of origin, and some of them equated their national identity with their religious identity. They have provided various reasons for their connection to their parents' country of origin. For example, the Pakistani-born girl Zulekha (aged 18), who lived in Holland before moving to Britain at the age of 12, considered herself to be a Pakistani:

> I believe I'm a Pakistani. I can't say I'm a white person or that I'm British because I don't like dressing up the way they do. I'm not saying they're wrong, I mean everybody has their own way of doing things. I don't fit in, I don't drink, I don't eat the same things, I don't listen to English songs, I don't watch television. So a lot of the things, even when I was in Holland, I didn't change, I think I'm quite happy with my identity. (Interview, London, 20 April 2008)

Though Zulekha attended a state school with mainstream British students, it did not have much impact on Zulekha's identity. Perhaps her home environment has helped her to retain her Pakistani identity. It is to be expected that frequent visits to one's country of origin would influence one's identity. Two British-born sisters of Bangladeshi background (aged 16 and 17) said that they felt connected to Bangladesh because they went back home every year where they have a big house and a swimming pool, and they have lots of fun there (Interview, 26 March 2008). These girls also lived in a predominantly Bangladeshi area in London, which presumably would reinforce their Bangladeshi identity.

Two British-born male respondents, Qutb and Khurshid (aged 18 and 19) of Pakistani background, lived in a predominantly Pakistani, economically deprived area in south Leeds. They visited Pakistan many times, spoke Urdu and English, and both said that their identity was Pakistani (Interviews, Leeds, 8 October 2008). The two respondents were both High School dropouts, and one had worked in his father's restaurant since the age of 13 and was married to a Pakistani-born girl in Pakistan at the age of 17; the other was unemployed. Initially, they were reluctant to talk to me because they thought that I was a media person and would misrepresent them. Regarding their media experience they said:

> [After 7/7] we feel normal but, what's it called when, obviously when the media comes and this and that starts, you know interviews of us, that's what just, you know, puts us off – we don't like it, we just walk off and that. Obviously it's [dis] stressing if they're coming to you every 10 minutes. One bunch comes to you then after that another comes, so you do get stressed from it. So we don't like that now. (Interviews, Leeds, 8 October 2008)

Though both respondents felt Pakistani (one through marriage and the other through heritage and neighbourhood) they were bicultural in music and sports. They liked hip-hop and rock, computer games, played cricket, volleyball and football, and 'chilling out' with friends. They spoke admiringly of the Indian cricket players Rama Pandi, Shamrez Marawat and Sachin Tendulkar, and were apparently more interested in the Indian cricket team than the Pakistani team. They also offered prayers in the mosque regularly. Khurshid said:

> I'm just straightforward Paki . . . My hope and dream is I want to become a sports-man player, whatever, play for a team and my dream is just to get in a car and just flex it – just drive around, I want to pass my driving test, that's my dream. (Interviews, Leeds, 8 October 2008)

I assume it could be natural to have a strong Pakistani identity if a person lived within that Pakistani environment. However, in Leicester, many Muslims lived in a very Asian (people of Indian, Pakistani, African-Gujrati background) area, segregated from mainstream British people. But Faraz, a British-born male (aged 18, who has a girlfriend of Pakistani background, and was also a fan of Manchester United), said:

> I feel more strongly as a Pakistani than as a British. I speak Urdu and Punjabi. Whenever things happen, for example the 9/11 incident, they [the media] were very harsh [with the Muslims]. Personally, I think British people do not like Muslims but we have to deal with that. Personally, I think we should not have to do anything. We should be ourself. Everyone has to agree with us. We are not different to anyone else. We just have different skin colour. They should get used to us. (Interview, Leicester, 10 April 2008)

I thought Faraz might say that he felt Asian or British-Asian, as some respondents in Leicester said. Perhaps Faraz's dislike of the British media stereotype against Muslims has drawn him closer to his Pakistani (Muslim) identity. Similar sentiments were echoed a week later by Kashfia, a Muslim girl in London. Kashfia is a 17-year-old British-born Pakistani girl; she said:

> I would feel British but because of all this 9/11, everything the way the media por-trays the Muslims, everyone sees Muslims as, you know, not good people I don't feel that British anymore. I'm more cultural like Pakistani. (Interview, London, 16 April 2008)

Arman, a 17-year-old British-born male student of Palestinian background, spoke very enthusiastically about his Palestinian identity. Arman was involved in organising Palestinian rallies and meetings, which revealed his patriotism towards his country of origin, which he considered 'occupied':

> I feel connected to Palestine and I feel that as a Muslim, it is the Muslim's duty to fight for that land cos obviously it's sort of an Islamic thing. I don't really feel con-nected to Britain . . . because you feel that the people just don't want you here.

I've never, ever, ever experienced any prejudice. I don't really look like an Arab. I was once waiting in a majority black area where a bit of crime goes on, an old white man came up to me and he swore actually, he said, 'Did you hear about that shooting up at there?', and then he turned around and said to me, 'Honestly we need to get rid of these F'ing black people'. He thought I was British, so he thought yeah I'd probably agree with him. (Interview, London, 16 April 2008)

Arman has merged his Palestinian identity with the collective *Ummah* identity, and with his minority identity he was sympathetic to the black people in Britain. He cited the political struggles of his imaginary homeland, lack of British government negotiations with the Palestinian government, prevalence of racism against the African-Caribbeans in Britain: all these factors seem to have impacted on his imaginary disconnection from Britain.

Finally, the 16-year-old British-born male student of Iraqi background Alamgir, who had never visited Iraq, desired to visit his imagined homeland one day. However, Alamgir supported Manchester United and was a fan of the Irish political activist Bob Geldof who constantly campaigned to 'Make Poverty History'. Alamgir also spoke of the Irish lead singer Bono of U2 music band and remarked, 'The [British] government in Britain do not do enough, they just want to meet their needs and forget about the rest of the world.' About his identity, Alamgir said:

I consider myself an Iraqi Muslim because I would never consider myself British because this country is really disgraceful . . . the way they act, the way they talk, it's not really something that I would want to be associated with. (Interview, London, 15 April 2008)

However, Alamgir's dislike for Britain was enigmatic, as the following remarks reveal an appreciation for life in Britain:

Even though I do sometimes tend to have negative thoughts about Britain but overall I think Britain is a good country like its food's great, lots of fun, like you could go to for example for the park if you want to take the kids out – Alton Towers, Chessington World of Adventures and I could go on for hours. London is a very pretty city; like nice landmarks, Shakespeare's Globe Theatre, the Tricycle Theatre. I mean London has huge, huge tourist attractions. (Interview, London 15 April 2008)

Why I am only Muslim?

Out of 216 respondents of this study, only 15 [Table 4.1] said that they felt exclusively Muslim, and did not want to connect themselves with any ethnicity or nationality. Some participants were tertiary students, who had never attended a faith school, but decided to be practising Muslims and wear the *hijab*. Typically the 'only Muslim' identity participants considered English music as *makrouh* (disliked or undesirable), listened to *nasheeds* (Islamic devotional songs) and did not watch television programmes. A few respondents were becoming Quran-e-Hafez (memorised the Quran) and had taken the *alima* course (Islamic studies course) in schools. However, despite their devotion to Islam these Muslim respondents did not completely detach themselves from British society. They were readers of English novels and watched British sports such as football, although two interviewees (female, Lateefa; and male, Aatif) felt hurt over British foreign policy on Iraq, and the Danish media's publication of Prophet Muhammad's [PBUH] cartoon, and have endorsed an exclusive Muslim identity.

Lateefa, a 16-year-old Pakistani-born girl who came to Britain at the age of eight, held a collective *Ummah* identity. Later, she shifted her *Ummah* identity to her Pakistani identity and refused to be associated with Britain. In the process of defining her identity, Lateefa was critical of British foreign policy:

> I hate the media and I hate being British. I would just want to be called a Muslim or the follower of the Prophet Muhammad [PBUH]. I mean I don't find anything good about Britain. All they do is go in different countries, go in Muslim countries especially, just for oil, they torture our people, and they kill the girls. I would rather say that I like Pakistan. (Interview, London 28 March 2008)

Regarding Muslim sentiments (for example, Lateefa's views), Salma Yaqoob, Head of Birmingham Stop the War Coalition, observed that Muslim anger and concern about injustices fellow-Muslims suffer in a far-away land such as Iraq was not new. Most British Muslims have grown up being familiar with Islamic networks in which fundraising for those suffering oppression in Palestine, Kashmir, Bosnia and Chechnya were commonplace. Many Muslims also travelled directly to those countries to do charity work (Yaqoob 2007: 280). I assume such bonding with the Muslim *Ummah* has encouraged some young Muslims to disassociate from British identity. Aatif, a British-born 30-year-old respondent of Pakistani background, held:

> Maybe after 9/11 and 7/7 and everything that's happened and you know Danish cartoons [of Prophet Muhammad, PBUH] and all these kind of things you hear about Muslim faith has probably drawn me closer to my faith really and made me a stronger person. So yeah I would identify myself first and foremost as a Muslim. (Interview, Leeds, 10 September 2008)

As discussed earlier, some Muslims felt targeted after the 9/11 and 7/7 tragedies. But Aatif's opinion that the Danish cartoon incident has drawn him closer to his faith shows the fluidity of one's identity. Prior to these incidents, Aatif never thought that he would prioritise his religious identity before his national identity. It should be noted that the English press refrained from reprinting the cartoons of Prophet Muhammad [PBUH]. British foreign Minister Jack Straw praised the British media's 'sensitivity' over the issue after UK newspapers declined to print the cartoons, which first appeared in the Danish *Jyllands-Posten* daily in September. However, the UK broadcasters, including the BBC and Channel 4, had shown brief glimpses of the images. The *Spectator* magazine briefly published them on its website, but they were quickly removed (*Guardian*, 3 February 2006, online). Only one newspaper – that of the University of Cardiff – reprinted the cartoons of Prophet Muhammad [PBUH], but it too was soon recalled. A church magazine that published these cartoons was also recalled (Interviews, Cardiff, 18 and 23 October 2008). Overall, the British press respected the sensibilities of the Muslim community. Nevertheless, Aatif (also a fan of the Liverpool football team) felt hurt over the mockery of Prophet Muhammad's [PBUH] cartoon by the Danish press, and that was the incident that tipped the scales towards him rejecting his national identity and endorsing his religious identity.

Identity and sports

In the previous two sections I have discussed how different factors have impacted on Muslims' identity. Now I discuss how sports have increased Muslims' bond with Britain. In this study, about one-third of respondents (15–30 years) said they were fans of British football. The other two-thirds said they watched cricket, tennis and boxing and Welsh rugby. Furthermore, two-thirds of the respondents (particularly males) played sports such as tennis, badminton, cage-fighting, kick-boxing, football (in their local clubs or schools); swimming and football were more popular among the female respondents.

Table 4.2 shows the respondents' support for different football teams. Forty-nine male and 25 female participants said that they supported different football teams. As outlined in Chapter 1, the total number of male respondents (15–30 years) was 94; and the total number of female respondents (15–30) was 109. Of the total male respondents, 52 per cent were fans of British football. But out of 109 total female respondents, only 23 per cent were fans of British football.

It is interesting to note that Muslims of different backgrounds felt so strongly about football. One British-born Muslim girl of Bangladeshi background, Muna (also wears a *niqab*, aged 15), said:

We live in a Bengali area. Yeah, I feel British 'cause we live here. I watch sports with my brothers . . . Manchester United. I wanna go [to] Old Trafford, you know Man United stadium, I want to go there, I want to play football! I want to go around the world and be a big fan of Manchester United Football Club. I want to be a good Muslim as well, yeah that's it. (Interview, London, 26 March 2008)

Table 4.2 British football fans, participants 15–30 years

Cities	Manchester United	Liverpool	Arsenal	Chelsea	Other
London	22	0	10	4	Tottenham 1 West Ham 1
Leicester	1	1	1	0	Leicester City 1 Bolton Wanderers 1
Bradford	2	6	0	1	0
Leeds	1	6	2	0	0
Cardiff	9	1	3	0	0
Total	35	14	16	5	4

Figure 4.1 Old Trafford Stadium, Manchester, 14 January 2009:
Manchester United v. Wigan Athletic. Table 4.2 shows that 35 Muslims
were supporters of Manchester United and many interviewees spoke highly
of No. 7, Cristiano Ronaldo. United won 1–0.
Courtesy: photo taken by Sakhawat Kabir, 14 January 2009.

The British-born Muslim girl of Pakistani background Farha (also a *hijab*, *jilbab* and *niqab* wearer who did not listen to English music but only *nasheeds*) said that she was a British Muslim. Regarding sports, she said:

> Manchester United, Liverpool, Arsenal and Chelsea; I like all of them. The best footballers, you've got Rio Ferdinand [Manchester United], Theo Walcott [Arsenal] who's a rising star, he's only 17, my age. (Interview, Bradford, 9 October 2008)

Humayun, a 15-year-old British-born male student of Bangladeshi background, said that his identity included all three: Bangladesh, British and Muslim, and he supported Manchester United:

> It's Manchester United. Cristiano Ronaldo, or Paul Scholes good Man U players. No there's always competition on the lead table because there's other tough teams as well like Chelsea and Liverpool. So there's all this competition but we [Manchester United] always end up at the top. (Interview, London, 31 March 2008)

A 15-year-old Pakistani-born Muslim male student, Mansoor, who came to England at the age of 10, defined his identity as 'British' because he said, 'I live here and I speak the language. My sad moment is when Manchester United loses' (Interview, Leeds, 13 October 2008). Paradoxically, Aatif, a British-born man of Pakistani background, said he no longer felt connected to Britain because of the 9/11 and 7/7 events, and Prophet Muhammad's [PBUH] cartoon incident (discussed earlier), but when it came to sports:

> I support Liverpool, like in the 80s they were the most successful team in Europe and so forth . . . so obviously young people want to support the best so . . . just affiliate yourself to whoever was the best team so . . . it's always been Liverpool, although recently they haven't been that successful apart from the last three or four years so . . . [now young people support Manchester United]. (Interview, Leeds, 10 September 2008)

In Cardiff, a female respondent of Somali background, Mehjabeen, who felt 'Welsh', said that she supported Arsenal because the team has many coloured players. So her 'Welshness' extended to 'Britishness' in the context of minorities' (colour) recognition in mainstream British society.

Smith and Porter (2004: 2) observe that ethnic minorities submerged within a majority national culture may identify more strongly in some circumstances with the nation-state that they or their parents have left rather than the one they actually inhabit. For example, in a cricket match between Pakistan and England, a British-Pakistani may support the Pakistani team. This might be a determining factor of their national identity. However, in my survey I found only a small minority of respondents from the Indian subcontinent (12 respondents, second or third generation) supported the Pakistani cricket team rather than the English team.

As discussed earlier, about one-third of respondents (36 per cent) explicitly said that they supported British football teams (Table 4.2). Hobsbawm (1992, cited in Smith and Porter 2004: 4) argues that sport, at least for males, has proved 'uniquely effective' in generating a sense of belonging to a nation. Hobsbawm (1992) accounts for this by recalling 'the ease with which even the least political or public individuals can identify with the nations as symbolised by young persons excelling at what practically every man wants, or at one time in his life has wanted, to be good at'. The national team thus becomes a focus for these powerful, if unrealisable fantasies:

> The imagined community of millions seems more real as a team of eleven named people. The individual, even the one who only cheers, becomes a symbol of his nation himself. (Hobsbawm 1992: 143)

Smith and Porter (2004: 5) emphasised that an exclusive sport feeling was essentially a male preserve, and that most (English) men dream of being David Beckham or Nasser Hussein. Similarly, in the Scottish context, Hopkins (2007a; 2007b) found that sports (football) was popular among Muslim men. However, in my survey I found that sports supporters were not restricted only to male (English) participants. Young Muslim women also appeared to be keen football fans, and spoke of their favourite players. Overall, many interviewees, both male and female (particularly a few Muslim girls), spoke highly of Cristiano Ronaldo.

Conclusion

Some scholars (Nairn 1981; Hobsbawm 1992; Smith and Porter 2004; Polley 2004; Douglas 2009) have noted that only sports can exhibit one's sense of loyalty and become a 'cultural marker of nationalism', or 'us' against 'them' mentality. In other words, affiliation with sports could reveal separateness or integration. For example, if a British-Iraqi supports the Iraqi soccer team against the British team, in that case his identity would be marked with Iraqi nationalism, or as Anderson (1991) said, that diasporic immigrants dream of returning to their homeland one day. On the other hand, a respondent of this study, Imran (British-born male of Bangladeshi background, aged 20), who said that his national identity was Bengali-Welsh, commented, 'I've never supported a team: Bengali, British or Welsh. But rugby, I think, is the only one where maybe I have some kind of personal or emotional investment – I want to see Wales win' (interview, Cardiff, 20 October 2008). According to the theorists above, it marked Imran's Welsh identity.

However, I think that attributing affiliation by sport alone is far too simplistic. Throughout this chapter I have noted that identity was not fixed. For example the 16-year-old British-born Iraqi, Alamgir, initially detested Britain, but as he discussed the landscape of Britain he reflected his admiration for the country. Similarly, Arman, the 17-year-old British-born student of Palestinian background, felt disconnected to Britain as he saw the disdain of the British government towards the ordeal of the Palestinians in their country, Palestine. However, when he spoke of his interfaith activities through school, Arman appeared to be a thoughtful British citizen. I have also pointed out that positive experience in the workforce can help in building a stronger British identity.

Whereas the focus of this chapter has been on young Muslims' affinity with Britain, it is important to note that the Muslim community also has responsibilities towards becoming responsible British citizens. Constructive criticism of British foreign policy is a citizenship right, but for Muslim parents constantly to talk negatively about British culture and politics may negatively impact on their children. Also, it is naïve to believe that children who were born and raised in Britain would one day return to their 'imagined homeland'. Parents should encourage their children to be connected with Britain. By the same token, the British government should be vigilant that its foreign policies, such as Iraqi occupation or aloofness to the Palestinian ordeal, could negatively impact on British Muslims' identity.

Finally, it is encouraging that all 216 respondents in the five cities (London, Leicester, Bradford, Leeds and Cardiff) were to some extent bicultural, which is a positive sign of British citizenship. However, the schools and colleges should give more recognition to their students' bicultural skills and respect their ethnic and religious cultural sensitivities. For example, if the wider community accepts a minority's culture, then the minorities will be more inclined to adopt the new (host) culture. For example, if Muslim girls wish to refrain from swimming with boys, their opinions should be respected. Many Muslim girls prefer to dress modestly. Swimming costumes can be quite revealing, so swimming with their male counterparts contradicts their belief in modesty. On the other hand, the Muslim students should be encouraged to participate in wider community/voluntary services and interfaith dialogues. Muslim youths are fond of English music and in Muslim schools they should not be forced to listen to *nasheeds*. Also many Muslim students are bilingual. At home they speak their first language (mother tongue), which is a valuable source of other languages for the nation, so the schools should provide special classes to improve the English-language skills of the bilingual students if required. It is also important that parents recognise that if their children have a good knowledge of the English language, they will fare better in the wider society (further discussions in the last chapter – Conclusion).

CHAPTER

5

IS THE MEDIA BIASED AGAINST MUSLIMS?

Yeah, a long time before 7/7 people shouted 'Paki' at us. But after 7/7 that has changed. The only thing is that now – the media, the demonisation, well obviously if you see every day in newspapers, hundreds of articles, on the news every day something bad saying, Muslims they do this and Muslims they do that. They blame Muslims, they are killing everyone. Somewhere in their [wider society's] mind, someone is going to say, I don't like these [Muslim] people because I am afraid of them. (Interview, London, 15 April 2008)

The interviewee, Shujauddin (male, aged 18), identified himself as 'mixed race' and British because he was born in Britain. Shujauddin's parents were from Pakistani and English backgrounds. He noted that since the 7/7 London bombings, the word 'Paki' has been replaced by 'Muslim' and the British media have been responsible for this change in the wider society's perception. Another interviewee, the British-born student of Palestinian background Sadaat (male, aged 18), thought that after the 7/7 incident the British media have become more influenced by the right-wing ideology of the British National Party. Sadaat was overseas for a few years but when he returned to London after the 7/7 London bombings, he noticed a sudden change in people's perception: Muslim equates with terrorists. Sadaat believed:

The BNP, they feed off those kinds of things. Obviously the media, I mean in my opinion the media blatantly is as biased as you can be against Muslims and obviously they feed off that kind of thing. I mean when the government feeds off it. They [media] use it as an excuse to sort of spread their hate against the Muslim community . . .

If you ask me the real victims of 7/7 were not the 52 people who died, it was actually the 1.6 million Muslims in Britain who are feeling the consequences of it. (Interview, London, 16 April 2008)

Sadaat's observation that the BNP has capitalised on the 7/7 incident has some justification. For example, for their upcoming by-election in Barking, East London in July 2005, the BNP distributed a leaflet with a photograph of the bomb-blasted number 30 bus, with the slogan, 'Maybe now it's time to start listening to the BNP' (*Mail Online,* 12 July 2005). As discussed in Chapter 3, the BNP was against 'coloured' immigration, but the leaflet shows that their target had shifted to the Muslims. In the report, 'In Defence of British Muslims', the author Lucy James (2009) notes that around 2005 the British National Party shifted its focus from general racism against the Asian and the Black to a religious group, Muslims. Since the Muslims cannot be protected, James states:

> Now there was a change in tactic. Feeding on the general atmosphere of suspicion post 7/7, fed by the relentless tabloid press, the BNP initiated a vicious targeted attack against Britain's Muslim communities . . . In 2006 Nick Griffin, Chairman of the BNP since 1999, boldly stated that 'the British National party is positioned very firmly to benefit politically from ever-growing popular concern about the rise of Islam'. Perhaps this was an attempt to avoid prosecution for inciting racial hatred; under British law Muslims do not exist as an ethnic group, so cannot be victims of racial discrimination on the basis of their faith. (James 2009: 6)

In other words, James (2009: 6, 20–34) observes that British Muslims could be doubly disadvantaged. On the one hand, the BNP, encouraged by the tabloid media, is making derogatory statements against the Muslims, and on the other hand, Muslims as a religious group cannot file complaints against the BNP (or the media) under the anti-discrimination laws because Muslims do not form an enthic group like the Jews and Sikhs (see also Modood 2005).

In this chapter I argue that the media plays an important role in the formation of one's identity. Based on previous research, I hypothesise that if the national media targets one particular group through constant derogatory depictions in reporting, images, headlines, etc., that group feels marginalised. I apply this hypothesis to the case of Muslims in Britain (2006–8), drawing on evidence from my field study and with reference to social identity theory. I begin with the aforementioned Jenkins (2008) observation (see Chapter 1):

> Individuals, in using stereotypical categories to define themselves, thus bring into being human collective life. Jenkins (2008: 112–13)

In this context, I argue that respondents of this study frequently invoked media stereotypes to define themselves, for example, that 'we' (the Muslims) are detested by 'them' (the British media). Thus the British media has induced the Muslim interviewees to think as a collective group (though they were ethnically very diverse). Arguably, by collectively resisting what they saw as unfair stereotyping by the media, Muslims actually strengthened their Islamic identity.

I begin the rest of this chapter, first, with a brief discussion of some academics' observations on the British media's representation of the minorities, including Muslims, in order to understand the 'Us' (the mainstream British people/media) and 'Them' (the ethnic/religious minority) debate. Second, I display the pattern of responses of 216 respondents on the British media in Table 5.1. Third, I examine the representation of Muslims in the British print media. I examine the language (headlines and content) used in the newspapers in terms of what these signified to readers (O'Shaughnessy and Stadler, 2002: 41–3 and 55). I also examine the photographic and other images associated with the news reports/content, which are designed to further the audience's understanding and to engage readers more deeply with the people, events and issues in the news. Finally, I make a snapshot analysis of some British newspapers published on three anniversaries of the 7/7 London bombings to review the 'Us' and 'Them' press rhetoric.

Academics' observations

Just as the arrival of immigrants in the 1960s, '70s and '80s was viewed as undesirable by a section of British society, some British media took every opportunity to express mainstream British superiority in the divide between 'Us' and 'Them'. However, the 'Us' and 'Them' divide is not only restricted to the British media. In *Covering Islam*, Said (1997) observed that there are many troubling incidents associated with the Muslim world, such as the killing of 240 American marines by a Muslim group in Lebanon in 1983, the Lockerbie bombing of Pan Am flight 103 in 1988, and Khomeini's *fatwa* against Salman Rushdie in 1989; but when the Western mass media apply a blanket label of 'Islam' to an event, either as an explanation or indiscriminately to condemn 'Islam', this is usually a form of attack against the Islamic world (Said 1997: ix–xvi).

In the Australian context, Kabir (2006; 2008a) observes that in times of crisis, the *Australian* and *West Australian* newspapers have generally leaned towards the mainstream Australian/Western worldview; for example, in the aftermath of the 11 September 2001 tragedy and the Cronulla riots in December 2005, it labelled Muslims as the 'Other'. In the UK context, in *Media Audiences*, Herbert (2005: 114) suggests that through the use of powerful headlines, the print media overtly influences its mainstream British audience on any critical issue. One example of this might be the *Sun* newspaper's headline on the day of the 1992 UK General Election (9 April) which stated, 'If Kinnock wins today, will the last person to leave Britain please turn out the lights' (Herbert 2005: 115). Arguably, this may have influenced undecided voters against the Labour Party leader, Neil Kinnock, and affected the outcome of the election (Herbert, 2005: 114–15).

Earlier in 1991, Van Dijk analysed 2,700 British newspaper articles that were written on ethnic issues in the period 1985–6. He recognised the importance of unequal power relations in society (in this instance, of reduced power relations associated with ethnicity); media content; and public or audience attitudes and beliefs. The study sought to explain how 'white in-group' members expressed and communicated their ethnic and racial attitudes within the group, and how such attitudes were adopted in the wider society. Van Dijk (1991: 176–7, see also Devereux 2003: 130) noted that the editorials of some newspapers conformed to a right-wing ideology about ethnic issues; for example, from an editorial published in the *Mail* newspaper (28 November 1985), Van Dijk (cited in Devereux 2003: 130) identified the following themes: First, 'the editorial "presupposes" that "we [British] are hospitable and tolerant"'; and secondly, '[the editorial] employs a number of euphemisms when applied to how "we" should deal with immigrants. We (or us) the tolerant and hospitable British must be "brisk", "in saying no", "in showing the door" to them (the immigrants)' (Van Dijk 1991: 176–7, cited in Devereux 2003: 130).

In the Scottish context, Douglas (2009: 50–2, 59) observed that newspapers have a powerful and 'exclusive' relationship with their readers based largely on a sense of shared community and national consciousness. Newspapers need readers, and for their commercial purpose they need to develop a 'core loyal readership' who will continue to buy the same newspaper on a regular basis. Therefore to retain a community feeling the newspapers promote their exclusive national character against the 'Other' (the English). For example, the terms 'we' and 'us' (we the Scots, to we in the UK, or we in Scotland and in the UK as a whole or so on) are used within or between Scottish newspaper discourse.

However, in his book *Islamic Britain*, Lewis noted that the British press became particularly interested in the Muslims after the Honeyford affair in 1984–5 (Lewis 1994: 2–3). Ray Honeyford was the headteacher of Drummond Road Middle School in Bradford, which had a majority of Muslim pupils of Pakistani background. He publicly deplored the concessions made by the education authority to accommodate the special needs of Muslim parents such as single-sex education and extended leave for children to visit South Asia. He considered this gave 'priority to the preservation of cultural identity over the promotion of social integration and social cohesion' (Lewis 2002: 71). When Honeyford published his article in a right-wing journal, the *Salisbury Review*, in 1984, it attracted condemnation from the Islamic and Pakistani society in Bradford. The unhappy episode dragged on for eighteen months and was only resolved at the end of 1985 when Honeyford was persuaded to take early retirement and given a generous financial settlement. Lewis (2002: 2–3) observed:

In retrospect, the 'Honeyford affair' assumed additional importance. It represented 'the first major public campaigning victory of any Muslim community in Britain'. Muslims could no longer be ignored and were attracting national media interest. Throughout the campaign, pictures of angry crowds picketing the school and holding aloft inflammatory placards were flashed across the nation's television screens. Ominously, the term 'fundamentalist' had also entered the journalistic lexicon to describe Muslims.

Arguably at best, this 'victory' was a muted one because the Muslims were then framed within the media rhetoric of 'Us' and 'Them'. Later in 1997, the Runnymede Trust report gathered data on examples of Islamophobia in the UK, noting that since the early 1980s, the Honeyford Affair, the Rushdie Affair, and issues such as *halal* meat in schools and the first Gulf War had pushed Islam into the national arena. These events suggested that Muslims were desperate to preserve their culture, which in turn promoted separatism and posed a threat to traditional British values. Poole (2002) discussed how the British broadsheet press had covered Islam and Muslims since the Salman Rushdie affair (1989), when a *fatwa* of death warrant was issued against Rushdie by Iran's Ayatollah Khomeini following the 1988 publication of *The Satanic Verses*. Poole (2002: 57) observed that in the late 1990s, many of the international events dominating the news media's attention in places like Algeria, Afghanistan, Bosnia, Chechnya, Kashmir and Kosovo had involved the 'Muslim Other', for example, the Taliban's atrocities against Muslim women, and the Chechen militants' fight for independence from Russia.

Poole (2002) observed that coverage by *The Guardian* appeared generously disposed towards British Muslims, giving voice and space to a range of commentators who raised the West's treatment of Islam and Muslims as instances of 'Other'-ing. Commentators such as Edward Said, Salman Rushdie, Ziauddin Sardar and Tariq Modood were given space in this newspaper's opinion section. *The Guardian* also provided sympathetic coverage in cultural issues raised since 9/11, including, for example, the choice of some Western Muslim women to wear the *hijab*. *The Times* also covered some Muslim issues sympathetically, but the approach of *The Guardian* was usually from a secular perspective highlighting civil liberties and freedom of speech. *The Times* was more likely to adopt a 'Christian perspective' and focus on Muslim extremism (Poole 2002: 5–7), setting up a clash of cultures/clash of faiths discourse. However, Poole (2002: 84; see also Green and Kabir 2007: 2–3) identified some defining themes in Britain's broadsheet coverage of Muslims and Islam prior to the 2005 bombings, as follows:

- Muslim involvement in deviant activities threatens security in the UK
- Muslims are a threat to British 'mainstream' values and thus provoke concerns about integration
- There are inherent cultural differences between Muslims and the host community, which create tensions in interpersonal relations
- Muslims are increasingly making their presence felt in the public sphere

Gillespie (2006: 908) observed, 'media create spaces in which identity, belonging, and security are continually questioned, negotiated, reinforced and revised'. So the media reporting and representation of current issues could impact on the audience of both Muslims and non-Muslims in different ways. For example, Matar (2006) noted that the 9/11 tragedy reinforced the views of many Palestinians in Britain that the British media was biased. For example, the BBC, ITV, Channel 4, Sky and Channel Five reported the same news every day, exactly in the same order and at the same time. If there was news of five Palestinians killed by Israel, they never showed the graphics, which would be damaging to Britain's ally, Israel, and they usually portrayed the Palestinians as 'terrorists' (Matar 2006: 1039). However, when the September 11th tragedy occurred, Knightly (2001, cited in Harb and Bessaiso 2006: 1064) noted that, by continuing to refer to them as 'Muslim and Islamic terrorists', the perpetrators were seen as 'products of a fanatical strain of Islam'. As a result, the associated negative behaviour was seen to evolve out of something inherent in the religion, rendering any Muslim a potential terrorist (Knightly 2001, cited in Harb and Bessaiso 2006: 1064).

According to Harb and Bessaiso (2006: 1064), the cultural politics of 'us and them' in news discourses create and reinforce fears of white audiences towards ethnic groups. Wilson and Gutierrez (1995: 44) believed that in the absence of alternative media portrayals and broadened news coverage, one-sided portrayals and news articles could easily become 'the reality in the minds of the audience'. In that respect the media has a greater influence over the opinions of their audience. For example, after the 9/11 Twin Towers tragedy a member of the mainstream British audience, Andrea (aged 35–45), expressed her anger against the Muslims:

> . . . I must admit, if I was walking down the street and I would see one of these, you know those dresses that they wear from head to toe, I'd get angry cause I'd think, you know, 'your bloody beliefs and all the rest of it, that did all that' . . . (Cited in Adams and Burke 2006: 992)

Of course, the media does not make news. It is a mirror to reality. The perpetrators of the 9/11 tragedy and the 7/7 London bombings were Muslims but they represented minority militant Muslim groups. But this distinction was soon lost because the media relentlessly represented Muslims as the 'Other' through their choice of words, images and headlines.

In Table 5.1, I extract the key points of the responses of the 216 participants on the British media, and in the later sections I examine interview responses of the participants along with examples of the British media's (press) representation of Muslims.

Table 5.1 shows that most of the 216 respondents said that the British media was biased or negative towards Muslims. I separated their responses

Table 5.1 Key points of 216 responses, aged 15–30 and over [male 105; female 111]

Number of participants	Responses	Key points
71 (30 males, 41 females)	Media is biased	Media conveys the wrong message. They take some verses of the Quran that is against humanity, and then highlight it. Media is biased. So many Iraqis are dying, but if one British soldier dies, it is big news. Gordon Brown is biased. He does not say anything to the media.
14 (6 males, 8 females)	Media since 7/7	We live in an English area. The media made it difficult for me after the 7/7 London bombings. After 7/7, media's hostile reporting. Media is so biased that it didn't report British National Party's bomb-making equipments.
11 (4 males, 7 females)	Muslims as terrorists	About 10–15 years ago there was nothing on Muslims, now you turn on the news it is Muslims, terrorists.
6 females	Media is ignorant	Media always associate Muslims with arranged marriage, forced marriage, female circumcision and honour killing.
6 (4 males, 2 females)	Media stereotype	Media provides extreme view. Everyone who has a beard has a bomb under their beard.
13 (6 males, 7 females)	Media has lost our trust	Even the moderate newspapers *The Independent* and *The Guardian*, they blatantly lied over Archbishop's comments. From that day I lost my faith in British media. 'Media has wrongly portrayed the alleged terrorist, Babar Ahmed of Tooting, South London.' Media does not bring educated Muslim women in their programmes.
2 (1 male, 1 female)	Media radicalises Muslim youth	Media finger points at you, radicalised Muslim youth. Media, the British National Party factor, politicians targeting Muslim students, and indirectly creating radicalisation.
13 (4 males, 9 females)	Biased newspapers	Negative against Muslims, e.g. *Metro* newspaper; *The Sun* and *The Star* are gossip newspapers; the *Evening Standard*, the *Daily Star*, *Daily Mirror*; *Daily Mail*, *Leicester Mercury* portrays Muslims negatively.
10 (5 males, 5 females)	Reference to electronic media	In Sky news, every single story was about terrorism. Channel 4 wants to make all rules. Media misrepresents Muslims. It takes the views of Muslims with extreme views, e.g. *Dispatches*. Channel 4 has a programme on Islam, it becomes controversial, but there is no controversy on *The DaVinci Code*.

Table 5.1 (continued)

Number of participants	Responses	Key points
11 (9 males, 2 females)	Muslims are at fault	There are too many tensions in the Muslim community. I think media has put Islam proper back.
15 (12 males, 3 females)	Media culture	Media is business; media is propaganda; media is politics; media is racist; media is double-standard; media is rumour and gossip.
5 (2 males 3 females)	Media needs to improve	Media needs a bit of improvement. Media should advise us how to be good Muslims.
10 (7 males 3 females)	Positive comments	British media is good. Media is allowing Muslim voice. Channel 4 shows Muslim programmes.
2 (1 male, 1 female)	Selective audience	I only watch sports.
3 (2 males, 1 female)	No time for media	No time for media, however, media should investigate more rather than twist news.
2 (1 male, 1 female)	No impact from the media	Media does not affect me.
22 (11 males, 11 females)	No comments	No comments on the media.

into the following categories: Seventy-one respondents said that the British media was biased, and some of them also gave examples. Fourteen respondents explicitly spoke of the repercussions of the 7/7 London bombings upon them as 'Muslims'. Eleven people said that the media portrayed them as terrorists. Six spoke of the media's ignorance, and another six respondents remarked on the stereotypical representation of Muslims, for example, associating Muslim news with men with beards. Thirteen people said that they had lost their trust in the media because of the heavy focus on radical Muslims. Two participants thought that the media's constant negative news of Muslims would radicalise Muslim youths. Twenty-three interviewees made particular reference to the press and electronic media, which they thought portrayed Muslims negatively, and delivered one-sided news.

On the other hand, eleven respondents were self-critical and recognised that the Muslims were not doing enough to present a positive image in society. For example, there were questionable cultural issues within the Muslim community such as forced marriages and lack of Muslim leadership (discussed in Chapter 3). It was noted that through better integration, Muslims could create a more positive image in the wider society.

Surprisingly, ten respondents had positive comments on the media in that they suggested the British media has given space to Muslim voices such as Shaykh Ibrahim Mogra (more in Chapter 7), whereas five participants suggested the media needs to improve its reporting style. Of the rest: fifteen interviewees spoke in neutral terms of media culture; two respondents said that they were a selective audience; three participants did not have time for the media; and two interviewees said that the media did not have an impact on them. Finally, twenty-two respondents did not make any comments on the media. In the next section, I examine some of the observations of the respondents of this study.

Representation of Muslims in the British print media

As indicated above, many respondents in this study said that the British media was biased. I categorise their observations in separate subheadings as follows:

Muslims are labelled as the 'Other'

The *Tower Hamlets Recorder* (5 March 2008: 1) had a big headline, 'Muslims are at war', with a small headline, 'Men accused of supporting terrorism'. The headline was associated with the photos of two alleged terrorists who had beards and were wearing Muslim caps (*topi*). It was a report on eight alleged terrorists, three of whom were locals from Tower Hamlets. It cited a Muslim, Abdul Saleem, aged 31, of Mellish Street, Isle of Dogs, who insisted in the Kingston Crown Court that Muslims are 'at war', and were entitled to target those 'tyrant oppressors' who occupy their lands. He further said that it was the 'obligation' of British Muslims to support all Muslims across the world, including insurgents in Iraq, Pakistan and Afghanistan. Saleem said, 'We are all Muslim brothers and we must support them physically, verbally or financially. An attack on Muslims in Pakistan is an attack on Osama bin Laden is an attack on me because he is a Muslim'.

The *Tower Hamlets Recorder* is a local subedition of the weekly tabloid newspaper the *Newham Recorder* for the London Borough of Tower Hamlets. In 2007 Tower Hamlets was a home for 71,389 Muslims, which amounted to 36.4 per cent of the population of Tower Hamlets (Lewis 2007: 21). Since three of the alleged terrorists were from Tower Hamlets, it would certainly be a matter of great concern for all the people of Tower Hamlets (including Muslims). But the headline 'Muslims are at war' accused all Muslims in general of terrorism. This sort of headline, where a specific religious group is labelled, impacts in a negative manner on the general Muslim population. I have interviewed some Muslim male students, aged 15–16, in the London Borough of Tower Hamlets. They attended a Muslim school and as a part of their school uniform they had to wear a Muslim cap (*topi*) and a Muslim shirt (*kurta*). In order to avoid being seen as a Muslim, one interviewee, Yunus (British-born of Bangladeshi background, male, aged 15), remarked:

After school they [the boys] tuck their *kurta* into their trousers, put their jacket on and take this hat [*topi*] off and they put another hat on. So they [the wider society] don't see them as an obvious Muslim. Because sometimes it's for your [the boys'] own safety. (Interview, London, 30 March 2008)

Another British-born male school student of Bangladeshi background in Tower Hamlets, Saqer, aged 15, said:

You're walking down the street if you have a head scarf or if you're a normal Muslim brother with a beard and the cap, they would criticise you right in front of your face because they just imagine that 'Oh you're going to bomb us as well aren't you? So we want to kick you out of our country, you don't deserve to stay here'. (Interview, London, 30 March 2008)

These young Muslims identified themselves as British Bangladeshi Muslims, but when it came to the British values of freedom of movement, their movement, they were under constant surveillance because the media has constructed their image as the 'Other'.

Two weeks later, the national tabloid newspaper, *The Sun* (18 March 2008: 29), had a big headline, 'MOSQUE FIEND'. Underneath it was written, 'Muslim who raped girl claimed he was preaching'. The headline was associated with a photograph of the East London mosque, and the caption read: 'Mosque . . . 7 members lied'. *The Sun* (18 March 2008: 29) reported that, 'A Muslim leader who claimed he was preaching at a mosque when he was really carrying out a brutal rape was jailed for ten years yesterday.' It was alleged that Abdul Mukin Khalisadar, aged 26, held a knife to his victim's throat and attacked her in her home. Abdul persuaded seven men to back up his claim that he had been in the mosque at that time. However, the DNA sample proved that Abdul was guilty of rape. When Judge Timothy King gave his verdict against Abdul, *The Sun* (18 March 2008: 29) reported, the 'Burka-clad women [victim's relatives] in the gallery yelled at the judge – and one screamed that the victim was a prostitute'.

Of course, rape is a heinous crime, and rapists should be punished. However, rape is not specific to any religion: in linking a rapist with his religion and place of worship, *The Sun* (18 March 2008: 29) appeared to imply that rape was synonymous with Muslims. In 2009, the UK Equality and Human Rights Commission said that every year an estimated 3 million women experience rape, domestic violence, stalking or some other kind of abuse (*Guardian*, 30 January 2009: 1). Regarding the British media, the British-born interviewee of Bangladeshi background Suraj, aged 16, observed:

The British media is fairer in portraying the Muslims than other types of media like the American media or the French media. The British media will portray the Muslims' bad things as well as the non-Muslim things. But one thing I don't like about the British media is when, suppose there's a rapist and his name is John Allen, they will not say a Christian rapist, they will [say] John Allen is a rapist. But if his name is Muhammad Abdullah, and he was a rapist, they would say a Muslim rapist. Again, they will say, 'Oh, four white men jailed over Islamophobic attack'. Likewise they will say, 'Four Muslim men jailed over you know homophobic attack, they will say in this sense effect. (Interview, London, 31 March 2008)

As an example of what Suraj asserted: under the headline, 'Muslim man convicted of killing BNP activist after years of "racial hostility"', the *Independent* newspaper (30 August 2008: 12) reported that a Muslim man, Habib Khan, was jailed for eight years for killing his BNP activist neighbour Keith Brown. The report was accompanied by the murderer's photo (a bearded man) and the caption read: 'Habib Khan: Stabbed next-door neighbour, Keith Brown'. The incident was obviously a race-relations issue, but the headline indicated 'a Muslim man', which was inappropriate and likely to generate mainstream fear of the British Muslim population.

The problematic Muslims

In March 2008, the *Muslim News* ('Distorted Media Reports on Muslim Doctors' Hygiene widely Condemned', 28 March 2008: 1) claimed that the *Liverpool Echo* 'inaccurately' reported that female medical students at Alder Hey Hospital 'objected to rolling up their sleeves when washing their hands and removing arm coverings in theatre, claiming that it is regarded as immodest'. The story originally appeared online on 26 February 2008 with the headline, 'Muslim Medics in Alder Hey Stand-Off'; it was subsequently picked up by the *Daily Mail*, which reported that 'Muslim Medics refuse to roll up their sleeves in hygiene crack down – because it's against their religion', and by the *Daily Telegraph,* which alleged that 'Female Muslim medics "disobey hygiene rules"' (see *Muslim News*, 28 March 2008: 1). Alder Hey's Medical Director, Dr Steve Ryan, told the *Muslim News*:

> As part of our Single Equality Scheme we continue to consult with minority groups on a range of issues, uniform being just one. We have not received any complaints from our staff in relation to this stipulation which is part of our wide-ranging infection control policy. (*Muslim News*, 28 March 2008: 1)

A spokeswoman for the Royal Liverpool Children NHS Trust (in Alder Hey) also fervently refuted the allegations made in the *Liverpool Echo*, which she said left the staff and students 'very distressed'. She further added:

> The *Liverpool Echo* ran a story that was frankly misleading, inaccurate, untrue and racist in our view. We have taken this up with them and made a formal complaint

about their very poor covering of this subject, which has no foundation or substance to it. (*Muslim News*, 28 March 2008: 1)

On the other hand, the *Liverpool Echo* correspondent Caroline Innes defended her reporting ('Muslim Medics in Alder Hey Stand-Off', 26 March 2008). She told the *Muslim News* that her newspaper had responded to a complaint by the Royal Liverpool Children's NHS Trust and that 'lots of things they had said, they have actually withdrawn'. Subsequently, the wider community reacted to the female Muslim medics news, whereupon only one of the 53 postings on the *Daily Mail* website was favourable to Muslims, with a majority calling for the medics to resign (see *Muslim News*, 28 March 2008: 1). The *Daily Mail*'s strategy reminded me of Nawsheen's (a British-born female interviewee of Pakistani background) comment that 'the media is negative because it wants a bigger reaction' (Interview, Bradford, 7 October 2008).

A few months later, over a different incident, the *Daily Express* (16 October 2008: 7), under the headline, 'Muslim postal workers demand extra breaks to pray five times a shift', reminded its readers about the 'problematic' Muslims in Britain. The postal workers soon withdrew their case because they were told they had no chance of winning: they were already provided with breaks (along with other non-Muslim colleagues) when they could offer their prayers. Thus the *Daily Express* (16 October 2008: 7) report was mischievous because the case was withdrawn by the postal workers.

That the Muslims were a 'problem' was again indicated in November by the *Daily Mail* (3 November 2008: 5) under the headline, 'Muslim chef sues police for asking him to cook pork'. The article reported that Hasanali Khoja had accused Scotland Yard of refusing to guarantee that he would not have to handle pork, which is forbidden in Islam. Khoja complained that he was placed on special unpaid leave for a year after refusing to work without the guarantee that he would not have to handle pork. Later he was given work at another section where he did not have to handle pork, but he had been down-graded to higher catering manager. Along with this report, the *Daily Mail* (3 November 2008: 5) reminded readers of other issues about Muslims under a subheading, 'The clash of cultures':

- In June this year Bushra Noah, a Muslim, was awarded £4,000 after suing a hair salon which turned her down for a job because she wore a veil covering her hair.
- In January 2007, a female Muslim police cadet refused to shake the hand of former Scotland Yard chief Sir Ian Blair at her passing-out ceremony because it was against her faith to touch a man who was not her husband or a close relative.
- In November 2006, Aishah Azmi, a Muslim teaching assistant from Dewsbury in West Yorkshire, was sacked for refusing to remove her veil in class. In a hugely controversial case, she sued for discrimination but the claim was dismissed.

- Alexander Omar Basha, a 24-year-old Muslim policeman, was excused from guarding the Israeli embassy on 'moral grounds' in 2006 after he expressed concerns over the bombing of Lebanon.
- Sainsbury's permits Muslim checkout staff to refuse to sell alcohol, allowing them to call in a colleague when customers are buying wine, beer or spirits. (*Daily Mail*, 3 November 2008: 5)

There is no doubt that the incidents (including chef Khoja's case) noted above indicate 'a clash of cultures'. However, such cultural restrictions cannot be imposed in mainstream workplaces unless these are Islamic institutions. Nevertheless, when these isolated incidents are reported in the media they are bound to generate fear among mainstream readers and cast Muslims as the 'Other'. The next discussion shows that too much focus on Muslims elsewhere in the world negatively impacts on British Muslim readers as well.

Reference to the Quran

On 25 March 2008, the *Daily Express* had a huge headline, covering almost the whole of the cover page: 'Fury over plan to teach the Koran in schools'. It reported that a National Union of Teachers (NUT) representative at a conference said that 'state schools should be forced to open their doors to Islamic preachers teaching the Koran'. It also suggested that the 'existing religious schools – almost all of them Christian – should have to admit pupils from other faiths'. The union's general secretary Steve Sinnott thought that 'allowing Muslim imams to preach in schools would be a way to reunite divided communities' (*Daily Express*, 25 March 2008: 1). The proposal was immediately criticised by Conservative Party backbencher Mark Pritchard, who said, 'This is just further appeasement of Muslim militants. We should just follow the existing laws on religious education, which state that it should be of a predominantly Christian character . . .'

On page 7, the report (*Daily Express*, 25 March 2008) continued. It was associated with another headline, 'Call to let imams preach in schools', and an image of a *madrasah* in Dhaka, Bangladesh where an imam was teaching young Muslim girls wearing the *burqa* and boys wearing a turban and *topi*. The caption read: 'Holy orders: Children reading the Koran at school in Dhaka, Bangladesh. British schools should follow suit, says the NUT' (*Daily Express*, 25 March 2008: 7).

When I read the report (*Daily Express*, 25 March 2008: 1 and 7), I thought that since there was so much negativity associated with radical Muslims, the NUT was well intentioned by allowing the imams in state schools to teach Muslim students. In that way, non-Muslims would understand that Islam is not a destructive religion, and that not all imams are radicals. But the *Daily Express* (25 March 2008) was bent on sensationalising the news, accentuated by a *madrasah* photo from Bangladesh, and thus generating fear among the British audience.

Christians are victims

On 21 October 2008, *The Independent*'s cover page had the headline, 'Killed for being Christian', which implied Christians were victims. It reported that Gayle Williams, a 34-year-old British woman, who worked with the poorest and most unfortunate children in Afghanistan who had lost limbs to landmines and bombs, was killed by the Taliban in Afghanistan. The Taliban spokesperson said that she was executed 'because she was working for an organisation which was preaching Christianity in Afghanistan'. *The Independent* (21 October 2008: 1–2) failed to report that the Taliban were not only the enemy of Westerners, but they were also the enemies of most Muslims and particularly Muslim women (see Chapter 7). With its headline, *The Independent* further damaged the image of mainstream Muslims living in Britain.

Islam as a political tool

In April 2008, the tabloid *Evening Standard* accused the former Mayor of London, Ken Livingstone, of playing politics to win over the Muslim voters in East London by 'smearing his rival Boris Johnson as a Muslim hater'. On its cover page, it ran a headline covering half the page: 'Suicide bomb backer runs Ken campaign' (16 April 2008: 1). It reported to its readers in bullet point (as the key point), 'Islamic leaders try to win 200,000 Muslim votes to "swing it for Mayor"'. It was associated with images of Muslim leader Azzam Tamini of the group Muslims 4 Ken, and the controversial cleric Yusuf al-Qaradawi, who had behind them posters saying, 'Freedom for Palestine' and 'Don't attack Iraq'. Then on page 18, under the headline, 'Embracing Islam gives Ken new election hope' (16 April 2008: 18), the *Evening Standard* reported that nearly half a million Muslim voters were urged to support Ken Livingstone against Boris Johnson in the upcoming mayoral election. It also reported that the London Development Agency, often referred to as 'Ken's piggy bank', gave £700,000 to help set up the London Muslim Centre in Whitechapel. It alleged that the centre and the adjoining East London Mosque were the geographical heartland of the Muslim campaign to re-elect Ken. Furthermore, it reported that the group called Muslims 4 Ken could be as large as 450,000, and that it persuaded every voter to register and vote for Ken Livingstone. To feed more fear about Ken Livingstone's voters, the newspaper reported that the prospective Muslim voters were supporters of the Sunni scholar Yusuf al-Qaradawi, who was welcomed to City Hall by Ken Livingstone. Al-Qaradawi was alleged to have spoken in defence of suicide bombers, female circumcision and persecution of homosexuals, although he has denounced terrorism for political goals (*Evening Standard*,16 April 2008: 18). The report was accompanied by photographs of Ken Livingstone hugging a Muslim leader at City Hall and of the East London mosque. The captions read: 'Warm welcome: Ken Livingstone greets Yusuf al-Qaradawi at City Hall' and 'Above [photo] the East London Mosque, epicentre of the Muslim campaign to re-elect Ken as Mayor'. The messages of the *Evening Standard* (16 April 2008: 1, 18–19) were clear: the mosque, the radical Muslim leaders and supporters of the Muslim leaders are a threat to 'our' society; should Ken Livingstone win the election, then our society would be doomed to radicalism.

Abu Hamza's case

The Egyptian-born Abu Hamza al-Masri was an influential imam at the Finsbury mosque, which has been visited by convicted 9/11 conspirator Zacarias Moussaoui and the attempted shoe bomber, Richard Reid ('Bombers next door', *Newsweek*, 8 August 2005: 32; O'Neill and McGrory 2006: 215–34). Having allegedly sustained injuries during his time in post-war Afghanistan in the 1990s, Hamza was fitted with a distinctive false arm and hooked hand that the tabloid media seized upon (Baxter 2007: 75). The respondents of my study spoke of Abu Hamza as the 'Hook Imam' because the media always showed his image with his metallic hooked hand exposed. In 2004 the United States requested his extradition over the construction of ter-rorist training camps in the US, recruitment for *jihadi* activities in Afghanistan, and attacks in Yemen. He was arrested but released again in August 2005 and finally charged with 16 offences relating to terrorism and incitement to racial hatred in October 2005. With the conclusion of his trial in January 2006, Hamza was found guilty of 11 counts, including solicitation of murder and stirring up of racial hatred. He has been sentenced to seven years in a UK prison (*The Times*, 8 February 2008: 4). Abu Hamza news dominated the British media, and any association with Abu Hamza was considered highly suspicious. As the British-born Somali male student Sohrab (aged 15) recalled:

> Oh! I remember, he [Abu Hamza] was near my house! You know Finsbury Park is also in North London? And we used to live near him but you know then people started saying that if you go there you're going to get in trouble and so many people just they got in trouble just for listening to him. (Interview, London, 25 March 2008)

A British-born female of Bangladeshi background, Taslima (aged 22), noted:

> Abu Hamza gets promoted a lot, rather than the actual, the mainstream view of Muslims. That gets put to the side. And you get to hear the really extreme views, well actually the extreme two sides of the spectrum . . . Yeah we can say he's extreme, but we don't know – that is fed into us by the media. He could be a really nice person

for all we know. But all we see is this guy with a hook. (Interviews, London, 8 April 2008)

Similarly, three more British-born female respondents of Bangladehi back-round (aged 22–3) thought the British media had some hidden agenda behind their representation of Abu Hamza (that Islam is a bad religion). For example, the *Daily Telegraph* (12 January 2006: 1) had a headline, 'Hamza "had Big Ben as terror target"', along with the photo of Abu Hamza with his hooked hand exposed. The photo caption ran: 'Abu Hamza: "terror blueprint"'. Even though Abu Hamza has been convicted on terror charges, the respondents did not trust the media because the media had caricatured him a lot. It's like the boy who cried wolf. Since the media blows up news out of proportion, these four respondents had reasonable doubts about the real threat posed by Abu Hamza. An overseas-born male respondent of Arab background, Khaled, aged 21, also thought that the media went overboard with Abu Hamza's case, noting that Hamza did not represent all Muslims. Khaled said, 'For me he is no one and he doesn't influence me when he speaks and I don't see why he is the face of Islam in Britain' (Interview, London, 20 April 2008). Similarly, Habib, a Syrian-born 30-year-old male respondent in Cardiff, commented:

I was in London last time and in the Metro [railway station], you know. As I opened the *Metro* newspaper the only news about Muslims was Abu Hamza Al-Masri and his [hooked] photograph. Actually nobody agrees with him, nobody accepts him. (Interview, Cardiff, 23 October 2008)

Two British-born female respondents of Indian-Kenyan and Bangladeshi backgrounds thought that the media ridiculed a disabled person. The 24-year-old female respondent of Bangladeshi background, Nuzhat, pointed out, 'If somebody rapes a woman and he's disabled, you would still treat him as a disabled person. The point I'm trying to make is that this guy [Abu Hamza] is a hate preacher [who] was disabled and he was treated badly by the press' (Interview, London, 27 April 2008).

'Muslim equals terrorist'?

Hakem, a British-born male interviewee of Pakistani background, aged 29, observed:

There's a big drive at the moment to expose Islam as being some sort of monster, right. So there is also a counter effort to expose Islam in a positive manner as a peaceful loving religion. The leaders in Deoband in India have already issued an une-quivocal statement against terrorism. This doesn't get into the news. You won't see the positive things in the news, all you'll see is effectively through subliminal brain washing, the two words that you'll get associated now with each other are 'Muslim' equals 'terrorist', and that is what people on the ground 'Joe Public' thinks and the media has been 90 per cent responsible for this and the other 10 per cent would go to our esteemed government for playing to the media and making unprofessional statements and not doing too many good things for community relations. (Interview, Bradford, 26 August 2008)

Other respondents also expressed their concern that Muslims were perceived as terrorists, particularly if it was a man with beard and a *topi* (Table 5.1). To examine the validity of these remarks, I looked into eight newspapers (four broadsheets, four tabloids) dated 4 April 2008, which reported on an alleged terrorism case, as follows.

In August 2006, British police arrested eight British men who allegedly planned to detonate suicide bombs on seven transatlantic flights over North America. Almost two years later, on 4 April 2008, Peter Wright, QC, opened the prosecution case against the eight men accused of the plot, and told Woolwich Crown Court that the attacks would have 'a truly global picture'. Mr Wright said that the eight defendants shared a common interest in 'inflicting heavy casualties upon an innocent civilian population, all in the name of Islam'. The defendants denied charges of conspiracy to murder and conspiracy to cause an explosion on an aircraft (*The Times*, 4 April 2008: 1). However, five months later, in September 2008, three men, Abdulla Ahmed Ali, Assad Sarwar and Tanvir Hussain, were convicted of the conspiracy to commit mass murder through suicide bomb explosions, but the jury at Woolwich Crown Court failed to convict any of the eight defendants, Abdulla Ahmed Ali, Assad Sarwar, Tanvir Hussain, Umar Islam, Waheed Zaman, Arafat Waheed Khan, Ibrahim Savant and Mohammed Gulzar, of conspiring to murder people by blowing up an aircraft. The one defendant, Mohammed Gulzar, whom the Crown alleged flew into Britain from Pakistan to oversee the plot, was acquitted of all charges (*Guardian*, 9 September 2008: 1).

The point I wish to make is that in this case some print media labelled these Muslims as terrorists as soon as the Crown case started in April 2008. It appeared to be trial by the media. For example, the *Daily Telegraph* (4 April 2008: 1) had a headline in quotation marks, implying it had been cited by the Crown prosecuter Mr Wright: '"British suicide bombers planned to blow airliners out of the sky"'. But subheadlines marked in bullets – 'Muslims plotted to kill thousands in the name of Islam' and 'Ingredients for liquid explosives "were to be designed as soft drinks"' – implied that all Muslim people were terrorists. The same day, *The Independent* ('Court told of plot to bomb transatlantic airliners', 4 April 2008: 13) informed its readers:

Eight British Muslims potentially came within days of blowing up at least seven transatlantic airliners using liquid bombs disguised as soft drinks in a suicide plot, which would have led to 'death on an almost unprecedented scale', a court was told yesterday. The men were described by the prosecutors as 'cold-eyed fanatics' . . .

Clearly, the tabloid newspapers picked up the most negative words from Peter Wright's statements in the Court and passed them on to their readers. For example, the *Daily Mail* (4 April 2008: 1), with its headlines, 'British Muslim gang planned worst atrocity since 9/11, jury said' and 'Plot to blow seven planes from the sky', once again associated British Muslims with terrorism. On the other hand, the *Daily Express* ('Carnage in Lucozade bottle', 4 April 2008: 4–5) did not include 'Muslims' in its headline, but the article commenced with these words: 'Eight Muslim fanatics plotted to kill thousands of travellers by smuggling suicide bombs disguised as fizzy drinks on the transatlantic jets, a court heard yesterday.' Similarly, *The Sun* ('Brit fanatics "plotted" to murder thousands', 4 April 2008: 6–7) did not label Muslims in its headline, though it did report, 'An Islamic plot to blow up seven airliners with bottle bombs would have caused civilian deaths on an "unprecedented scale", a court heard yesterday.' But the *Daily Mirror* (4 April 2008: 4–5) had the most sensational headline. It did not label the Muslims in its headline, but its headline, '7 planes, 8 bombers, 1000s dead', implied that the alleged terrorism had already occurred.

I found only one broadsheet paper, *The Guardian* ('Eight deny plot to blow up planes over Atlantic', 4 April 2008: 1, 4–5), which had a balanced report in the sense that it decided to quote very little of the prosecutor's anti-Muslim words. The general trend of the press was to portray Muslims as terrorists, though it turned out the jury could not convict the eight accused men as being guilty of blowing up planes, and one defendant, Mohammad Gulzar, was set free.

A few respondents of this study observed that the *Metro* newspaper also views Muslims as 'terrorists' (Table 5.1). For example, Majd al Din, a British-born male student of Libyan background, aged 15, said:

Yeah, you hear a news headline, and even on the *Metro*, a Muslim terrorist, terrorist always comes after the word Muslim. Because the *Metro* [free newspaper] is given out in the train station. Sometimes they just go back to the history of 7/7, 9/11, and they bring it up. (Interview, London, 15 April 2008)

Majd al Din said that he felt uneasy at train stations because of the negative Muslim news published in the *Metro*. I examined a few *Metro* newspapers when I was in London. I was surprised to find out that the *Metro* (4 April 2008: 1) had the headline, 'Suicide plot to bomb 7 planes', and its reporting was as balanced as *The Guardian*. However, a week later, I noticed that the *Metro* (11 April 2008: 5) dedicated an entire page to news related to the 7/7 London bombers, which confirms the point made by Majd al Din. The *Metro* reported on the trial of three men, Sadeer Saleem, Mohammed Shakil and Waheed Ali, who were alleged to have assisted the 7/7 London bombers and published the photographs of the three accused men. Furthermore, the *Metro* (11 April 2008: 5) published a video image of a London bomber (probably Hasib Hussain) with a banner where the first pillar of Islam was written (*La ilaha illal la hu Muhammadur Rasul ullah*: There is no God but Allah and Muhammad His messenger) as shown during the trial of the three accused men. It further reported the farewell message of the mastermind Mohammad Siddique Khan that he delivered to his daughter ('Bomber's farewell message', 11 April 2008: 5), and how he introduced her to her 'uncles' – fellow suicide bombers Shezhad Tanweer and Hasib Hussain.

Of course, the media does not make news. It delivers news as it takes place. The alleged 7/7 London bombers happened to be from the Islamic faith, so any news made by them has attracted the attention of newspapers (including the *Metro*). But with every news story about the alleged terrorists, their photographs were also published and most of them had a visibly Muslim appearance because of their beards. Therefore, the image of a terrorist has been constructed by the media. It was fair for the *Metro* to print the latest news on the trial of the accused men, Sadeer Saleem, Mohammed Shakil and Waheed Ali because the trial was going on during that period, but to show the video image of the 7/7 London bomber was unnecessary. Under these circumstances, many Muslims travelling on trains felt uncomfortable with the negative news, and in general many Muslims in Britain were uneasy because of the media's sustained association of Muslims with terrorism (for example, Hakem's views).

Muslims' image since 7/7

Some respondents of this study said that they were directly affected by the 7/7 London bombings, particularly some young Muslim males in Beeston in Leeds who told me that the media haunted them after the 7/7 tragedy (Table 5.1). Three of the 7/7 bombers lived in Beeston, so the area became a media focus. A Muslim woman in Leeds, Nadira (Pakistani background, aged 30), said that after the 7/7 incident the media was so hostile that 'the police activity in Beeston and in Leeds 6, and around the Grand Mosque was very much heightened', and Muslims felt that they were under surveillance all the time (Interview, Leeds, 30 August 2008). Nadira provided further anecdotes regarding the 'bias' of the British media:

> The media has been so biased in its reporting. I mean it's just incredible that they're allowed to get away with it really. For example, the biggest raid on the bomb equipment came from a BNP person that the police found so much bomb making equipment in his house. If this person had been a Muslim everybody would [have] known what had happened. (Interview, Leeds, 30 August 2008)

After the 7/7 London bombings, Nadira noted that sometimes the future of innocent Muslims had been jeopardised by the media's extensive coverage:

You know there was somebody at the time of the 7/7 bombing who was an Egyptian student who was accused of being one of the bombers in Leeds 6. The whole house that he lived in was sealed off and everything and his face was all over the newspapers. They ruined his life, you know. He couldn't have got a job anywhere in the UK after that and he was, in the end, he wasn't even charged with anything and yet there's no reporting of that. (Interview, Leeds, 30 August 2008)

I assume Nadira spoke of the Egyptian chemistry student Magdy Elnashar, aged 33, who lived in Leeds, but was arrested and detained in Cairo on 15 July 2005. A few days later, the Egyptian authorities cleared Magdy Elnashar of any link to the July 7th London bombings (*Daily Telegraph*, 21 July 2005: 23). Similar views were shared by an 18-year-old British-born female respondent of Pakistani background, Mustaeenah, that the media had wrongly portrayed Babar Ahmed of Tooting, South London. Mustaeenah comments, 'It is so wrong in Britain, whenever they are talking about terrorists they [the media] always focus on Muslims. They are not thinking there are other terrorists out there as well like the Irish' (Interview, London, 24 April 2008). In 2009, Babar Ahmed was acquitted and won 60,000 from Scotland Yard for being assaulted by the police who arrested him (*Daily Mirror*, 19 March 2009: 39). In Cardiff, a young British Muslim girl of Iraqi heritage, Mahinoor, aged 21, pointed out that since the 7/7 London bombings the media was 'mostly bad':

It's very saddening. Every time you look in the news you see an article about people who have blown themselves up and obviously they've identified them as Muslims, practising Muslims, for example the July 7th bombings and after that a few other enquiries have taken place. And that in itself, you know, it doesn't reflect the proper Islamic society as a whole.

It's like picking the Ku Klux Klan [in America] and saying that this represents the whole of the white [American] population. (Interview, Cardiff, 23 October 2008)

Nadira, Mustaeenah and Mahinoor pointed out that the British media's coverage of Muslims since the 7/7 London bombings has been generally negative. On the other hand, British media do not have extensive coverage on the British National Party, though the BNP has engaged in anti-Muslim activities. For example, in July 2009, the *Sunday Times* reported 'England's largest seizure of a suspected terrorist arsenal since the IRA mainland bombings in the early 1990s from the homes of White-supremacists in the north of England, along with the maps of British mosques' (cited in James 2009: 9). This is just one report and may not continue for days, as is done with the Muslim news.

I now examine how four broadsheets, *The Times*, *Guardian*, *Daily Telegraph* and *Independent*, and four tabloids, *The Sun*, *Daily Mirror*, *Daily Express* and *Daily Mail*, represented the Muslims during the first, second and third anniversaries of the 7/7 London bombings and whether these newspapers labelled Muslims as the 'Other'.

A snapshot observation of eight newspapers published on the three anniversaries of the London bombing

Broadsheets

The Times

On the first anniversary of the London bombings, *The Times* (7 July 2006) dedicated pages 1–7 to the events of the previous year and their aftermath. The cover page juxtaposed the images of 22-year-old bomber, Shehzad Tanweer, and 20-year-old Muslim victim, Shahara Islam. It revealed two faces of Islam through its headlines: the militant Islam of the terrorist, and the moderate Islam of Shahara, a victim of the attacks. *The Times* also made explicit reference to Christian values and, in an article titled 'Faiths unite against terrorism', it implied that Judeo-Christian values were superior to others (*The Times*, 7 July 2006: 3; see also Green and Kabir 2007).

On the second anniversary of the 7/7 bombing, *The Times* was somewhat distracted by the Glasgow bombings that had occurred recently (30 June 2007). Under the headline 'Bomb plot suspect "had engineering expertise to construct explosive"' (*The Times*, 7 July 2007: 2), it focused on news of the alleged terrorist Glasgow airport bomb plot. Only at the bottom section of page 2 was there mention of the 7/7 London bombings, stating that more than 120 of the victims injured in 2005 were still waiting for full compensation.

On the other hand, pages 6 and 7 of *The Times* had a banner headline, 'Turning to jihad', which indicated the theme of that section of the paper. On page 6 there was a bigger headline, 'Average age: 26. From a caring family, married, with children, graduate. The unexpected profile of the modern terrorist' (*The Times*, 7 July 2007: 6). It conveyed the message, 'We expect suicide bombers to be uneducated social outcasts who have been twisted by fanatics. But the reality can be very different.' The article (page 6) discussed Dr Marc Sageman's research findings, published in 2004 in *Understanding terrorist networks*, which concluded that most terrorists were 'upwardly and geographically mobile'. The article (page 6) was associated with the images of Ayman al-Zahahiri, surgeon and Osama bin Laden's deputy; Mohammad Atta, engineer and 9/11 terrorist; and Khalid Mohammed, another associate of Osama bin Laden, who was behind the murder of Daniel Pearl and the Bali bombings. There were also images of the Twin Towers burning and of

Wall Street Journal correspondent Daniel Pearl tied with a metal chain. The headlines and images seemed designed to create fear of the global threat of terrorism among readers, and especially so in the UK with Kafeel Ahmed and the recent bomb plots.

The Times (7 July 2007: 6) differentiated between the majority of good Muslims who do not condone violence and a few who endorse martyrdom through terrorism in the name of *jihad*. However, the aforementioned head-line, 'Average age: 26. From a caring family, married, with children, gradu-ate. The unexpected profile of the modern terrorist' (page 6), might have already induced fear among readers that there are suicide bombers ready and waiting, educated and young, among us. Thus the print media do not only promote the 'Us' and 'Them' rhetoric, they also indicate that we cannot necessarily distinguish 'Them' from 'Us' and promote fear and suspicion through headlines and television video footage (see also Christians, Rotzoll, Fackler, Makee and Woods 2004: 211; Kabir 2006; Kabir and Green 2008). However, on the third anniversary of the London bombings, *The Times* (7 July 2008: 4) had a brief report under the heading 'Bomb victim tribute', that a memorial was set up to pay tribute to Giles Hart, 'a lifelong cam-paigner for freedom and human rights', who died in the Tavistock Square bus bomb.

Daily Telegraph

The *Daily Telegraph*'s (7 July 2006: 15) reporting of the first anniversary of the 7/7 London bombings was sensational. It geographically linked its news with a photograph of the father of a London bomber, Hasib Hussain. This appeared to be irrelevant in the context, but Hussain's father had the appear-ance of a 'typical' Muslim man with beard and Islamic cap (*topi*); so at a glance it could have conveyed that 'Muslimness' equated with violence.

On the second anniversary, the *Daily Telegraph* (7 July 2007: 10–11, 19–20, 25) had the largest coverage of security issues, reminding readers of the current threats (Glasgow airport bomb plot and the 7/7 second anniver-sary). The newspaper retained its sensational stance with its headlines and images. The 'Britain on alert' pages (marked by banner headlines at the top of pages 10–11) had reports on the Glasgow airport attack with images of Kafeel Ahmed and Sabeel Ahmed (including a well-used photograph of the burned figure of Kafeel Ahmed being handcuffed by police). There was a report titled 'Few imams in British mosques born in the UK' (page 10). This article described research that indicates only 8 per cent of imams preaching in British mosques had been born in the United Kingdom, and just 6 per cent of them spoke English as a first language. Further, according to the research, most imams had been living in the UK for less than five years. The *Daily Telegraph* (7 July 2007: 10) further reported:

A study painted a picture of a deeply conservative body of individuals wedded to traditional languages who were still largely recruited from the Indian sub-continent. [. . .] Patrick Mercer, a Conservative MP, said the UK should adopt a tougher system [. . .] (page 10)

In this context, the newspaper was revisiting news reports that Muslim militants had been indoctrinated by fanatical imams. For example, as discussed above, the Egyptian-born cleric Abu Hamza al-Masri was alleged to have indoctrinated the 9/11 plotter Zacarias Moussaoui and 'shoe bomber' Richard Reid while he was the imam of the Finsbury Park mosque.

The *Daily Telegraph*'s report on 'The textbook terrorists' (7 July 2007: 19) was similar to that in *The Times*, noting that the terrorists were well educated. It published some graphics of the burning Jeep at Glasgow airport and the bearded terror suspect Mohammad Asha, holding his son. In its repeat of the previous year's coverage (7 July 2006: 15), the newspaper effectively primed readers about the probable physical appearance of a Muslim terrorist (in 2009, Mohammad Asha was acquitted of terrorism, see *Mail Online*, 10 August 2009). Finally, in the editorial section, the newspaper reiterated its conventional conservative approach with the headline: 'We must make Muslims loyal subjects once more' (*Daily Telegraph*, 7 July 2006: 25). The message conveyed became 'We' (the loyal British) must make the 'Other' (i.e. British Muslims) loyal subjects once more. In other words, Muslims were labelled as the 'Other'. However, on the third anniversary, the *Daily Telegraph* had just one headline: 'One in 10 7/7 victims still waiting for injury payout' (7 July 2008: 14). It was critical of the British government and the Criminal Injuries Compensation Authority for the irresponsible handling of payments for 700 people injured.

The Guardian

On the first anniversary of the London bombings, under the headline 'One year on, a London bomber issues a threat from the dead', *The Guardian* led heavily with an article featuring Shehzad Tanweer's suicide video image (7 July 2006: 1). However, on the second anniversary *The Guardian* aligned itself more with its anticipated stance, offering more balanced reporting of the 'Terror threat' than was the norm on that day. Alongside a report on the flaws in the emergency service response revealed during the 7/7 tragedy was a piece on how overseas doctors feared repercussions following Kafeel Ahmed's failed bomb plot. The newspaper emphasised that many overseas doctors had provided service to the victims of the 7/7 tragedy, and included an article on how the Australian federal police had dealt effectively with security issues. There was also a large photograph (covering almost half a page) of the burned Kafeel Ahmed being handcuffed by British police.

On the third anniversary of the London bombing, *The Guardian* (like *The Times*) had a brief report on the memorial for the human rights activist (*Guardian*, 7 July 2008: 12). However, on the page opposite it a headline read, 'Former member of Islamist group barred from becoming solicitor' (7 July 2008: 13). With the report was associated a photograph of the former member of the Islamist group, Maajid Nawaz, with the caption: 'Maajid Nawaz was jailed in Egypt for membership of Hizb ut-Tahrir'. Though the report was sympathetic to the cause of Maajid Nawaz, the headline and the photograph (a visible Muslim man with beard) were subtle reminders of the Muslim 'Other'.

The Independent

Unlike the other broadsheets, *The Independent*'s front page on the first anniversary of the 7/7 bombings did not have a scaremongering graphic or headline. However, in its follow-up nine-page *EXTRA* lift-out, *The Independent* had similar images of the London bombers to the other newspapers. On the second anniversary of the London bombings, *The Independent* carried the headline, 'Police identify bomb-maker as Iraqi becomes first man to be charged over terror attacks' (7 July 2007: 8). This article reported on the latest findings about the Glasgow bomb plotters (Kafeel Ahmed and his associates), and the story was associated with two small images of Bilal Abdulla and Kafeel Ahmed (page 9). On page 30, *The Independent* (7 July 2007) remarked that the current British Prime Minister Gordon Brown's language was restrained, and so was the language of Jacqui Smith, the Home Secretary. Apparently neither of them used the word 'Islam', 'Islamist' or 'Muslim'; and they were adamant that the perpetrators of the London and Glasgow attacks were criminals.

On the third anniversary of the London bombings, *The Independent* had a brief reminder of the 7/7 London bombings under the headline, 'Mother of 7 July bombing victim calls for inquiry' (7 July 2008: 16). However, it published an opinion piece in which the columnist Bruce Anderson (*Independent*, 7 July 2008: 29) discussed the complexities involving the *shariah* law debate enunciated by Archbishop Dr Rowan Williams and later supported by Justice Lord Nick Phillips (discussed further in Chapter 7) but emphasised, 'It is also necessary to remind some of them [Muslims] that respect is a mutual obligation.' It was said against the background of a Cheshire schoolmistress who made non-Muslim children kneel to worship Allah:

> Imagine if Islamic children had been ordered to kneel in Christian worship. The teacher would be sacked, if not indeed imprisoned, while 20 British Council offices would have been torched in riots around the Islamic world. (Anderson, *Independent*, 7 July 2008: 29)

As discussed earlier, the Taliban killed a British woman whom they accused of spreading Christianity (*Independent*, 21 October 2008: 1). Besides, over the Rushdie Affair and Prophet Muhammad's [PBUH] cartoon there was rage in the Muslim world. So it was not unlikely that some Muslims would have overreacted if Muslim children had been forced to kneel down and pray. Ironically, *The Independent* published another opinion piece ('The shameful Islamophobia at the heart of Britain's press', *Independent*, weekly media section, 7 July 2008: 10–11) where the columnist Peter Oborne criticised the tabloid newspaper, *The Sun*, as Islamophobic.

Overall, the reporting pattern of the broadsheet newspapers suggests that when there was a crisis, such as the 7/7 London bombings, the Glasgow airport terrorist attack and the *shariah* law debate, most newspapers represented the Muslims as the 'Other'. However, the representation of the Muslims as the 'Other' in the broadsheets appeared not to be as intense as the tabloid newspapers, as discussed next.

Tabloids

The Sun

Of all the tabloid papers, *The Sun* offered the maximum coverage of the first anniversary of the London bombings. As its cover image, *The Sun* carried the picture of a London double-decker bus, route 30: the service that was blown up by 18-year-old Hasib Mir Hussain. The headline '7/7: One year on' was complemented by the word in the bus's destination display: 'UNBEATEN' (*Sun*, 7 July 2006: 1). The reports (pages 4–6) in *The Sun* focused on the survivors' comments and strength, whereas a special inside report contained eight pages of tributes to the victims. The main news coverage (*Sun*, 7 July 2006: 4–5) carried headlines that echoed the front-page image, '7/7 ONE YEAR ON . . . WE ARE STILL NOT AFRAID', and used as a subheading a tagline from one of the people affected: 'They won't beat me and they won't beat Britain' (which may have inspired the 'UNBEATEN' destination indicator). *The Sun* used the comments of a victim's mother, Marie Fatayi-Williams, to indicate that the killer's (Hasib Hussain's) family was still in a state of denial. The story reported that 'Marie issued her plea [to Hussain's parents] as it was revealed Hussain's dad is STILL in denial over his son's involvement in the bloodbath. He insisted at his Leeds home: "No one has shown me any evidence that he did it"' ('Face truth, mum begs killer's family', *Sun*, 7 July 2006: 4).

On the second anniversary of the London bombings, *The Sun* did not have much coverage of the topic. Like other newspapers, it focused on the Glasgow airport attack. In a three-page story entitled 'Bomb fiend's £5k bill' (*Sun*, 7 July 2007: 1, 8, 9), *The Sun* commented that British people had become furious when it was revealed that the National Health Service was spending more than £5,000 a day in an attempt to save the life of alleged car bomber Kafeel Ahmed, who had 'plotted death' and turned himself into 'a human torch at Glasgow airport' (7 July 2007: 9). *The Sun* was very critical of spending such sums on a would-be bomber's medical treatment (see 'Terror madness', *Sun*, 7 July 2007: 5). It also ran a story on the terrorist conviction of Omar Altimimi (page 9).

However, on the third anniversary of the London bombings, *The Sun* suddenly woke up. Under the headline 'Terror peril' (7 July 2008: 6), *The Sun* commented, 'Three years ago today 52 people died in the 7/7 attacks on London. It would be a monumental mistake to think that it could never happen again.' Then under the headline, 'Islamophobia . . . or cold, hard truth?' (*Sun*, 7 July 2008: 6), the columnist Trevor Kavanagh criticised Peter Oborne, the columnist of the *Independent* newspaper (as discussed earlier) who branded *The Sun* as Islamophobic. Kavanagh argued that Muslim women were oppressed by Muslim men and forced marriages were common in Muslim families; honour killings and beatings were far from rare; and women were refused education and a chance to learn English.

I have discussed in Chapter 3 that some Muslim women remain disadvantaged in the Muslim community in Britain. In this context, Kavanagh's criticism should not be considered 'Islamophobic', because there are definitely issues within the Muslim community, such as forced marriages, that need to be addressed. However, Kavanagh's claim that honour killings are exclusive to Islam is unwarranted; they are also seen in non-Muslim Indian communities. Moreover, domestic violence and beating of women are, unfortunately, universal. But what was Islamophobic was the labelling of Muslims and their place of worship, for example. Earlier in this chapter I discussed how *The Sun* associated the mosque with an isolated rape incident in East London ('Mosque Fiend', *Sun*, 8 March 2008: 29). *The Sun* – a Murdoch publication – enjoys the highest circulation of any daily English-language newspaper in the world, with a readership of 3,047,527 a day between 2 and 29 April 2007 (NMA 2007). Under the circumstances, its representations of British Muslims in a negative manner are gratuitous and not helpful.

Daily Express

Under the headline 'Terror video that sickens the nation' (7 July 2006: 6–7), the *Daily Express* reported on the grief of the British people; and it targeted the frustrations and disappointment of a victim's mother with respect to the mother of bomber Hasib Mir Hussain – who did not repond to pleas to denounce terrorism; it also reported on Hussain's father who said that he had not known of his 'son's murderous plans' (7 July 2006: 7). In an editorial, 'We must pull the plug on the television terrorists' (7 July 2006: 12), the *Express* argued that since the *Al Jazeera* Arabic television broadcasting service was giving terrorists the 'oxygen of publicity' by screening Shehzad Tanweer's suicide video, the service should be banned.

On the second anniversary of the London bombings (7 July 2007), the *Daily Express* devoted four pages to topics about Muslims. Under the headline 'Suspect told mum: I will not fail' (pages 6–7), the *Daily Express* offered coverage of the Glasgow airport bombing. It also provided an image of the bomb plotter, Kafeel Ahmed, and his mother, who was pictured as a fully covered Muslim woman wearing the *burqa*, *hijab* and the *niqab*. The image of Kafeel Ahmed's mother can be interpreted as confirming prejudices because it has been established elsewhere that fully covered Muslim women carry negative connotations for Western audiences (Kabir 2006). There was a further headline, 'Attack fears grow on 7/7 anniversary' (*Daily Express*, 2007: 6), which reported, 'Police fear the terrorists could attack again in a sickening "celebration" of the outrage which left 52 people dead and 700 injured.' The *Daily Express* further commented, under the heading 'Multiculturalism has let terror flourish in Britain' (7 July 2007: 14):

> Today is the second anniversary of the London bombings when 52 innocent people died and hundreds were injured. In the aftermath of that atrocity we learned that the young bombers were British-born and appeared to have fallen under the evil spell of imams who preached hatred of the West. It was imperative that the Muslim community looked within itself and dug out this poison [. . .] As we now see this will be a mammoth task.

A few pages later there was further coverage featuring Muslims. This time the story was a report on a Muslim man who had demanded £150,000 compensation after claiming he was falsely branded a suicide bomber, presumably because he was 'profiled' as a result of wearing traditional Islamic dress. The article appeared under the headline '"Insulted" Muslim sues Homebase for £150,000 (That's £143,000 more than some 7/7 victims [received])' (*Daily Express*, 7 July 2007: 19). On this page the newspaper underlined its sympathy for the 7/7 bomb survivors by also including a second article under the headline 'Bomb survivors "are the forgotten people"' (7 July 2007: 19). Finally, the *Daily Express* allotted another two pages to the Glasgow airport bomb plot under the heading 'Accidental Hero' (*Daily Express*, 7 July 2007: 22–3). This coverage was associated with photographs of the burned and handcuffed Kafeel Ahmed, Osama bin Laden, and local hero John Smeaton, who had tackled the bomb suspect Kafeel Ahmed at the site of the failed Glasgow bombing. The images clearly depicted John Smeaton as one of 'Us': 'the accidental hero'.

On the third anniversary of the London bombings, the *Daily Express* reminded its readers of the Muslim 'Other' with its headline, 'Bootees for sniffer dogs are just not necessary says imam' (*Daily Express*, 7 July 2008: 7).

It reported that dogs were regarded as unclean in Islamic culture and many avoided direct contact with the animal. So in an effort to respect such cultural sensitivities, the Association of Chief Police Officers suggested providing rubber booties which sniffer dogs could wear on their paws. A few pages later, under the headline, 'Official pandering to the Islamic hardliners is political cowardice' (7 July 2008: 12), the *Daily Express* published the columnist Leo McKinstry's opinion piece:

> In recent years we have had to endure a constant threat to our society from Muslim extremists who kill, maim and brutalise in the name of Allah. Yet, in the inverted moral universe created by our Left-wing political establishment, any criticism of Islam provokes indignant cries of 'racism' or 'Islamophobia' . . . In the light of today's third anniversary of the July bombings in 2005, the eagerness of Muslim representatives to don the mantle of victimhood is truly sickening. Last week, Minister for International Development and Dewsbury MP Shahid Malik had the nerve to claim that 'Muslims feel like the Jews of Europe' because of supposed persecution.

McKinstry's opinion piece (7 July 2008: 12) was associated with a photograph of Muslim men in *sijda* (third prayer position of prostration: forehead on the ground facing Mecca). The caption read, 'VICTIMS? Muslim activists on a demo against Islamophobia pray in Trafalgar Square'.

I note that the *Daily Express* has maintained a double standard in its observations. For example, it has been critical of the Muslims on page 12, while on page 19 it published a report on the Reverend Christopher Walker who was drunk and was jailed because he kicked his wife in the face over an argument. Of course, it was an isolated case, as were other Muslim cases reported by the *Daily Express* earlier in this chapter, but the difference was that the Reverend Walker's case was not labelled with any religious affiliation (see 'Jailed, vicar who beat up wife in row over dinner', *Daily Express*, 7 July 2008: 19). It could be argued that the word 'Reverend or Vicar' implied an Anglican minister, and the *Daily Express* was critical of Christians too, but the difference is that there were criticisms of Muslims on several pages of the same edition (*Daily Express*, 7 July 2008), whereas there was mention of only one Christian case: the Vicar's case.

Apart from discussions on Muslims on pages 7 and 12, the *Daily Express* (7 July 2008) published two letters on page 48. The first letter (Anonymous, 'Wrong to punish people for refusing to worship Allah', *Daily Express*, 7 July 2008: 48) was critical of an incident where a Muslim religious education teacher forced their non-Muslim students to pray, and pointed out that 'if Muslims were forced to pray in our style, there would be an almighty outcry resulting in charges of racial harassment'. The second letter ('Prayer row is a symptom of Christianity in retreat') brings out the 'Us' and 'Them' rhetoric:

. . .What is it about Islam that makes this government and certain individuals favour the Muslim community over the rest of the population. We have a great deal of freedom here and no one wants to see this minority so unhappy in what is a Christian country. May I suggest to any person, Muslim or otherwise, who feels this way that they use the basic right of freedom – the freedom to leave? (S. Rodas, *Daily Express*, 7 July 2008: 48)

Daily Mail

On the first anniversary of the London bombings, the *Daily Mail* published an image of each of the 52 victims on its cover page (7 July 2006: 1). The headline on the front page declared: 'Yesterday, those behind the 7/7 atrocity released a video of one of the bombers. Their aim, on this poignant anniversary, was to keep the victims of their evil act off our front page. They failed.' Having honoured the dead, much of the internal *Mail* coverage (pages 4–5) concentrated on images of, and stories from, the survivors. The final comment of the coverage was that of Arshad Choudhry, a member of the Leeds Muslim Forum: 'It's very upsetting for Muslims for it [the Tanweer video] to come at this time, especially when we are trying to look ahead. It's very sad for the people who knew those who lost their lives' (7 July 2006: 5). In an editorial entitled 'A squalid stunt as a nation remembers' (7 July 2006: 14), the *Daily Mail* commented that 'while most decent Muslims were horrified by Tanweer's crime, polls suggest that 13 per cent regard the killers as "martyrs"'. The overall theme of the day was that some British Muslims are violent and still remain a threat.

On the second anniversary of the 7/7 London bombings, the *Daily Mail* appears to have tried to instil the greatest fear among readers that 'We' are living with our 'enemy'. Under the headline, 'Al Qaeda fanatics working in politics', the *Daily Mail* (7 July 2007: 1 and 8) informed its readers that up to eight police officers and civilian staff (in the UK) were suspected of having links to extremist groups, including Al-Qaeda. Some of them are even believed to have attended terror camps in Pakistan or Afghanistan. On the third anniversary of the London bombings, the *Daily Mail* reminded readers of the anniversary with the headline, 'Brother of 7/7 bomber is given a free trip to Pakistan' (7 July 2008: 11). It was critical of a project run by James Caan which was trying to build a bridge between British-Pakistanis and the wider society. This issue (*Daily Mail*, 7 July 2008) also had two reports on the vicar David Cameron's short-tempered behaviour at a wedding ceremony ('Vicar throws out a boy of two as his parents wed', *Daily Mail*, 7 July 2008: 23); and the Reverend Christopher Walker's abusive behaviour to his wife ('Vicar kicked wife in the face as they rowed over what to have for dinner', 7 July 2008: 27). But none of the reports labelled the religion of the perpetrators. I thought it was inconsistent with the newspaper's reporting style, where it tends to label

Muslims on every occasion (discussed earlier on 'the problematic Muslims' issue).

Daily Mirror

On the first anniversary of the London bombings, the *Daily Mirror* used a still photograph of Shehzad Tanweer from the *Al Jazeera* broadcast on its front page. The headline read: 'On the day we remember the victims of 7/7, al-Qaeda releases this video of a London suicide bomber taunting Britain. We say "DAMN YOU TO HELL"'. Inside (*Daily Mirror*, 7 July 2006: 4–5), the *Mirror* also carried a threatening image from the suicide tape of Mohammad Siddique Khan. John Falding, partner of bombing victim Anat Rosenberg (who died in the 7/7 attacks), commented: 'If this [Tanweer's] video is meant to twist the knife and wreck the anniversary, I have one message for al-Qaeda. IT WON'T.' The paper also carried an article about British Muslims, including a comment from the Muslim Council of Britain which (the *Mirror* said) 'appears to confirm the bombers were radicalised due to aspects of our country's foreign policy and participation in wars against Afghanistan and Iraq' (*Daily Mirror*, 7 July 2006: 4). One might interpret this as commenting that British Muslims were blaming the British government's foreign policy for the atrocities, instead of the bombers' criminal acts.

On the second anniversary of the London bombing, the *Daily Mirror* headlined 'Terror "Sleeper" Jailed' (7 July 2007: 7). This story was about 'a failed asylum seeker [Omar Altimimi] who kept manuals on making car bombs [who] was jailed for nine years yesterday'. The conviction was an example of pre-emptive (or preventative) justice under the UK's controversial Terrorism Acts, where a person can be convicted on the grounds of the information they possess and the people with whom they associate. Altimimi had arrived in Britain from the Netherlands in 2002 with his wife and three children (*Daily Mirror*, 7 July 2007: 7). The brief report was accompanied by Altimimi's photograph, indicating he was a bearded Muslim man. It was an effective reminder that 'We' remain at risk from the threat created by the Muslim 'Other'. However, on the third anniversary of the London bombings (7 July 2008), the *Daily Mirror* was distracted by news of a knife crime, and there was no mention of the 7/7 London bombings.

Conclusion

In this chapter I have discussed the British print media. I have noted that the media is a mirror to reality. It does not make news but it relays news to its audience. But in the process of relaying news, it tends to take sides, revealed through its headlines, images, content and reporting, and it has been negative about mainstream Muslims, particularly Muslim men. As Radi (British-born engineer of Bangladeshi background, aged 27) noted, 'I think we're under the pressure in the sense of the media basically pointed the finger at you know, radicalised Muslim youth and so there's a lot more scrutiny on them [and it affects us because of our Muslim visibility]' (Interview, London, 28 March 2008). A few (11) respondents were self-critical (Table 5.1). They recognised that their cultural issues, such as forced marriages and conflict within the Muslim community, are likely to draw the mainstream media's interest. Radicalisation of some Muslim youth has taken place in some sections of the Muslim community. Ten respondents said that after the 7/7 London bombings, Muslim voices can be heard through the mainstream media. Overall, my impression of the majority of the 216 respondents of this study was that they were critical of the British media, but they felt very connected to Britain (discussed in Chapter 4). While expressing their frustrations about the media they momentarily felt 'Muslim', but as they shared their life stories with me I found that they wanted to move on, buoyed by their dual or multiple identities, and their hopes and aspirations for a better future.

Note

Some sections of this chapter (the first and second anniversary of the 7/7 London bombings, with co-author Lelia Green) appeared in ANZCA07 proceedings at http://www.latrobe.edu.au/ANZCA2007/proceedings.html, and in the ANZCA08 proceedings at http://anzca08.massey.ac.nz.

THE *NIQAB* DEBATE

With every crisis that has involved the Muslim *Ummah* in recent years, some British Muslims have exerted their exclusive identity by expressing their opinion over the issue. British Muslim identity politics had been activated by the *Satanic Verses* affair in 1989. It was a crisis that led many to identify themselves as 'Muslims' for the first time in a public way (Lewis 2002; Werbner 2002: 124–5; Werbner 2004b: 905; Modood 2007: 136). Some scholars (Werbner 2002: 162–3; Cressey 2006: 106) observed that during the First Gulf War (1990–1), even if Saddam Hussein was considered an 'evil tyrant' by the West, some Muslims considered him to be a hero. Even after 9/11 (2001) there were divided loyalties in regard to Osama bin Laden, whose image, at best, was constructed as a devout 'desert' Muslim sacrificing his millionaire Westernised lifestyle for the cause of Islam (Geaves 2005: 71–5), and there also prevailed conspiracy theories that exonerated bin Laden. Geaves (2005: 73) considered that 'Stop the War' protests by the Muslims (along with many non-Muslims) who believed it was an 'illegal occupation' during the Second Gulf War also gave the Muslims an opportunity to assert their Muslim identity and British citizenship. Some scholars (Werbner 2002; Ahsan 2003) believed that the British Muslims' alternative views should be seen as a legitimate demonstration of their democratic rights, rather than a questioning of their loyalties.

After the 7/7 London bombings, British Muslims were considered to be the 'Other' by some media (discussed in Chapter 5). This viewpoint impacted on some British Muslims so much that they started announcing their Muslim identity publicly, rather than keeping it private. For example, Farmida Bi, a New Labour parliamentary candidate in Mole Valley, formed a group called 'Progressive British Muslims' and launched the movement at the House of Commons on 10 November 2005. Farmida Bi believed that after the bombings on 7 July 2005, it was imperative that people who were comfortable with their combined identities as Britons and Muslims should participate in political debate (Modood 2007: 137). This notion of combined identity brings us to Tajfel's social identity theory (1978), which, as outlined in Chapter 1, refers to how people relate to their own group, and how their emotions can be influenced by other broader groups. So in one context a Muslim can relate to his Islamic identity and feel compassionately towards the *Ummah*, but there could be circumstances where a Muslim can overcome the subjectivities and apply some rational thinking, and absorb the British values of free speech and integration into their identity.

This chapter reflects the social identity of British Muslims. With the *niqab* debate, first initiated by the former British Foreign Secretary, Jack Straw, in Lancashire, and later continued with a separate case, Aishah Azmi's case in Dewsbury, some respondents of this study revealed their Muslim identity from different viewpoints. In this chapter I first discuss the initiation of the *niqab* (face veil) debate. Second, I discuss British politicians' intervention in the *niqab* issue. Third, I examine the Muslims' and the wider community's (including the media) reaction to the situation. Finally, I consider the views of 71 respondents of this study with regard to whether the *niqab* forms an integral part of Muslim women's identity. It should be noted that since the two completely unrelated incidents on the *niqab* issue (Jack Straw's comment and Mrs Azmi's workplace incident) occurred one after another in October 2006, the interviewees' comments have been mixed as some specifically mentioned Jack Straw's comments, while others had views about Mrs Azmi's case. Overall, the topic of discussion was: Muslim women's *niqab*.

Initiation of the *niqab* debate

Jack Straw's comment

On 5 October 2006, the Member of Parliament for Blackburn in Lancashire, Jack Straw, whose constituency contained nearly 20 per cent Muslims, wrote in his local paper, the *Lancashire Telegraph*, about a Muslim woman wearing the full veil, 'her eyes were uncovered but the rest of her face was covered in cloth'; she was accompanied by her husband (a professional man) and came to his office to discuss a problem (see Straw 2006). Jack Straw was impressed with her 'entirely English accent, the couple's education (wholly in the UK)', but he had serious reservations about her use of the *niqab*. Jack Straw commented:

> Now, I always ensure that a female member of my staff is with me. I explain that this is a country built on freedoms. I defend absolutely the right of any woman to wear a headscarf. As for the full veil, wearing it breaks no laws. (Straw 2006)

However, he felt the *niqab* 'was such a visible statement of separation and of difference' that he asked women wearing face veils to remove them when they visited his MP advice surgery at his constituency in Blackburn, Lancashire (Straw 2006). Jack Straw also mentioned that he was advised by Muslim scholars that a full veil was not obligatory at all. However, Jack Straw further commented that 'women as well as men went head uncovered the whole time when on their *hajj* – pilgrimage – in Mecca' (Straw 2006).

Being a member of a Muslim community, I understand that a woman can feel uncomfortable visiting a man alone in his office, so I appreciated that Jack Straw arranged for a female member of his staff to accompany him during the meetings. However, Jack Straw's generalised observation that 'Muslim women went head uncovered the whole time when on their Hajj' was wrong. During the *hajj*, which is performed in the Islamic month of *Zil Hajj*, it is obligatory for Muslim women to cover both their hair and their bodies with the *hijab* and *jilbab*. Even during the *Umrah Hajj*, which Muslims perform at times other than that prescribed for the *hajj*, Muslim women cannot expose their hair. I have performed *Umrah Hajj* four times and therefore I have experienced this requirement first hand.

Aishah Azmi's case

On 12 October 2006, another incident occurred concerning the *niqab* which intensified the debate: a 24-year-old Muslim classroom assistant (teaching aide), Aishah Azmi, of Gujrati-Indian background from Cardiff, was suspended at the Headfield Church of England Primary School in the Yorkshire town of Dewsbury for refusing to remove her *niqab* in class. Azmi was employed as a bilingual support worker to help British Pakistani children learn English. Azmi claimed she wore the veil only in the presence of men. It later emerged that students complained they could not hear her properly from behind her veil (*Daily Telegraph*, 28 October 2006: 1).

Azmi fought the suspension under rules set out in the Employment Equality (Religion or Belief) Regulations 2004, but lost after an employment tribunal ruled she was not the victim of discrimination. She was later sacked from her £15,000 a year job. Later the employment tribunal ruled Mrs Azmi had not been discriminated against but awarded her £1,100 for victimisation by Headfield Church of England Primary School in Dewsbury for 'injury to feelings' (*Birmingham Mail*, 24 November 2006: 4; *Guardian*, 25 November 2006: 10).

Politicians' intervention

On 17 October 2006, Prime Minister Tony Blair remarked that the veil worn by hundreds of Muslim women in the UK was a 'mark of separation' which made people of other ethnic backgrounds feel uncomfortable (*Western Mail*, 18 October 2006: 9). Blair's comment was his strongest intervention yet in the debate that had been sparked by his Cabinet colleague Jack Straw's assertion that the wearing of full veils or the *niqab* made community relations more difficult. Prime Minister Blair also backed the local education authority that suspended Mrs Azmi for refusing to remove her veil during lessons. Mr Blair said he could 'see the reason' why Kirklees Council chose to suspend 24-year-old Aishah Azmi for refusing to remove her veil. Blair also said that it was 'absurd' to suggest that Britain's foreign policy was to blame for the radicalisation of Muslim youth. Blair repeated pledges that British forces would not 'walk away' from Iraq or Afghanistan until their job was done. Blair denied that this put him at odds with the head of the Army, General Sir Richard Dannatt, who a week earlier had said that the British presence in Iraq was exacerbating the UK's problems around the world.

Soon after, the Culture Secretary, Tessa Jowell, described the veil as a 'symbol of women's subjugation to men', and suggested that women wearing it 'cannot take their full place in society' (*Western Mail*, 18 October 2006: 9). Harriet Harman, a minister in the Department of Constitutional Affairs and, like Straw, probably a candidate for the deputy leadership of the Labour Party, told the *New Statesman* that she would like to see an end to the *niqab* 'because I want women to be fully included. If you want equality, you have to be in society, not hidden away from it' (cited in Kristianasen, 1 November 2006). The Race Relations Minister Phil Woolas demanded Mrs Azmi be sacked, accusing her of 'denying the right of children to a full education' because her stand meant she could not 'do her job', and insisted that barring men from working with her would amount to 'sexual discrimination'. Later, Shadow Home Secretary David Davis launched a stinging attack on Muslim leaders for risking 'voluntary apartheid' in Britain, and allegedly expecting special protection from criticism (*Birmingham Mail*, 24 November 2006: 4).

A few weeks later, for his comments on the wearing of the *niqab*, Jack Straw was hailed as a hero by the wider members of his constituency. Later, when he fronted a meeting at Blackburn Town Hall, the heart of his constituency, hundreds turned up. He stood by his comments, and when the meeting was over the applause was overwhelming. As he headed towards his car, a woman's voice rang out, 'Well done, Jack. If they don't like it they should go home' (*Daily Telegraph*, 28 October 2006: 1). At the same time, Moulana Hanif, from the Blackburn Mosques Forum, commented, 'Jack Straw has insulted Islam and Muslims and has no right to do so. People are disgusted and insulted. We demand a full public apology' (*Daily Telegraph*, 28 October 2006: 1).

On 22 October 2006, the Chairman of the Commission for Racial Equity, Trevor Phillips, warned that if not handled correctly the issue could escalate into full-scale race riots of the like not seen in Britain since 2001 (BBC News, 2006c). Phillips said, 'What started as a perfectly reasonable and timely discussion about how we deal with aspects of our diversity in this society seems to have turned into something really quite ugly' (BBC News 2006c; *Daily Telegraph*, 28 October 2006: 1). Phillips said the debate was becoming dangerously polarised:

> On one side of the trenches we have those who want a fully fledged auto-da-fe against British Muslims, in which anything any Muslim does or says must be condemned as a signal of their wilful alienation and separation. On the other hand, the defensiveness of some in the Muslim communities has hardened into a sensitivity that turns the most neutral of comments into yet another act of persecution. This is not what anyone intended, and it is the last thing Britain needs. All the evidence shows that we are, as a society, becoming more socially polarised by race and faith. In many of our cities things cannot get any worse. (Cited in *Daily Telegraph*, 28 October 2006: 1)

Phillips was immediately criticised by some members of the wider community and there were also anti-Muslim sentiments expressed in the letters page of the *Sun* newspaper (see 'Veiled threat over race riot; The big issue; Dear Sun; Letter', *Sun*, Scotland, 26 October 2006: 73). On the other hand, critics believed that the *niqab* was an easy target and that a cultural attack had been made for political gain. Jack Straw's decision to raise the issue created a storm amplified by the media and used by politicians as Labour figures jockeyed for positions in the anticipated post-Blair era. Government discipline had broken down and Britain's disastrous foreign policies in Iraq were unravelling. Labour sensed it was losing the voters over Iraq and perhaps looked to the white working-class vote, while gambling on retaining the core of its previous massive Muslim vote (Kristianasen 2006). The tribunal that decided Aishah Azmi's case regretfully commented that it was 'most unfortunate' that politicians had made comments on this case while it was *sub judice* (*Birmingham Mail*, 24 November 2006: 4).

In his speech, 'The Duty to Integrate: Shared British Values', on 8 December 2006, Tony Blair re-entered the controversy over women wearing face veils by pointing out that Jack Straw's disclosure that he asked for them to be removed in constituency surgeries had been backed by the Mufti of Egypt, an interpreter of Islamic law. Tony Blair said, 'It is really a matter of plain common sense that when it is an essential part of someone's work to communicate directly with people, being able to see their face is important.' Though Tony Blair (2006) defined British values as 'belief in democracy, the rule of law, tolerance, equal treatment for all, respect for this country and its shared heritage', he did not equate the wearing of the *niqab* with the notion of freedom and tolerance.

Muslims and the wider community's reaction

It appeared that the 7/7 London bombings, and later the debate over veils, placed additional pressures on British Muslims, who had been complaining of discrimination since the 11 September 2001 Twin Towers tragedy (see Abbas 2005; Choudhury 2005). The debate on the veil merged with the old issue of assimilation. In a November 2006 poll, only 22 per cent of Britons said they thought Muslims had done enough to integrate, with 57 per cent saying Muslims should do more to fit in ('Behind the Veil Debate', *Scholastic Update*, 27 November 2006: 22). The most notable discovery from a survey of British attitudes to Muslim women in full veil was a morass of confusion and unease. One in three respondents thought that women should be banned from wearing the *niqab* in public, because it conceals everything but the eyes; just over half thought not; and one in ten didn't know. Only 41 per cent of people supported a general ban on the *niqab* in the workplace, which rose to 53 per cent if the workplace was a school or courtroom. And 61 per cent backed a ban at passport control unless the airport officials could be trained to identify travellers by their irises alone ('The Hidden Truth of the Veil, It's all Politics', *Sunday Telegraph*, 3 December 2006: 26).

There was also an outcry from some Christian groups against Muslim women wearing the *niqab*. Evangelical lobby group Christian Voice's Stephen Green said the alternative message will 'put people's backs up'. He added: 'The niqab is a veil of separation between Muslims and the indigenous Christian community. This will expose multi-culturalism for what it is – a bias against the Christian population' (*Daily Express*, 6 December 2006: 7). Pakistani-born Michael Nazir-Ali, the Bishop of Rochester and the Church of England's only Asian bishop, called for a complete ban on the veil to improve security and cohesion in Britain. His call for new laws to control the wearing of the veil in public came only days after it was revealed that Mustaf Jama, the Somali suspected of murdering policewoman Sharon Beshenivsky, was thought to have fled the country by dressing in a *niqab*. Bishop Nazir-Ali, whose father converted from Islam to Catholicism, said that the legislation should cover not only airports, but should extend to all areas of travel where an identity needs to be established, such as underground railway stations and ports (*Sunday Telegraph*, 24 December 2006: 1).

Perhaps surprisingly, there were Muslim voices for and against the *niqab*. As the debate was raging, some other Muslims sided with the mainstream British voices by not supporting the wearing of the *niqab* in British society. For example, Labour MP Shahid Malik, who represented Mrs Azmi's home town of Dewsbury, said the tribunal ruling was 'quite clearly a victory for common sense' (*Press Association National Newswire*, 20 October 2006, online). Yasmin Alibhai-Brown, a Muslim who was a columnist for *The Independent*, also saw it a little differently. 'What any of us does in our own lives is a private matter – a precious and inalienable right', she wrote. 'But once we enter the job market or national and local authority domains, or tread into places where there is interaction with different citizens, privacy and individual choice become contested – quite rightly, for there is such a thing as British society' (cited in *New York Times*, 27 October 2006: 3).

In December 2006, Mrs Ravat, aged 33, from Leicester, spoke in favour of the veil after ex-Foreign Secretary Jack Straw declared it made community relations more difficult. Mrs Ravat, who had worn a veil for ten years, said that rather than making women submissive, the veil empowered women to avoid domination by fashion and society and its pressures. She said she wore the veil when teaching adults because it helped them to concentrate better. 'I know then that people are concentrating on what I'm writing on the board', she explained. She expressed strong views that Muslims were being persecuted in Britain. Mrs Ravat also rejected allegations that Islamic schools have been instrumental in the rise of Muslim radicals in Britain (*Daily Express*, 6 December 2006: 7).

However, Lord Nazir Ahmed of Rotherham called for a rational and sensitive debate among Muslims on whether veils were needed in today's society. The Labour peer said he did not want the *niqab* to be banned by law but asserted it was meant to be worn so women would not be harassed, yet it was now having the opposite effect in Britain. Lord Ahmed, who became the first Muslim peer in 1988, told the *Yorkshire Post*:

The veil is now a mark of separation, segregation and defiance against mainstream British culture. But there's nothing in the Koran to say that the wearing of a niqab is desirable, let alone compulsory. It's purely cultural. It's an identity thing which has been misinterpreted. They were supposed to be worn so that women wouldn't be harassed. But my argument is that women, and communities as a whole, are now being harassed because they are wearing them. (Cited in *Press Association Regional Newswire – Yorkshire and Humberside*, 20 February 2007, online)

The debate continued for the next six months, as in March 2007, Massoud Shadjareh, chairman of the Islamic Human Rights Commission, discussing the question of whether Muslim women should wear the veil, argued that the government has blown up the question out of all proportion. Shadjareh said:

The whole thing has become an issue that goes far beyond the veil. When 99.9% of the Muslim community does not wear the veil, how does it become an issue of integration – unless there are really other issues that people are hiding behind? (*Press Association National Newswire*, 20 March 2007, online)

At the time when British Muslim voices were heard, the non-Muslims also expressed their views. For example, the Archbishop of Canterbury, Dr Rowan Williams, who has always been sympathetic to the Muslim cause (discussed in Chapter 7), cautioned that 'an outwardly secular society would be politically dangerous', arguing that the state had never been seen as a source of morality. Dr Williams said, 'The ideal of a society where no visible public signs of religion would be seen – no crosses around necks, no sidelocks, turbans or veils – is a politically dangerous one' (*Western Mail*, 28 October 2006: 10). But not all mainstream British people agreed to accept the *niqab* in public places. There were some letters to the editor where British people expressed their feelings on the *niqab* debate. For example, one wrote:

> Jack Straw is right. My deaf daughter needs to lip-read and can't communicate if she can't see someone's face. (Desmond Connelly (Stafford), 'Veil women have to see our side too', *People*, 22 October 2006: 37)

One person wrote, 'It makes my blood boil how people like Aishah Azmi can get Pounds [£]1,100 for hurt feelings. How pathetic' (A.S. {Leicester}, 'Txt us; Dear Sun; Letter', *The Sun*, 23 October 2006: 37). Another person wrote:

> I'll be surprised if the Muslim community actually take part in an open debate. They seem too busy making out they are being picked on over issues such as the wearing of veils to sit down and talk about it – but I'd like to be proved wrong. (Sarah McIntyre {Aberdeen}, 'Veiled threat over race riot; The big issue; Dear Sun; Letter', *Sun*, Scotland, 26 October 2006: 73)

Another reader wrote:

> It is preposterous that veil wearer Aishah Azmi (October 20) should be awarded anything (£1,000 for injured feelings) after her suspension.
>   When she was interviewed for her job, she didn't wear a veil, nor did she say she would later wear one. In my opinion wearing the niqab in a school has nothing to do with religious beliefs but is purely political. The Political Correctness and Human Rights laws should be scrapped and rewritten to include some common sense, a thing that seems to be lacking (together with freedom of speech) in this country. (A. R. Jackson {Oulton Close, North Hykeham}, 'Wearing a veil was purely political', *Lincolnshire Echo*, 28 October 2006: 12)

Some mainstream British media ('Niqab nonsense', *Daily Telegraph*, 20 October 2006: 25) perceived Azmi's motives as 'political', as it noted that Azmi's £1,100 award was 'some sort of victory' for Azmi and her supporters 'in an undeclared Holy War'. They perceived that the wearing of a veil was a political and cultural statement, not a religious one, and the sooner this was more widely recognised, the less likely it will be that 'we have a repeat of this nonsense'. One Muslim reader (Zafer Iqbal, 'Faith in Humanity Need not Depend on Religion', *Sunday Times*, 29 October 2006: 20) agreed that these days Islam was more than a religion or a theology; rather, it was a rising political ideology that is faith based. This is the cause of the tensions Muslims saw in British (and European) societies. However, the best way was not to target or label Aishah Azmi or institutions (schools) but 'to begin a debate on the values of this society and the Islamic values in order to achieve consensus. Instead, politicians take the easier route of vilifying the Muslim community.'

Tablighi Jamaat targeted

Through Azmi's case, Tablighi Jamaat, a Muslim group, became the focus of some British media attention (different Muslim sects are discussed in Chapter 3). Azmi's legal team held that she insisted on wearing a veil in class because a *fatwa* (religious ruling) was issued personally to her by an Islamic cleric belonging to a hard-line sect, Mufti Yusuf Sacha, in West Yorkshire. However, Azmi maintained that her decision to wear the veil was driven entirely by her personal beliefs, rather than the advice or instruction of a third party ('Veil teacher was obeying a fatwa', *Sunday Times*, 29 October 2006: 4).

Mufti Sacha followed the teachings of the Tablighi Jamaat, a hard-line Muslim group, elements of which are suspected by Western intelligence agencies of having links with terrorism (*Sunday Times*, 29 October 2006: 4). It was reported in the *Sunday Times* (29 October 2006: 4) that the majority of Tablighis are regarded as moderate. However, Mohammad Sidique Khan and Shehzad Tanweer, two of the 7/7 London bombers, were said to have been regular attendees at Sacha's mosque. Sacha's *fatwa* (religious ruling) on the veil was disputed by other Muslims. Mufti Abdul Kadir Barkatullah, who was affiliated to the Muslim Council of Britain, said: 'I am 100% sure that wearing the niqab is not obligatory for Muslim women – it is a matter of choice. It's more about habit than religion. The Tablighis observe the niqab very strictly' (*Sunday Times*, 29 October 2006: 4).

It appears that some Muslims were offended by the ongoing labelling of Tablighi Jamaat as extremist by some media. A Muslim woman, Sumiya Mann, wrote to *The Independent* (Sumiya Mann, 'Letter: Kindly Muslims, not terrorists' Batley, West Yorkshire, *Independent*, 27 October 2006: 50) not to label a religious group, Tablighi Jamaat, as 'terrorists'. Sumiya Mann assured them:

Although it [Tablighi Jamaat] is centred on Dewsbury, it also involves people from Batley, the neighbouring town just to the north. I know several of the people associated with the Tabligh movement personally: they are kindly men, not terrorists. It is a very loose association, mostly of local businessmen, but anyone from the Muslim community here can join them on their trips abroad, where they preach reform, not terrorism. For instance, they try to persuade their fellow Muslims to observe the five daily prayers . . . When I was speaking to one of them [Tablighi Jamaat people] on Thursday, he raised the issue of the veiled teacher, Aishah Azmi. He agreed that it was right to dismiss her, as it was inappropriate for her to cover her face in a junior school classroom.

However, a year later *The Times* ('Muslim group behind "mega-mosque" seeks to convert all Britain', 10 September 2007: 32) again reminded its readers of the danger posed by the Tablighi Jamaat people. It was reported that the Tablighi Jamaat aimed to build an Islamic complex near to the site of the 2012 Olympic stadium, with a mosque for 12,000 people, by far the largest religious building in Britain. The intelligence agencies had cautioned against the group's ability to influence young men over jihadist terrorism. *The Times* (10 September 2007: 32) reminded its readers that Kafeel Ahmed, the Indian engineer who died from burns in August 2007 after trying to set off a car bomb at Glasgow airport, was the latest in a line of terrorists for whose initial radicalisation Tablighi Jamaat has been blamed. One of the suicide bombers who attacked London in July 2005, Shehzad Tanweer, studied at the Deobandi seminary in Dewsbury, and Mohammad Sidique Khan, the leader of the 7/7 terrorist plot, was a regular worshipper at the adjoining (Tablighi Jamaat) mosque. Richard Reid, the shoe bomber, was said to have been influenced by Tablighi Jamaat, several of whose adherents were also among those arrested in 2006 over an alleged plot to blow up transatlantic airliners. *The Times* (10 September 2007: 32) again reminded its readers that it was on the advice of a Tablighi Jamaat scholar that Aishah Azmi, a Dewsbury teaching assistant, refused to remove her full-face veil in the classroom while helping young children who were learning to speak English.

The Times (10 September 2007: 32) also reported that some British Deobandis preach that non-Muslims are an evil and corrupting influence. One leading advocate, Ebrahim Rangooni, was alleged to have said that the movement seeks to 'rescue the ummah [the global Muslim community] from the culture and civilisation of the Jews, the Christians and [other] enemies of Islam'. Its aim, he wrote, was to 'create such hatred for their ways as human beings have for urine and excreta'. Mr Rangooni was alleged to have warned parents that non-Muslim schools 'turn humans into animals' and that sending a Muslim child to a British college 'is as dangerous as throwing them into hell with your own hands'. In the same report it was also alleged that the Tablighi Jamaat's long-term mission was to win 'the whole of Britain to Islam' (*The Times*, 10 September 2007: 32). It should be noted that the Tablighi Jamaat follows the Deobandi interpretation of Islam (discussed in Chapter 3).

Yoginder Sikand, a Muslim expert on the Tablighi Jamaat movement, says that its ethos of 'social and cultural separatism and insularity' seeks 'to minimise contacts with people of other faiths' (*The Times*, 10 September 2007: 32). On the other hand, Shabbir Daji, a trustee and secretary of the Tablighi Jamaat mosque in Dewsbury, said that the movement's aim was 'unity among all humanity'. He said that it had no hidden agenda. 'We never come out on demonstrations against the Government', he said. 'Our aim is to make each and everyone . . . a better Muslim' (*The Times*, 10 September 2007: 32). Irfan al-Alawi, international director of the Centre for Islamic Pluralism, says the missionary work of Tablighi Jamaat acts as 'a recruitment agency for jihad' in Afghanistan, the occupied territories and Iraq. They go around deprived areas of British towns and cities, knocking on doors and urging young Muslims to come to their gatherings (*The Times*, 10 September 2007: 32).

However, my personal experience with Tablighi Jamaat is that they visit Muslims' homes and advise them to be better practising Muslims. They prefer to talk to the male members of the family, and refuse to engage in dialogue with Muslim women or have any eye contact with women. They normally knock at Muslim doors during prayer time, for example *Maghrib* (sunset prayer time), and request the Muslims to join them in prayer. In other words, they want to transform the nominal, non-practising Muslims to practising Muslims. The Tablighi men sometimes leave their families behind and go on a retreat for 40 days for their spiritual self-reformation, which is called *chilla*. Cesari (2004: 93) observes that the Tablighis take a traditionalist and legalistic approach to Islam, and are sometimes referred to as the 'Jehovah's Witnesses of Islam'. The Tablighi is usually described as a pietist and apolitical movement whose primary aim is to strengthen Muslim orthodoxy. It appears *The Times* (10 September 2007: 32) selectively chose to publish the comments of some Muslim extremists to show the danger of the existing 'Other', and the danger of the establishment of another mosque near the Olympic stadium.

Since 9/11 it has been debated by Muslim and non-Muslim leaders in Britain whether Muslims should be allowed to live in isolation or if they should work towards social cohesion (Choudhury 2005: 82–3). I assume that it is important that both Muslims and non-Muslims feel an 'institutional belonging', with an attachment to key political and legal institutions. Developing a 'sense of belonging' requires an understanding of different cultures, communications, compromise and adjustment by all parties. However, from the mainstream British media, often only one-sided mainstream British people's voices were heard. For the above discussion on the *niqab*, it appears that Muslims are a problem: Muslim women wearing the *niqab* is a barrier to integration; a Muslim woman (Aishah Azmi) received undue harassment compensation (£1,100); Tablighi Jammat is a source of all ills; the fact that Mrs Ravat wore her *niqab* while she taught adults was objectionable; human rights laws should be rewritten 'to include some common sense'. However, there were significant comments from some Muslims such as Lord Nazir Ahmed, Labour MP Shahid Malik, and journalist Yasmin. As Jenkins (2008: 112–13) pointed out (see Chapter 1), one of the criteria of the social identity theory was that individuals will self-categorise themselves differently together with the contingencies they are faced with, thus Lord Ahmed, MP Malik and journalist Yasmin who worked with the wider community perceived that the wearing of the *niqab* at work was a barrier to social cohesion. Their comments also fit into Geaves' (2005: 74) definition of identity, when he argued that identity was not only about who a person was but where that person was placed, and in that perspective both space and place become important to one's sense of identity (Geaves 2005: 74).

Respondents' opinion on the wearing of the *niqab*

I did not engage all 216 respondents of this study (as I did in some chapters) in a discussion on the *niqab*, for reasons given in Chapter 1. However, from the 71 people with whom I managed to discuss the *niqab*, I received a fair idea how it affected their identity. The interviewees are given fictitious names. First, I discuss the responses of 12 Muslim adults (20–50 years) who were directly involved in Muslim community affairs in their respective cities. Next, I discuss 59 young Muslims' (15–30 years) views on the *niqab* issue who were mere observers.

Muslims engaged directly with the Islamic community, 20–50 years

A youth worker in Leeds, Sobhan (male, aged 24, British-born of Indian background), observed:

> I don't think the issue that Jack Straw raised was that bad. It's the way he raised the issue. I think it's a debate that needs to take place within the Muslim community itself first as *niqab* itself is a contentious issue within Muslims. (Interview, Leeds, 6 October 2008)

Sobhan suggested a debate within the Muslim community would be worthwhile, but would such a debate be possible? The Muslim community itself is composed of diverse sects and ethnicities: some are moderate, some are orthodox, some are tribal, and some are rural and urban. Furthermore, some are Sunni, and some Shia. In fact this division goes further (as discussed in Chapter 3): within the Sunnis there are Deobandis, Tabligh Jamaat, Brelwi and Sufi. Could such diverse people possibly reach an agreement?

That the wearing of the *niqab* is a contentious issue within the Muslim community was confirmed by a Pakistani-born Muslim teacher in an Islamic school, Nazneen, aged 28, who migrated to Britain at the age of six, attended a state school and later received a British university degree. Nazneen said her family lived in a wealthy English suburb and had a very Western lifestyle when they were young. However, she said:

> When we [my sister and I] put on *hijab* it was a shock for our parents . . . in fact, it was such a shock for them and for other people in our family they tried to stop us from wearing it. Some people actually went a bit violent when it came to stopping us and when we put on *niqab*, which you know the face veil, then it was just a bit schwoop . . . it was a bit much for them. (Interview, London, 26 March 2008)

Later, in 2008, when I asked a Pakistani-born Muslim leader in Cardiff, Zulfikar (male, over 40) about the *niqab* debate, he said that in Cardiff the majority of the women who wore the *niqab* were new Muslims. They were very articulate, and also very educated (for example, Jack Straw himself admitted that the woman who came to his MP surgery had an English education). The Muslim leader further noted that the *niqabi* women were not forced to wear it; they were wearing it because it was their choice. So this was an expression of the British values of freedom. The leader commented that no one was forced to wear a *niqab*, but if they wanted to wear it, why should one stop them? Regarding the Muslim teacher in Dewsbury, Aishah Azmi, Zulfikar believed that the teacher was prepared to take off her *niqab* in front of the children, or women. It was only when the men were coming in that she put it on. Zulfikar further noted:

> I'm certain and I know a lot of doctors who wear *niqabs* but when they're in the hospital or seeing a patient they don't wear *niqab*. When girls check in at the airport, they [airport security] want them to take off their *hijab*, they take you in a cabin or kiosk for security check. When girls want to wear it [*hijab*, *niqab*], it is okay. Yes, if they force other people to wear it, that's an issue then; obviously this is not right. (Interview, Cardiff, 20 October 2008)

Another Muslim respondent, Habib (male, over 30, overseas-born of Arab background), said that some people look at his wife in a different way because she wears a *niqab*. Perhaps people are not used to this form of dress but 'when a man like Jack Straw says [about the *niqab*], this is what we expect from normal people, you know it's very strange [for a politician to comment on the *niqab*]' (Interview, Cardiff, 22 October 2008). A British-born councillor from London's East End, Fatima (female, aged 22, Bangladeshi background), commented:

> I mean there was a big hoo-ha about the fact that there was this girl [Aishah Azmi] working at a primary school and she used to wear *niqab* and there was this thing where she took it to the Court and she wanted to stand up for her rights at wearing the *niqab* but there was a big thing in the media about that. But the point was, I thought to myself, how can you teach, because I am teacher myself – how can you teach with a *niqab* on? They can't see your facial expressions and things and it is not possible. (Interview, London, 29 March 2008)

Another British-born participant, a schoolteacher in London's East End, Faizul (male, aged 30, Bangladeshi background), commented:

> My personal opinion, in a way I did agree with Jack Straw when he said you know the woman who came to his chambers for advice should take off the *niqab* because we live in a society, we shouldn't be people who are dressed in a strange way cos we give more tension to other people and they will find it very strange so it would be hard to interact. So the basic garment is head gear [*hijab*], is fine you know when you

speak to someone they can see who you are. *Niqab* I personally think if you are back home it's fine. (Interview, Tower Hamlets, London, 31 March 2008)

Not everyone in London's East End shared similar views. A British-born schoolteacher, Nuzhat (female, aged 24, Bangladeshi background), said:

If I wore the *niqab* and I went to a job interview and they asked me to take my *niqab* off in order to get the job, I would say, 'No, thank you'. Because if I wear the *niqab* my reason for wearing the *niqab* would be I'm doing it to attain Allah's pleasure. It's not part of an identity thing, it's because I'm trying to do it for Allah. Now, if, there's society and there's God; for me if I have to choose between I'd choose God.

[What] I'm also saying is that, just because you're wearing a *niqab* doesn't mean you can't be an active part of society. A job isn't the only way that you can be an active part of society, do you understand? Going up to a random person in the streets, when they've got shopping, carrying their shopping, that's being a good citizen. (Interview, Tower Hamlets, London, 28 March 2008)

Nuzhat herself did not wear the *niqab*, she just wore the *hijab,* but she said that she had friends who work in Islamic schools and wear the *niqab*. Nuzhat contended that women wish to wear the *niqab* for 'Allah's pleasure', but she emphasised the need for integration, the importance of helping other people and trying to be good citizens. Similarly, Zayed (male, aged 25, British-born of Bangladeshi background) had this to say:

The *niqab* is not an obligatory, it's a matter of personal choice. We have a sister who works here, she's very functional in society, but she wears the *niqab*. Jack Straw's comments were a bit naïve and unconstructive to say the least. It's a matter of 1) the Muslims who wear their *niqab* extended themselves out to the community, and 2) on the part of the community itself to try to understand, come to terms with it. (Interview, London, 30 March 2008)

Zayed runs a weekend Islamic school where one of his women employees (an administrative officer) wore the *niqab*. I argue that since the woman worked in an Islamic environment and also in the administrative section, and her employer had no objection to her veil, then it should be acceptable as she had no direct contact with the schoolchildren.

A respondent in Leicester, Nargis (female, aged 30, British-born of Pakistani background), also commented that the *niqab* should be a matter of personal choice. I myself find the wearing of the *niqab* causes Muslim women to separate themselves from society at a time when there are already so many misconceptions about Muslims. People who wear it may regard it as important to their religion, but some respondents in this study believed that wearing it is not obligatory (Table 6.1, discussed later).

People are familiar with the *niqab* in Bangladesh (my country of origin) because it is predominantly a Muslim country. In the Middle Eastern countries where I lived for ten years (with my husband and children), in Saudi Arabia and Oman, I observed the *niqab* was also an integral part of Arab culture. However, it appears that in Britain the *niqab* is worn by a minority of Muslim people. For example, in this chapter, only four female respondents (15–18 years) wore the *niqab* and the rest (except one) wore the *hijab*. Among the female adult Muslims so far discussed, only Nazneen wore it. But when a politician raises such an issue, Muslims construe it as an attack on their community, no matter how diverse the community may be. A British-born Muslim observer in Leeds, Rukhsana (female, over 40), noted:

It was part of this broader feeling that it was legitimate to undermine the Muslim community and to criticise them and to stop them from practising things that were part of their religion. So I mean 1 per cent of Muslim women in the UK wear the *niqab* and yet it became headline news everywhere because of his comments. So he [Jack Straw] actually gave the green light to anybody who wanted to say this is unacceptable in British culture. I know that some people actually started to wear the *niqab* because of what he has said, what he'd done . . . If a Muslim public figure said people shouldn't wear mini skirts there'd be an uproar. (Interview, Leeds, 12 September 2008)

The interviewee pointed out two things: first, to begin to wear the *niqab* changed Muslim women's identity; second, Jack Straw's comment gave the green light to anybody (news media) who wanted to say this is unacceptable in British culture. Regarding Rukhsana's first comment that some Muslim women began wearing the *niqab* as a mark of protest against Jack Straw's attack on Muslim identity, it seems that an identity becomes stronger when it is under attack. While researching the Pakistani Muslims in Manchester, Werbner (2002: 267) observed identities are not simply pre-given or inherited; they are formed, made and remade; they exist in practice, dialogically, through collective action and interaction. Identities constitute subjective narratives of virtue and moral commitment. Thus, identities are reflected '*in context*'. Werbner (2004b) also observed that the international humiliations against Muslims since 9/11, and their sense of powerlessness, were assisting Muslims to be drawn towards their identity. I assume in this context, the *niqab* stands as an identity marker for some Muslim women (as discussed by the Muslim observer Rukhsana). Regarding changing identities, Brah (2007: 143–4) observed, 'To have a sense of being, say, Muslim is therefore different when confronted with non-Muslims . . . This sense of self will vary depending on whether the non-Muslims are friendly or hostile'.

Rukhsana's second observation also appears to be accurate, though it was not based on Jack Straw's comment but on the Aishah Azmi *niqab* issue. *The Times* (2 November 2006: 27) published an opinion piece by Mary Ann Sieghart, 'Can't Muslim men control their urges?', where she noted that the Quran instructed the women 'to guard their private parts, and reveal not their adornment save such as is outward', and to dress modestly, so Sieghart argued, perhaps it is the Muslim men who are a part of the problem. Sieghart quoted the former Australian Mufti Sheikh Taj El-din al-Hilali's comments that he made in September 2006 during his *Ramadan* sermon at the Lakemba mosque in Sydney, and linked his comments with an unrelated incident of gang rape in Sydney. As I have carried out some research on the al-Hilali issue (Kabir 2008b), I was surprised when I read Sieghart's opinion piece.

In September 2006, al-Hilali was criticised by some sections of the Muslim community (including men) and a large section of the wider society for equating scantily dressed women with uncovered meat and blaming them for inciting men to rape (Kolig and Kabir 2008: 278–9). Though Sheikh Taj subsequently offered an unreserved apology in saying that he meant to protect women's honour, his statement sparked a heated debate in the Australian media, which continued for two weeks. Supporters of al-Hilali argued that the statement was taken out of context. They claimed he was discouraging sex outside marriage, and warning young women not to roam near the mosque after prayers, which might entice men to rape them. But critics (some politicians) said that Australia was a free society, where men and women are equal and that Muslim men's attitudes to women are culturally unacceptable because they treat women as unequal (Kolig and Kabir 2008: 278–9).

As discussed, *The Times*' columnist, Sieghart, linked Sheikh Taj's (2 November 2006: 27) comments with a completely unrelated horrendous gang rape incident that occurred in 2000 by two Australian-born brothers of Lebanese-Muslim background, while 14 Muslim youths watched. Both the brothers are serving long terms of imprisonment (Kolig and Kabir 2008: 278–9). Sieghart (*The Times*, 2 November 2006: 27) commented, 'Of course only a minuscule fraction of Muslim men are rapists; the rest are upright, law-abiding citizens'. Sieghart (*The Times*, 2 November 2006: 27) concluded that British values were superior to Muslim values:

> It takes time for cultural change to take its course. I don't blame Muslim men who were brought up in more traditional countries, such as Pakistan, for holding traditional views about women's garb. But it is incumbent on the next generation, born and brought up here, to re-examine their parents' prejudices in the context of this country's values . . .

As can be seen from the foregoing discussions, the *niqab* debate, commenced by Jack Straw and later continued through Mrs Azmi's case, turned out to be a complex one.

Some second-generation Muslim women (for example, Nazneen in London) wear the *niqab* as their choice because they consider British society to be a free one, but most are willing to compromise by de-veiling at workplaces. Another interviewee, a Pakistani-born teacher in Bradford, Zainab (female, aged 30), said, 'sometimes the traditional strict families, the fathers and the mothers, there is the first generation, particularly within the Pathan family, expect their second-generation daughters to wear *niqab*' (different Pakistani ethnic groups are discussed in Chapter 3). However, Zainab noted that her colleague who works in an Islamic school and does not belong to the Pathan family, wears it because it was her religious choice. Zainab says:

She's [her friend] educated, she's very outgoing, she attends meetings, mixed meetings and she goes. However, she's very well aware that when she goes to certain meetings she will wear, she may take the *niqab* off because, just to avoid the kind of tension. (Interview, Leeds, 10 October 2008)

Zainab's colleague works in an Islamic school where the environment could be considered appropriate for the *niqab*. In other situations, as Zainab pointed out, her colleague makes a compromise. The point is that some politicians and the media look at the situation with a non-compromising attitude. A community worker in Leeds, Sayeed (male, aged 40, Pakistani background), said:

It was a calculated political statement, and I didn't like it! The point is as an MP who has a constituent coming to see you, who you are there to represent, the idea that somehow that person will make you feel uncomfortable is just nonsense. You're the MP, you are the person who has the power in that situation and possibly has the power to help that person. Clearly the fact that woman was there in his office meant she wasn't segregating herself from society.

I think there is something that people feel about faces being covered and that preventing communication. Having that experience he [Jack Straw] wanted to encourage a debate about this and make people aware of it. I think there are different ways of doing that [rather] than going to a newspaper and saying 'this is an issue that concerns me', and giving an interview to make this point. (Interview, Leeds, 12 September 2008)

Of the 12 respondents in the category of Muslim leaders, only two, Fatima and Faizul, appeared to be critical of the wearing of the *niqab* (in the workplace and in general society), and five respondents (Sobhan, Zayed, Habib, Rukhsana and Sayeed) thought it was inappropriate for a politician to comment on Muslim women's attire, whereas four respondents (Zulfikar, Zainab, Nazneen and Nargis) held it was a matter of choice, and British values were about freedom. Zayed also commented that the *niqab* was not obligatory, but a matter of choice. Only one Muslim woman, Nuzhat, said that if one wishes to wear it for Allah or for God's pleasure, one should be allowed to do so. In the next section, I examine young (15–30) Muslims' views who were not associated with any Muslim organisation or youth centre.

Young Muslims' views on the wearing of the niqab (15–30 years)

I asked 59 participants (15–30 years), mostly British-born, about their views on the *niqab*, Jack Straw's comments and Aishah Azmi's case. Many respondents appeared to have heard Jack Straw's comments, but in some cases I told them about the incident. The overwhelming response was, 'wearing of *niqab* was a matter of choice, however, it was not compulsory' and 'it would bring alienation'. The key points of the responses are shown in Table 6.1. Later, I will elaborate on some relevant interviews.

Table 6.1 shows the general trend of the young Muslims' views. As the reader can see, there were voices of:

choice and freedom, reflecting the intrinsic British values;
reason within the 'choice' group;
niqab was not obligatory;
views for and against Jack Straw's comments;
reason and communication;
strong religious beliefs;
ignoring Islamophobia;
media, peer pressure, and human rights;
criticism of *niqab*.

Discussion

Diverse opinion

The 59 participants (15–30 years) provided a wide range of opinion on the *niqab* issue. Some young Muslims observed that the media and the politicians built up in-group (Muslim) feelings. When the British-born university student Yusuf (male, aged 20, Pakistani background) spoke of Jack Straw's political agenda, he drew attention to how Jack Straw conveyed the message of superior British values against the Muslim 'Other', and turned the discourse to 'Them' and 'Us':

> I think he [Straw] was only doing it for the sake of publicity and trying to stand up for British values. I don't have a very good opinion of politicians in general. I think they're not really down to earth. (Interview, Cardiff, 20 October 2008)

Josna in Bradford (female, aged 18, British-born of Pakistani background, state school) said:

Table 6.1 Key points of 59 responses, aged 15–30

Number of participants	Responses	Key points
22 (7 males, 15 females)	*Niqab* is one's personal choice	*Niqab* is multicultural. *Niqab* is freedom of religion. 'Why is it that he [Jack Straw] has any right to question a woman's wardrobe right to start with? *Niqab* is not compulsory, not obligatory.
5 (2 males, 3 females)	Jack Straw was political	All agreed: Jack Straw has tacitly reinforced Muslim identity. 'He was very calculated, he knows that the general atmosphere is anti-Muslim, so he knows that when he says something like that, yes it's going to spark controversy and I think the majority of the people would be with the *niqab* ban.'
5 (2 males, 3 females)	Jack Straw was right	Wearing *niqab* was incorrect in this society.
1 female	Human rights	'It is very, very hypocritical to ban someone from wearing the *niqab* when the whole point of the European Court of Human Justice and all this kind of thing, human rights.'
2 males	Be grateful	'If you want to cover up you can wear a *hijab* . . . you should be glad that you are allowed to do that.'
1 female	Angry at Muslims	'When they're wearing the *niqab*, they're walking past us they're still loud so it doesn't really make a difference . . . they are not doing what they ought to do . . . be modest.'
1 female	*Niqab* not necessary	'It is not a Muslim country.'
2 females	No jobs for women	'Some can be racist and they don't give you a job.'
1 male and few girls (below)	Islamophobia	All five *niqab*-wearing girls (next column) faced harassment and name-calling, such as 'penguin'. One male participant's mother was harassed.
5 females	*Niqab* is religious	'Yeah he [Jack Straw] goes it should be banned so I think that's wrong because it's our religion for the women to wear, cover themselves, and there's no problem with other people so he shouldn't ban that for no reason. Communication was possible through telephone, brick walls and eyes.'
3 females	Peer pressure	'My cousin wears a black *niqab* because of peer pressure.' 'Women wear it for *purdah* when they go to mosques.'

Table 6.1 (continued)

Number of participants	Responses	Key points
2 (1 male, 1 female)	Media	Media is reinforcing Muslim identity.
7 (1 male, 6 females)	Reason and communication	Muslims should compromise in their jobs. Get the right job, for example, Islamic school. For security reason, it should not be allowed. Islam emphasises modesty, so *hijab* should serve the purpose.
2 females	No comments	No comments

I didn't appreciate the negative media it received and also I felt that it was very judg-mental in what he [Jack Straw] said because I personally felt that he implied that it [*niqab*] was quite oppressive. (Interview, Bradford, 7 October 2008)

Dawood, a British-born professional (male, aged 25, Pakistani back-ground), believed that the media was impacting on Muslim identity to the extent that women started wearing the *niqab*:

Yeah I think the trend [of wearing the *niqab*] may be increasing because of certain, the media may be using themselves to kind of alienate us but in effect it's making peo-ple's *iman* [faith] stronger and it's making people who maybe wouldn't necessarily normally favour Islam move towards it just because of such negativity towards it and they feel that they're backed up into a corner and they may wear a *niqab*. (Interview, Cardiff, 20 October 2008)

Jenkins (2008: 112–13) observed that society is structured categorically, and organised by inequalities of power and resources. In this case, I assume both the media and the politicians were powerful agents in reinforcing a negative Muslim identity (as Dawood said; and Rukhsana noted earlier). A British-born girl, Firoza (female, aged 15, Indian/East African background, state school), argued:

Jack Straw shouldn't really be commenting. We're not complaining that there's no *Eid* holidays, like for two weeks there's Christmas [holidays], so why should he [Jack Straw] comment about our religion when already we've taken less? (Interview, Leeds, 14 October 2008)

So here, Firoza's threat to her identity reminded her that as a religious minority Muslims are overlooked. Some respondents of this study (Table 6.1) thought the wearing of the *niqab* was a matter of choice, while others thought it was purely religious. The respondents also realised that wearing the *niqab* in Britain was a difficult choice because the *niqabi* women were often subjected to humiliation by some members of the wider community. As Mussaret, a British-born woman (aged 18, Pakistani background, state school), said when she was in Pakistan she wore the *niqab*, where it was her choice, and nobody forced her to; but when she was back in Britain, she wore a long coat, and the *hijab*. Her mother regularly wears the *niqab* in Leeds, and when 'she's driving her car, she seems to get a lot more attention' (interview, Leeds, 15 October 2008). Similarly, a British-born young boy, Haneef (aged 15, Pakistani background, state school), commented:

> My mum wears one so I'm not bothered really. I just don't like it when people call my mum names just because she's wearing that. Well, there's quite a lot of people who wear that in our neighbourhood so they can't say anything. (Interview, Leeds, 15 October 2008)

Reason and communication

A British-born student, Mikal (male, aged 15, Somali background), who had heard about the *niqab* debate from his Somali teacher, said, 'The Arabs used to wear *niqab* so they [Muslim women in Britain] just copied them but *hijab* [for Muslim women] is compulsory' (Interview, Cardiff, 22 October 2008). Four respondents from three cities – Josna, Sufia, Sarah and Nafeesa – illustrate their negotiation with British society. British-born Josna (female, aged 18, Pakistani background, state school) in Bradford suggests:

> . . . It's much better if you work in a school where there is an environment, where you are able to remove that *niqab,* so hence an all-female environment for example, a Muslim school. (Interview, Bradford, 7 October 2008)

Similarly, a Bangladeshi-born student, Sufia (aged 15, state school), in Leeds thought the appearance of the *niqab* created a risk, which outweighed the benefit:

> At the end of the day, if you go to your job, you're just concentrating on one person [yourself] but you're not thinking about the non-Muslim community . . . if you think the risk is outweighing the benefit, so why would I wear *niqab*? (Interview, Leeds, 15 October 2008)

British-born Sarah (female, 30 years, Pakistani background, homemaker, Cardiff) said:

> First, I don't wear a *niqab*, it's completely up to whoever wants to wear them. I have found difficulty when I bump into sisters who wear *niqab* on the street – I don't

know who they are. We're not living in a Muslim country, you have to make allowances for that. (Interview, Cardiff, 18 October 2008)

Nafeesa (female, 22, British-born of Pakistani background, university student, Cardiff) pointed out the security issue, and that wearing the *niqab* would bring alienation when she said:

> In my personal opinions I feel, the *niqab* is not compulsory. Yeah the covering of the *awrah* [body shape], a *jilbab* is compulsory, a *hijab* is compulsory. I can understand the barrier debate because in this age where there are so many people who deceive, so many people use it for the wrong purpose. For example, I read a story where some men in London put the *niqab* on to go and rob a petrol station.
>
> Also the Psychology teachers say when you meet somebody it's all about facial expressions, it's all about eye contact, it's all about how you display your emotions. Now if you wear a *niqab*, the only thing showing is your eyes.

Nafeesa added:

> If I was a non-Muslim and I was to be in a *niqabi* room to a certain degree I think it would be a little uncomfortable but also from the *niqabi*'s point of view I'd feel quite alienated as well . . . If you're doing it for your religion, there are many good things you can do. You don't have to put yourself in a situation which really, really does alienate you. (Interview, Cardiff, 20 October 2008).

As the interviews revealed, some Muslims have argued the *niqab* issue with reason and negotiation. Stuart Hall (1995: 47–8, cited in Batrouney and Goldlust 2005: 23–4) described diasporic communities as:

> 'fashioning new kinds of cultural identity by . . . drawing on more than one culture' . . . They 'speak more than one language (literally and metaphorically), inhabit more than one identity, have more than one home' and 'have learned to "negotiate and translate" between cultures.' They 'represent new kinds of identities' and relate 'to culture and place in these more open ways'.

However, these respondents did not represent a typical diasporic community because they were second- or third-generation British-born people (except the overseas-born Sufia) and had lived all their lives in Britain, so I assume their negotiation was connected with rationality rather than emotion.

Strong religious conviction

In London, most respondents said that wearing the *niqab* was a matter of choice; however, some spoke of the harassment people face because of the *niqab*. Aaleyah (female, aged 17, British-born of Bangladeshi background, Islamic school) said:

> There was a Somali sister and she went into a shop and the man just came roaring at her to get out of his shop. Then she went to the police to report it and the police turned around and said to her, 'Do you always dress like that?' (Interview, London, 26 March 2008)

However, some schoolgirls felt strongly about their *niqab* on religious grounds. Muna, who wears the *niqab* (female, aged 15, British-born of Bangladeshi background, Islamic school), said:

> I did have a couple of times racist abuse. Once I was in a car, and a guy yelled 'Paki' to me; we were coming to school with our *niqabs* on. Once an English man threw water from a water can. This English man called me and my friend penguins – it's quite rude. (Interview, London, 27 March 2008)

Farhana (female, aged 15, British-born of Bangladeshi background, Islamic school), said she wore the *niqab* for Allah.

> Allah says that they will never be pleased with you until you accept their religion. So I'm thinking, you know, I'm pleased in my Lord, why should it bother me what they say to me? So it doesn't affect me, actually it makes me more stronger, *al Humdilallah* [thank God], I feel better. (Interview, London, 28 March 2008)

Muzna also wears the *niqab* on a regular basis (female, aged 15, British-born of Bangladeshi background, Islamic school). She said:

> There's Islamophobia, etc., but you have to learn to ignore it . . . Our Prophet Peace be Upon Him, he got abused a lot, but he never retaliated, he just allowed them to do that kind of thing. But he prayed for them, *Inshallah* [God willing] one day they'll become Muslims. (Interview, London, 28 March 2008)

Finally, Afroza (female, aged 17, Bangladeshi background, Islamic school) defended her wearing of the *niqab*:

> You hear people calling you 'Ninja Turtles' and all these names but it doesn't really bother me because I know that they don't understand the real purpose of wearing it. If they don't have the knowledge, then how will they understand? (Interview, London, 28 March 2008)

Afrosa found Jack Straw's comments on the *niqab* rude, and she remarked:

Yeah because there's a lot of people that speak on the radio and you can't see their faces so you know it works! . . . Even the eyes [reflect your state of mind]; when you're smiling you can tell by the eyes. I don't think it's a serious barrier to communication. (Interview, London, 28 March 2008)

The girls who wore the *niqab* felt strongly about it, partly because they go to a Muslim school and their uniform is the black *jilbab*, *hijab* and the *niqab*. Clearly, there is nothing anti-social about this. On another occasion, I (Kabir 2007) argued that it is alright for Muslims to have an exclusive Muslim identity, and to be devoted to *Ummah,* as long as they do it peacefully. Modood (2007: 200) noted that 'Muslims get self-pride and oppositional energy from their personal faith and collective solidarity'. For example, when the Muslim girls (Muna, Farhana, Muzna and Afrosa) saw that they were harassed by the wider community because they wore their *niqab*, they reaffirmed their moral commitment and became more determined not to give up their visible identity.

Modood (2007: 202) observed that 'Muslim schools' were under Britain's media scrutiny. They came to be linked with notions of divided cities, cultural backwardness, riots, lack of Britishness and a breeding ground for militant Islam. Modood asserted that Muslim-run schools were unfairly labelled with negativity, because none of their students (mainly junior girls) have a record of engaging themselves in riots and terrorism. However, the British-born professional Dawood (male, aged 25, Pakistani background), who earlier noted that the media was inducing a tendency for Muslims to adopt an exclusive identity and stereotypical representation of Islam and Muslims, later argued that any form of extreme Muslim identity could be counter-productive to the Muslim community (as they were relatively powerless in their host country):

Yeah, we should be thankful that in countries like this women can wear the *hijab* and it isn't an issue. If women try and maintain this *niqab* and try and work under these conditions they will have the same situation where say in France, where women won't be able to even go to school with them [wider community] and at least we've got that benefit you know now. And then it won't be a matter of whether you like it or not, it will be a matter of national security. (Interview, Cardiff, 20 October 2008)

Dawood, being a member of the Muslim *Ummah,* expressed his collective solidarity with Muslim women when he spoke against the media, but he also foresaw the danger of exclusion by the wider community (by giving the French example where Muslim girls who wear the *hijab* have been banned from attending state schools). In this case, the sense of powerlessness suggested to Dawood that there could be problems for the *Ummah* if British Muslims were drawn into an exclusive form of identity. However, Rupali (female, aged 20, Pakistani background) spoke of reason and communication: 'You can't just always blame the government and you can't always blame the *niqabis*.

Everyone has to pull together in this matter and figure out a way that we could all live together.' (Interview, 17 October, Cardiff)

Conclusion

The *niqab* issue was a contentious one among the respondents. Most of the female interviewees referred to in this chapter wore the *hijab*. Five respondents in London wore the *niqab,* whereas two interviewees in Cardiff did not wear Islamic attire (neither *hijab* nor *niqab*). It appeared that the *niqab* was still a minority Muslim women's dress. For example, there were 43 females (15–30 years, Table 6.1) and only five of them said that they wore the *niqab* in public places. However, both male and female respondents (except two, who did not comment) had strong views on this issue. The 12 Muslim leaders and community workers were closely associated with the Muslim community, so they gave their responses from that perspective, and the young Muslims (Table 6.1) had individual opinions on the topic. There were some common themes in the responses, such as 'choice', 'politics' and 'media'.

Jack Straw's claims concentrated on integration and loyalty. I assume that all respondents of this study have integrated into British society, as most of them were born in Britain, and they all spoke English. Tony Blair himself asserted that English-language skills meant Britishness (Chapter 1). Most of the 216 respondents of this study identified themselves as British Muslims with their heritage in the background (Chapter 4), and that is a further reflection of their integration and loyalty. Aishah Azmi's case was a local matter, which could have been dealt with locally rather than being blown up out of proportion with media headlines and discussion. It would seem that Tony Blair's comment, as the Prime Minister of the country, was un-statesmanlike in that in his intervention he sided with the majority against the minority.

I found that in some predominantly Muslim areas of Britain the wearing of the *niqab* was very common. I did not find it confronting, as in my country of origin some Muslim women wear Islamic attire including the *niqab*. I also found Muslim women wore the *niqab* in Saudi Arabia, as it is also considered a part of their culture. Personally, I found the Goths' appearance (with lots of piercings in the face, Gothic hairstyle, and black eye and lip make-up) more confronting, but I accept that they are a minority of Western culture. I believe that some members of the Muslim community need to understand and accept that Britain's mainstream culture is very different from its minority cultures. After the 7/7 London bombing, when there has been so much suspicion and Islamophobia in the wider community, there is bound to be a tightening of tolerance for diversity. The reality is that the wearing of the *niqab* in some situations does create communication barriers, and this goes against the integration process. On the other hand, whereas it is appropriate for the British politicians and media to have constructive debates about multiculturalism and integration, it is not acceptable to misrepresent a religion or deliberately feed false information to the public (for example, as discussed in the *Sunday Times*, 29 October 2006: 4; *The Times*, 2 November 2006: 27; also see Chapter 5). These interventions are bound to invigorate people's cultural identity, and emphasis on differences slows down the process of integration.

INDIGNATION ABOUT THE PROPOSAL TO INCLUDE *SHARIAH* LAW IN BRITAIN

Islamic law or *shariah* is interpreted according to four schools of law (*fiqh*, or jurisprudence), but the basic elements are the same throughout the Islamic world, especially where religious rites are concerned. These rites consist of: the five daily prayers performed in Arabic, whether one is in Malaysia or Bosnia; the tithes paid to the poor; the fast during the month of *Ramadan* carried out by all healthy adult Muslims; the annual pilgrimage (*hajj*) made from all parts of the Islamic world; and other religious acts that bind Muslims together wherever they might be. Over the ages the ethical norms related to *shariah* have been the injunctions of the Quran and *sunnah* (manners and deeds of Prophet Muhammad, PBUH) (see Nasr 2002: 59). In other words, *shariah* is practising Islam in one's everyday life, or, as Tariq Ramadan (2004: 32) points out, the *shariah* shows us 'how to be and remain Muslim'.

In its deeper meaning, the *shariah* is concerned with ordinances, or *hudud*, which literally means 'limits' set by Allah (God). The Muslims' holy book the Quran says, 'He [God] is the most swift of reckoners' (6:62), and many verses of the Quran are concerned with the *hudud* (Nasr 2002: 154). For example, verse 4:14 of the Quran says, 'Those who disobey God and His Messenger and transgress His limits will be admitted to a fire, to abide therein: and they shall have a humiliating punishment' (Nasr 2002: 154; see also Ali n.d.). Nasr (2002: 154) observes that the Quranic punishment, based on the concept that God is just and the reckoner of our deeds, concerns acts forbidden in the 'Sacred Text'; therefore, such acts are both illegal and sacrilegious. These acts include illicit sexual intercourse (*zina*) and false accusations of *zina*, alcoholic drinks, theft, robbery and murder, and the punishments by *shariah* (*hudud*) are severe. According to *shariah* (*hudud* or limits set by Allah), the punishment for adultery is stoning, but guilt must be established either by a confession by the party or parties involved or with evidence from four just witnesses. Punishment for theft and highway robbery, if it involves homicide, is death by sword or hanging, or amputation of a finger or, in extreme cases, a hand and a foot. For lesser cases there is flogging (Nasr 2002: 152–3). However, Nasr (2002: 154) notes that these punishments are rare in traditional Islamic societies as most of them are now under foreign influence and have blended their laws with the foreign laws. For example, by the middle of the nineteenth century in many Islamic countries, the rule of the *shariah* as a legal system was either limited to personal laws governing the family and inheritance, or replaced by Napoleonic codes or English common law and European-style courts. By the time most Islamic countries gained their independence after World War II, the full *shariah* was applied only in a few countries such as Saudi Arabia, Yemen and Afghanistan. These countries did not face the tension between two different legal systems and philosophies that other Muslim countries did (Nasr 2002: 154).

Sheikh Suhaib Hasan, secretary of the Islamic Shariah Council in Britain, said that *shariah* law is used by Muslim countries in different ways. There are 57 Muslim countries in the world and only two or three of them impose full *shariah* criminal law (*hudud*). There are also widely differing interpretations of *shariah*, both within the four classical Sunni and one Shi'ite schools of jurisprudence and between traditional and modern thinkers (Heneghan 2008). Egypt says *shariah* is the main source of its legislation but has penal and civil codes based mostly on nineteenth-century French law. *Hudud*, the corporal and capital punishments outlined in the Quran, has not been applied in modern-day Egypt. Pakistan has a similar split between civil and penal codes carried over from the British colonial period and Muslim personal law. It also has a Federal Shariah Court to decide if laws passed by Parliament conform to Islam. Indonesia is the world's largest Muslim nation and quite moderate in Islamic terms. Its western province of Aceh uses *shariah* law as part of a local autonomy deal granted by Jakarta, and people have been caned for adultery, gambling and stealing (Heneghan 2008). Yemen abides by the *hudud* (divinely prescribed fixed offences and punishments), including for apostasy and adultery, where the punishment is death by stoning. Nigeria's northern states adopted a harsh *shariah* code (*hudud*) in 2000; the Taliban in Afghanistan (which since 2009 includes Swat in Pakistan) abide by *hudud*. Sudan has also incorporated the *shariah* law (*hudud*), and in Saudi Arabia and Iran *hudud* applies to both Muslims and non-Muslims.

However, most Muslim states limit the use of *shariah* to 'personal law', which deals with issues such as marriage, divorce, inheritance and child custody. Western critics say most Muslim personal law limits women's rights and introduces inequality before the law, and sometimes Westerners perceive the personal law and *hudud* as the same. In this chapter, first I discuss the Archbishop of Canterbury, Dr Rowan Williams' comments on *shariah* law in the context of British law. Second, I examine the reporting of the *shariah* law in the British press (*The Times* and *Sun*) and the validity of society's anger, and finally, I examine young Muslims' (15–30 years) and a few Muslim adults' (30 years and over) comments on the *shariah* implications and its impact on their identity.

The Archbishop of Canterbury's comments on *shariah* law

On 7 February 2008, in his foundation lecture at the Royal Courts of Justice (a series on Islam and English law organised by the Temple Church and London University), the head of the Church of England, the Archbishop of Canterbury, Dr Rowan Williams, suggested that one way to accommodate alienated Muslims in Britain would be to introduce some version of *shariah* law. Dr Rowan Williams placed emphasis on 'personal laws' and rejected the ultra-orthodox model (practised in places such as Saudi Arabia). Dr Williams recognised that for a lot of people *shariah* or Islamic law prompts images of stonings, beheadings and a system that subjugates women, and there are parts of the Islamic world where such practices are law. Dr Williams said:

> Among the manifold anxieties that haunt the discussion of the place of Muslims in British society, one of the strongest, reinforced from time to time by the sensational reporting of opinion polls, is that Muslim communities in this country seek the freedom to live under *sharia* law. And what most people think they know of *sharia* is that it is repressive towards women and wedded to archaic and brutal physical punishments; just a few days ago, it was reported that a 'forced marriage' involving a young woman with learning difficulties had been 'sanctioned under *sharia* law' – the kind of story that, in its assumption that we all 'really' know what is involved in the practice of *sharia*, powerfully reinforces the image of – at best – a pre-modern system in which human rights have no role. (Archbishop's lecture, 2008)

Later, in a BBC News interview, Dr Williams said that already certain provisions of *shariah*, for example Islamic no-interest mortgages and contracts, were recognised in British society and under British law. So it was not as if Britain would be incorporating 'an alien and rival system' (BBC 2008). Next the reporter asked him:

> One of the examples you give where *shariah* might be applied is in relation to marriage. What would that look like? What would that mean, for example a British Muslim woman suddenly given the choice to settle a dispute via a *shariah* route as opposed to the existing British legal system? (BBC 2008)

Dr Williams replied:

> It's very important that you mention there the word 'choice'. I think it would be quite wrong to say that we could ever licence, so to speak, a system of law for some

community which gave people no right of appeal, no way of exercising the rights that are guaranteed to them as citizens in general, so that a woman in such circumstances would have to know that she was not signing away anything for good and all.

I'm simply saying that there are ways of looking at marital dispute, for example, which provide an alternative to the divorce courts as we understand them. In some cultural and religious settings they would seem more appropriate. (BBC 2008)

Furthermore, Dr Williams said that there are orthodox Jewish courts operating in Britain; likewise Catholics, Anglicans and others who have difficulty about issues like abortion were accommodated within the law; 'so the whole idea that there are perfectly proper ways in which the law of the land pays respect to custom and community – that's already there' (BBC 2008). In this context, I (the author) assume Archbishop Rowan Williams expressed good intentions to accommodate some elements of the *shariah* law within the British law (similar to the Jewish court, Beth Din), but he is ahead of his time and his comments on this topic have created confusion in British society. The media has also blown up his comments out of all proportion. A British-Bangladeshi male respondent of this study, Ejaz, aged 28, who studied law in London and later the *shariah* law in Syria for four years, observed:

If you actually read the Archbishop's speech, he was very philosophical throughout. He was addressing the issue of *shariah* in a much more philosophical way than most people realise. And, of course, he did say that the corporal and capital punishments in the *shariah* would not be applied in this country. What he was saying is what we need to do is we need to look at how we can learn from the *shariah* and at the end of his speech he actually said that we need to rethink the idea of the Enlightenment. So this is a very philosophical statement . . .

And in fact if you look at English law many of the provisions of English law, English jurisprudence comes from the *shariah*. (Interview, London, 1 April 2008)

Shariah *law in the British context*

In theory, *shariah* law is a voluntary code when it concerns marriage and divorce, which is binding if both parties agree. That is, if both parties want a divorce and were married under *shariah* law, and both agree to seek a divorce under *shariah* law, then the tribunal would make a binding decision.

Muslims argue that they have set up *shariah* councils in Britain for several years to help Muslim women who were having difficulties when their husbands refused them a religious divorce. Even if a woman does receive a civil divorce, she is unable to remarry. But if *shariah* law is affiliated with British law in matters of marriage, divorce, inheritance, occasionally child custody, and other family matters, then the paperwork can be speeded up. Muslims want a similar procedure as the Jewish people have in family matters. Muslims argue that aspects of Jewish divorce law have long been part of English law and it would be reasonable for Muslims to have the same opportunities (*National Public Radio*, 2008; *Guardian*, 4 July 2008: 4).

Jewish people seek divorce through Beth Din. Even if they get a legal secular divorce through the civil courts, they want to comply with Orthodox Jewish requirements to divorce and marry again. The divorce part of the proceedings is simply in order to make sure that they are freed and able to be remarried in a religious sense. Anybody who obtains a religious divorce has to go to a secular court in order to receive a civil divorce. Although if it is a recognised Beth Din, or if there's a binding arbitration agreement, the civil courts would normally pass that through very quickly (*National Public Radio*, 2008).

Sheikh Suhaib Hasan, secretary of the Islamic Shariah Council in Britain, said that the *shariah* council offers divorces that are cheaper and quicker than those available in the British courts, though a civil decree is still needed for legal dissolution of the marriage, and in the case of any property or child custody disputes. Sheikh Hasan said, 'A woman can get a divorce from the civil court, but she will still come to us . . . because she has to satisfy her conscience as well. And in this way, we are providing a service to the Muslim community, and complementing the British legal system' (cited in *Los Angeles Times*, 20 June 2008, online).

Though the Islamic Shariah Council in Britain claims that Muslim women have benefited by the *shariah* councils, there were grievances from some women who considered that the *shariah* council was run by a panel of men, who were not sympathetic to their cause. In some cases, women felt intimidated or basically not able – if she was unhappy in her marriage – to go to the courts, to approach male *shariah* judges and seek a divorce. There have been cases where a Muslim woman faced extreme domestic violence and approached the mosque (where the *shariah* council operates), but was turned down by these men. They said that women could not seek a divorce. It has to be the man (*National Public Radio*, 2008). I assume if that is a part of *shariah* justice, it would obviously be completely unacceptable in British society, as it would highlight the patriarchal structure of Muslim society. Later, it was reported in the *Los Angeles Times* (20 June 2008, online) that in some cases, women have no trouble obtaining a divorce in a British civil court but run into unforeseen difficulties when they approach Muslim scholars to seal it with their blessing. For example, a Somali woman whose husband had been wounded and sub-sequently disappeared during the civil war in her homeland for several years, approached the *shariah* council in North London. She was accompanied by her neighbour, a Muslim man, who had been helping her care for her children, and had offered to marry her if she obtained an Islamic divorce in addition to her civil divorce. Instead of the expected rubber stamp, the couple received 'a tongue lashing'. The judges told the woman to find a Somali cleric, who might help her prove her husband was dead, or had abandoned her. Should that happen, they said, she could have her divorce, and marry whom she pleased (*Los Angeles Times*, 20 June 2008, online).

It was noted above that Muslim women could benefit from the *shariah* council in divorce cases because the process is faster. So if the British law approves the mediation process or conflict resolution in family issues carried out by the *shariah* council (as done by Jewish Beth Din), then some Muslim families might benefit. As discussed in Chapter 3, some Muslim women remain disadvantaged in their family and community lives, so by accommodating provisions of British law in the *shariah* council or elements of *shariah* law in the civil courts, Muslim women's issues could be properly addressed. On the other hand, I was interested to learn from an interviewee, Sarfaraz (British-born male of Bangladeshi background, aged over 30), (also as the Archbishop Dr Williams said) that some elements of the *shariah* law already existed in British finance:

> You know when the current Prime Minister [Gordon Brown] was a Chancellor of Exchequer, he himself brought in legislation which facilitated Islamic financial transactions to be enacted, but this is because the country felt that there is an interest here, there is a tremendous amount of money floating around in the world investment market which is Islamic orientated and Britain can potentially become a major centre for some of those investments to be processed. Fair enough, so here is a way in which we are taking values of the *shariah* and using them to benefit everybody, it's a win/win situation. (Interview, 12 April, Leicester, 2008)

Later, through newspaper research, I learned that in 2003, UK tax authorities removed double taxation on Islamic mortgages and began offering tax relief for Islamic mortgage companies and consumers (see *Epoch Times*, 14 February 2008, online). In 2004, Mohammed Nazir set up the Halal Fund in Birmingham (linked to the Islamic Bank of Britain, in Edgbaston) to provide small-scale funding for small businesses in the city. The fund offered loans that were acceptable under Islamic law; which forbade charging interest. The loans are based on the fund taking control of a percentage of the firm as collateral, which can be bought back at any time (*Birmingham Post*, 20 February 2008: 22). On a larger scale, various applications of *shariah* law have proved successful in Britain since 2003. The Islamic Bank of Britain, European Islamic Investment Bank, the Bank of London and the Middle East (BLME) and Barclays Bank all provide *shariah*-compliant products in the UK. Additionally, there are nine fund managers and a number of law firms specialising in Islamic finance. A vibrant secondary market exists for *Sukuk* – an Islamic form of bonds – which reached $2 billion a month in 2007. The UK's education system, such as universities and business schools, is one of the only systems in Europe offering classes and training in Islamic financial products and its Chartered Institute of Management Accountants is the only one worldwide that has a Certificate in Islamic Finance. The UK Treasury and Britain's Financial Services Authority actively provide legal and regulatory venues for the growth of Islamic financial products and monitor for compliance within UK law (*Epoch Times*, 14 February 2008, online).

Archbishop Dr Rowan Williams' *shariah* debate recommenced. In July 2008, in his speech in an East London Mosque, the Lord Chief Justice, Lord Nicholas Phillips, said that there was 'widespread misunderstanding' of the nature of *shariah* law, and he argued:

> There is no reason why sharia principles, or any other religious code, should not be the basis for mediation or other forms of alternative dispute resolution [with the understanding] . . . that any sanctions for a failure to comply with the agreed terms of mediation would be drawn from the Laws of England and Wales. (*Mail Online*, 4 July 2008)

Lord Phillips signalled approval of *shariah* principles as long as punishments – and divorce rulings – complied with the law of the land. But his remarks, which backed the informal *shariah* courts operated by numerous mosques, provoked a barrage of criticism. Lawyers warned that family and marital disputes settled by *shariah* could disadvantage women (*Mail Online*, 4 July 2008). Tory Member of Parliament, Philip Davies, said:

> This is totally unacceptable. There is no place for sharia law or any aspect of it in the legal system. We have our own legal system here and anyone in this country should accept our laws and the way we do things. The Lord Chief Justice does not understand how damaging these kinds of remarks are to community cohesion. (*Daily Express*, 4 July 2008: 19)

In the same article, Labour Member of Parliament, Khalid Mahmood, was quoted as saying:

> My real concern is that this will further alienate and segregate the Muslim community, and give those who want to radicalise more leverage. It is very frustrating and all this does is focus on it and start to bring resentment from other communities. (*Daily Express*, 4 July 2008: 19)

Prime Minister Gordon Brown's office produced the same reaction as it did over the Archbishop of Canterbury's comments. 'We think British law should be based on British values and determined by the British Parliament', said a government spokesman (*Daily Express*, 4 July 2008: 19). This overlooks the fact that *shariah* law components had long been incorporated with British finance; therefore, when Prime Minister Gordon Brown's office pretended that *shariah* was an alien concept, he was guilty of a double standard. I assume that when it comes to politics, both Muslim and non-Muslim British politicians are capable of emphasising the dangers inherent in *shariah* law to suit their purpose.

Reporting of *shariah* law by the British press

In this section, I examine how Archbishop Dr Rowan Williams' views were conveyed by the British press. I include an examination of the media, because some respondents of this study believed that the media had blown up Dr Williams' comments out of proportion, which thereby evoked the collective identity issue that 'They' (the British media) are against 'Us' (the Muslims). I draw on four British broadsheets – *The Times, Guardian, Daily Telegraph* and *The Independent* – and four tabloids – *The Sun, Daily Express, Daily Mail* and *Daily Mirror* – all published on 8 February 2008, to present a snapshot analysis of the media's next-day reporting of the archbishop's speech (similar media research on the anniversaries of the 7/7 London bombings is discussed in Chapter 5). I found the news reporting pattern in all newspapers was similar; for example, there was a big headline on the cover page of all the newspapers (except *The Independent* and the *Daily Mirror*). *The Guardian* was compassionate towards Muslims, as the cartoon below indicates, but the columnist (Brown, *Guardian*, 8 February 2008: 39) in his opinion piece confused the *shariah* issue on marriage and divorce with 'forced marriages, female circumcision, and other evils' which are cultural issues, and also practised by non-Muslims. Of all the newspapers, I found *The Times* and *The Sun* most condemnatory of the *shariah* issue (discussed next).

On 8 February 2008, *The Times* headlined its front page, 'Archbishop argues for Islamic law in Britain'. It reported that there were nearly 1.6 million Muslims in Britain, representing 2.7 per cent of the total population; it noted that *shariah* courts did exist (with no legal standing) and that some *shariah* elements had been incorporated into financial dealings. However, the main thrust was that 'the Archbishop of Canterbury came under fierce attack from the government, his own Church and other religions' for suggesting the adoption of parts of *shariah* or Islamic law in Britain and it reported criticisms made by both Muslims and non-Muslims against the archbishop. For example, it quoted the controversial Pakistani-born Bishop of Rochester, Dr Michael Nazir-Ali, who a few weeks earlier had claimed that parts of Britain were no-go areas for non-Muslims:

> English law is rooted in the Judaeo-Christian tradition and our notions of human freedoms derive from that tradition. It would be impossible to introduce a tradition like Sharia into the corpus without fundamentally affecting its integrity. (*The Times*, 8 February 2008: 4)

Furthermore, *The Times* (8 February 2008), through its headline 'From Leyton to Dewsbury – Sharia courts are already settling disputes' on page 4, informed its readers of the definition of the *shariah*, and the vulnerability of

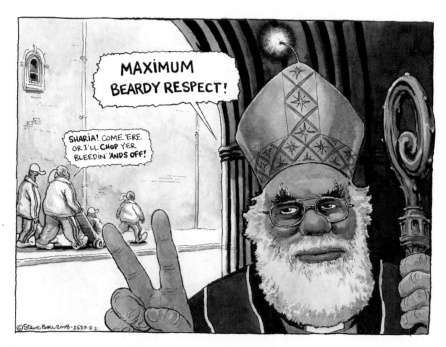

Figure 7.1 'Maximum Beardy Respect!' I interpret this cartoon as conveying
an ironical or satirical suggestion that Islamic values have become part
of British lower-class life! The other part of the message is that there is
disharmony between the Muslims and non-Muslims in Britain, and the
archbishop is trying to reconcile them.
Courtesy: cartoonist Steve Bell, Guardian, *8 February 2008, p. 39.*

women in times of divorce and adultery or *zina* (which in Pakistan carries
the death penalty). It also reported that unofficial courts run by the *shariah*
council existed in Britain, and discussed an isolated criminal case of a Somali
youth which was being settled by such a 'court'. Overall, through its reporting
this article appeared to indicate that the *shariah* council was dealing with all
Muslim criminal cases from 'Leyton to Dewsbury'. *The Times* warned:

> Sharia cannot trump the basic principles of English law. Muslims can decide to
> have disputes settled according to Sharia in private arbitration, but cannot ignore or
> abandon the human rights and responsibilities entrenched in the laws of this country.
> (*The Times*, 8 February 2008: 4)

It is important to note that in 2004 almost 10 per cent of the prison population in Britain were Muslim, two-thirds of whom were young men aged
18–30 (Prison Service statistics, 2004, cited in National Youth Agency 2004).
Surely they had been tried through the British criminal courts, so *The Times*

(8 February 2008: 4) was misrepresenting the situation and unnecessarily incit-ing fear among mainstream readers who were already stressed by the archbish-op's speech. The percentage of Muslim prisoners was further confirmed by a respondent of this study who was doing part-time mentoring work in a British prison. A British-born imam of Bangladeshi background, Muttaqi (male, aged 25) said:

> I work in a prison service as an imam. Ah, put it this way there are 510 inmates and 60 of them are Muslims. But you will find that out of those 60 all of them they will come for the *Jum'ah* (Friday prayers).
> . . . their crime, it's petty crime, stealing . . . when we take local prisoners it could be a driving licence offence or it could be drinking or stuff like that. Their average age starts from 18. (Interview, London, 5 April 2008)

The point I want to make is that the Somali youth's case could have been a one-off case, but through its headline and reporting, *The Times* (8 February 2008: 4) created a reasonable doubt among its readers that all *shariah* coun-cils from Leyton to Dewsbury have been bypassing the British criminal laws. The irony of the conservative British paper, *The Times*', reporting (8 February 2008: 4) is that it sympathises with the ordeal of Muslim women, but it labels all Muslims as 'the Muslim other'. As discussed, it has generalised the criminal case of the Somali youth with all Muslims. With its images and discussions, *The Times* has further reinforced the category of the 'Muslim Other'; for example, on page 4 (*Times*, 8 February 2008), there was a photograph of the Quran with the caption, 'Sharia rulings cannot trump the basic fundamental principles of English law'; then there was a cartoon which stated, 'Shoplifters will have their hands cut off'; and, finally, there was the image and report of the radical imam Abu Hamza, who is serving seven years in a British prison for inciting his followers to kill non-Muslims, which appeared to suggest that Muslims posed a big threat to Britain. In its editorial, *The Times* (8 February 2008: 16) stated:

> People of many faiths – Jews, Hindus, Sikhs – have settled happily in Britain without demanding a new set of laws for themselves. It would be more useful to ask how to help more Muslims to integrate successfully into what is a tolerant culture, than to urge a change in that culture to suit a notion that some parts of the Muslim com-munity feel more comfortable with . . . this is an act of appeasement. It threatens to undermine the practice of all faiths in Britain and the strength of our parliamentary democracy.

The Times (8 February 2008: 16) identified 'Us' as mainstream British, whereas the Muslims and the archbishop were 'the Other'. I assume the news-paper was not aware that certain sections of Jewish family laws have been incorporated into British laws (Beth Din), and that in some construction sites, Sikhs in Britain were exempted from wearing motorcycle crash helmets and hard hats.

Rupert Murdoch's tabloid newspaper, *The Sun* (8 February 2008: 1), went even further in sensationalising the news. Its front page was headed, 'What a Burkha', with photographs of Archbishop Dr Rowan Williams and a woman wearing the *burqa* and the *niqab* with her victory finger signs. Next to her left-hand side was a photograph of the radical Muslim cleric Abu Hamza with the caption, 'Hamza sent to America'. On the next page, *The Sun* ('Hook Slung: Hate preacher faces 99 years in US prison', *Sun*, 8 February 2008: 2) printed the full story of Shiekh Abu Hamza with his photograph showing his hooked hand (which he lost in Afghanistan). Next to this page (page 3) was a full-sized picture of a topless 20-year-old girl. By placing the photographs of the Muslim cleric and the topless model next to each other (pages 2 and 3), *The Sun* showed complete disregard for Muslims' notion of modesty. In its editorial, 'Dangerous rant' (*Sun*, 8 February 2008: 8), *The Sun* suggested that the archbishop was unfit for his job, and asked, 'Why doesn't he [the archbishop] condemn "honour" killings and forced marriages?' Other comments included, 'Gordon Brown rightly lost no time in slapping down Williams.' Then this provocative question was posed: 'Why is our Archbishop promoting a law under which women are stoned to death and shoplifters barbarically dismembered?' (*Sun*, 8 February 2008: 8). Pages 8 and 9 showed some images associated with Dr Williams, such as a picture of a bus destroyed in the 7/7 bombings, the flogging of a Muslim man (who was later hanged), and a man with an amputated hand (chopped off because of a *shariah* verdict). Finally, *The Sun* printed the headline, 'Archbishop says UK must accept Islamic Sharia law. He claims it's "unavoidable". His outburst is a . . . Victory for terrorism' (*Sun*, 8 February 2008: 8).

As discussed in Chapter 5, in times of crisis or when the media perceives that its mainstream 'superior values' are under attack, it lumps all Muslims together through conventional representation and reporting as 'the dangerous other'. With regard to the *shariah* law debate, I asked some Muslim adults 30 years and over about this question. One Muslim leader in Cardiff, Zulfikar, noted, 'On TV the *shariah* is shown as chopping hands, flogging and throwing stones, which is the very part of the *hudud* law that people normally react to' (Interview, Cardiff, 23 October 2008). A British-Bangladeshi Muslim respondent, Sarfaraz (male, over 30 years), explained:

I think there are two issues here: what did the Archbishop actually say? and what did the debate then become? I think the Archbishop actually wasn't advocating *shariah* law in the way that people presumed he was. I think what he was saying was that in a mature legal system there is always room for morality and experimentation and for thinking about how to accommodate the need for different groups of people.

His speech was a very articulate sort of intellectual interjection as he often does, but what that became in the media was unfortunately a reaction to the word *shariah* and what it showed us is that people don't understand what this term means in the public discourse. (Interview, Leicester, 12 April 2008)

But why so much negativity?

Muslims living in Britain are already enjoying the benefits of *shariah* law in their everyday lives. They can arrange to have animals slaughtered in *halal* fashion. They can set up Islamic financial institutions. They can build mosques. As discussed, it appears that the only remaining vacuum is women's right to divorce through the proceedings of the *shariah* council. However, Dr Williams' comments created anger among many people because some Muslims elsewhere have acted too severely. For example, in 2000 Nigeria's northern states adopted a harsh *shariah* code. The first victim who made worldwide news was a woman convicted of adultery, Amina Lawal. In 2002, Lawal was sentenced to death by stoning, and Ms Lawal's pregnancy was taken as proof of the adultery. Worldwide condemnation of the case, and a campaign mounted by human-rights organisations, eventually saw Ms Lawal's acquittal. If the sentence had been carried out, Amina would have been buried up to her neck in sand then pelted with rocks (*Mirror*, 6 August 2004: 5).

When the Taliban ruled Afghanistan from the mid-1990s until it was ousted by US-led forces in October 2001, the world witnessed several Taliban atrocities. The ultra-conservative Taliban espouses a very strict interpretation of Islam, which is unpopular among the majority of Afghans because it rejects all accommodation of Muslim moderation and the West. As Ahmed (2001: 94) says, 'The Taliban have given Islamic fundamentalism a new face and a new identity for the next millennium – one that refuses to accept any compromise or political system except their own.' The Taliban banned modern technology like the internet and TV in Afghanistan during its harsh 1996–2001 rule. Under Taliban rule, women were not allowed to work and girls and boys were not allowed to attend school. Men were beaten for trimming their beards and associating with women other than family members. The Taliban executed homosexuals by lapidation, bulldozing walls to crush their bodies (Ruthven 2004: 110–11, 121). In 1996, a group of 200 women, protesting against conditions in areas of Afghanistan run by the Taliban, delivered a letter to the United Nations office in Kabul, the capital. It said their human rights had been infringed by the Taliban as it closed more than 3,000 girls' schools and dismissed thousands of female teachers in Herat, a key city in Afghanistan ('In brief – Women demand UN protection', *Observer*, 8 September 1996: 20). The Taliban's punishment for adultery made worldwide news. In 1996, an Afghan woman called Nurbibi, aged 40, and her stepson and lover Turyalai, aged 38, were stoned to death under the provisions for stoning adulterers in the *shariah* ('They, who are with sin, are stoned . . . Two adulterers die under Taliban law', *Houston Chronicle*, 3 November 1996: 28). These vivid and frightening news items were often shown on television. In the same year, under Taliban rule, the first public execution which adhered to the strict version of the Islamic legal process was carried out. A convicted murderer was shot by the husband of the pregnant woman he killed. A thousand people gathered 'to watch justice in Afghanistan's capital, Taliban-style' ('Taliban-style execution carried out in Kabul', *Buffalo News*, 19 December 1996: 3). In 2001, the Taliban destroyed some 2,000-year-old Buddhist statues because they regarded them as an insult to Islam. The irony is that the Taliban interpreted those verses of the Holy Quran that suited them to prove their authority, while ignoring the verses that promote respect and tolerance for other religions. For example, *Sura Kafirun* (Sura CIX – Those who reject faith: 6289–91) says:

Say: O ye
That reject Faith!
I worship not that
Which ye worship,
Nor will ye worship
That which I worship.
And I will not worship
That which ye have been
Wont to worship,
Nor will ye worship
That which I worship
To you be your Way,
And to me mine.

In February 2009, Taliban rule in Swat in Pakistan received a boost when the Pakistan government struck a peace deal that suspended military action and allowed the introduction of *shariah* law. The Taliban aimed to raze Swat to the ground and begin again. To start with, they have destroyed 187 schools. Under the Taliban, girls' education is forbidden and 80,000 girls were confined to their homes. A Swat girl said: 'We will not go to school again, even if there is more security because we are scared. The Taliban are warning us they will bomb and destroy our school. The Taliban are very angry, the situation is getting worse everyday' (ABC *Four Corners*, 23 February 2009).

It is argued (Ahmed 2001: 111–12) that in the name of implementing Islamic law, the Taliban have used draconian measures against Muslim girls and women, and legitimised *shariah*. In an interview, the Taliban Attorney-General Moalvi Jalilullah Maulvizada said, 'The Koran cannot adjust itself to

other people's requirements, people should adjust themselves to the requirements of the Holy Koran' (Ahmed 2001: 111–12). Scholars of Islam (Mernissi
1987: 19; Nasr 2002: 193–4) say neither the Quran nor the *hadith* allows men
to subjugate women. The author of 'The Empowerment of Women in Islam'
(2000), Zeenat Shaukat Ali, challenges the stereotype that Islam considers
women inferior to men. Shaukat Ali (2000, cited in *The Times of India*, 22
February 2009: 1) says there are 805 verses and their derivatives in the Quran
that favour *ilm* (education). She adds that nowhere is it said that women
should be barred from seeking *ilm*. Akhtarul Wassey, who teaches Islamic
Studies at Delhi's Jamia Millia Islamia, explains that Prophet Muhammad
[PBUH] favoured educating girls. In a *hadith*, Prophet Muhammad [PBUH]
said, 'Acquire ilm right from the lap of your mother till you reach the grave.'
Wassey explains that this 'clearly means the Prophet laid great emphasis
on women's education because they become mothers'. But many *mullahs*
(imams), in the Indian subcontinent and elsewhere, believe it is sinful for the
parents to put girls beyond the ninth grade into co-education (*The Times of
India*, 22 February 2009: 1). (This issue was discussed in Chapter 3.)

Similarly, there are other cultural practices, such as female circumcision
(see Kabir 2006: 314–15) and honour killings, that have been committed
by both Muslims and non-Muslims, which have been labelled as exclusively
Islamic practices. For example, in 2003 a Muslim man in London was impris-
oned for life for murdering his 16-year-old daughter for 'dishonouring' his
Kurdish family ('Combat violence against women', *Herald Express*, 23 March
2004: 8). Then in 2008, another Muslim, Khan, was convicted of the 'alleged
honour killing' of Mehmood because Khan disapproved of his sister's relationship with Mehmood (*Yorkshire Post*, 25 June 2008, online). As discussed, it is
also a non-Muslim practice. In 2007, a non-Muslim Indian mother-in-law was
found guilty of honour killing her daughter-in-law, whose adultery she claimed
had brought shame on the family (*Independent*, 20 September 2007: 1).

In November 2007, a 54-year-old British international schoolteacher at
Unity High School in Sudan, Gillian Gibbons, was charged with 'inciting
religious hatred'. In Sudan, where the legal code is based on *shariah* law, it is
considered an insult and illegal to give the name Muhammad to an inanimate
object. The charge was that by giving this name to a toy bear in her second-
grade class, Ms Gibbons insulted Islam. She was arrested in Sudan and faced
the prospect of up to six months' jail, a fine and 40 lashes for 'blasphemy'.
Later, Ms Gibbons was spared the lashes, and the President of Sudan par-
doned her after two British Muslim members of the House of Lords, Baroness
Sayeeda Warsi and Lord Nazir Ahmed, pleaded for clemency on her behalf
(*Washington Post*, 4 December 2007: 16). It appears Ms Gibbons did not
mean to insult the Muslims. Perhaps Mohammad is a popular Muslim name,
and in Western culture children have special feelings for their teddy bears (soft
toy) and give it a special name. No doubt in that context Ms Gibbons thought

that it would be appropriate. But the reaction of the Muslims in Sudan had a strong impact on some mainstream British people. As one reader wrote to the editor of *The Guardian*, '. . . Salman Rushdie, the primary school teacher and the teddy bear, the Danish cartoonists et al. are testament that such laws [*shariah* law] are imposed upon non-believers' (Ken Walton, *Guardian*, 11 February 2008: 33). In other words, the letter writer suggests that Muslims are imperious and totalitarian.

There have been a few incidents in the Western world where some Muslims have been allowed to practise extreme forms of exclusion. For example, the *Washington Times* (12 February 2008: 15) reported that in Minnesota (United States) a Muslim cabdriver refused transportation to people he considered, under *shariah*, to be *haram* or unclean – including blind people with seeing-eye dogs and people carrying alcohol. I assume such negative news items are adding to the concerns of non-Muslims. The British-born participant Sarfaraz observed:

> Some Muslims have misused this word [*shariah*] themselves. I think when you settle here, when you become naturalised as a citizen, effectively for me, you are entering into a social contract. You have a relationship with the State, a legal relationship, you agree to abide by the law, you agree to pay your taxes, you agree to vote, to play a role as a citizen in the public life of a country and the State obliges, reciprocates by protecting you, providing you with services, the police will be there for you, the national health service will be there to look after you and so on and so forth . . . I think if certain things can be recognised, for example already non-interest bearing transactions have been recognised under English law, Islamic economics as it is sometimes called. (Interview, Leicester, 12 April 2008)

Of course, as Sarfaraz rightly said, British Muslims have a role to play as citizens, particularly when there is so much negativity associated with the *hudud*. However, it cannot be denied that in some media, Islam or Muslim in a generalised sense has been labelled as the 'Other'. As Edward Said (1997: xii–xvi) observed, there have indeed been many provocations and troubling incidents by Muslims, especially in Iran, Sudan, Iraq, Somalia, Afghanistan and Libya, but he argued, 'My concern . . . is that the mere use of the label "Islam" either to explain or indiscriminately condemn "Islam" actually ends up becoming a form of attack [against all Muslims].' I observe that sometimes the media does not overtly attack or label Islam as the 'Other', but through its headlines, reporting and images, it tends to condemn Islam (as discussed earlier in reference to *The Times* and *The Sun*, 8 February 2008). A British-Pakistani observer in Cardiff, Zulfikar (male, over 30), noted that critics of British Muslims (including the media) often ignore horrendous incidents, such as those committed by non-Muslims (Hindus) against Christians recently in India, but highlight anything negative that is related to Islam:

I don't know whether you saw there were thousands of Christians killed in India. [Pakistani-born] Bishop Nazir-Ali stirs a lot [against Muslims], but he never mentioned any statement about what happened in India and this is because if they [British politicians or the media] do [criticise] much their business [with India] will be affected, the money will be affected. (Interview, Cardiff, 23 October 2008)

Zulfikar was referring to what occurred in the first week of October 2008, when some Christians were killed and churches were destroyed in Orissa in India (see 'Holy war strikes India', *The Independent*, 9 October 2008: 19). During that period I was in Britain and I noticed that the British press reported the incidents, but they were not major news items and the discussion also did not linger day after day as it did with Dr Williams' comments. As Zulfikar observed, the media did not want to disrupt the commercial links of Great Britain with India for the sake of the national interest.

The other claim made by Zulfikar was that the British press gave undue attention to Pakistani-born Bishop Nazir-Ali's comment that some Muslim areas in Britain have become a 'no-go zone'. I assume, in this context, Zulfikar meant that both Bishop Nazir-Ali and some British newspapers have a common target – 'the Muslims' – and they label them as the 'Other'. Regarding the cultural superiority of Western-Christian values, a reader, Malcolm Wild, wrote a letter to the editor of his local newspaper (*Journal*, Newcastle, 12 February 2008: 10):

When a British schoolteacher was jailed in Sudan last year for breaking Sharia law by allowing her class to name their teddy-bear Mohammad, there was a massive outcry in this country that the authorities should have made allowances for the fact that she had been brought up to Western or Christian laws and values . . .

Yet when the Archbishop of Canterbury suggests that similar understanding and accommodation should apply over here for Muslim people brought up under Sharia law and values, he is roundly pilloried.

It seems to me that we in the West are brainwashed into believing our values are always superior to those of alternative cultures.

Earlier, Edward Said (1995: 237) argued that Western scholars (or Orientalists) would boast that 'We (Europeans and Christians) are this, and they (the Arabs and Muslims) are that.' However, critics of Edward Said's book *Orientalism* (1995) suggest that Said has generalised all Western scholars as guilty of depicting the 'Muslim Other', and boastful of their cultural superiority, and that his observation is far from true. I would add that several Western scholars (Poole 2002; Poole and Richardson 2004; Werbner 2002; Lewis 2007) have been sympathetic to the British Muslim cause. Similarly, the above letter of Malcolm Wild illustrates that Westerners are capable of compassion and able to see through so-called superior values (see also Daniel

Hannan, 'Muslims are trying to prove their loyalty', *Daily Telegraph*, 27 February 2008: 23). In the next section, I examine young Muslims' (15–30 years) views on the *shariah* debate, and how it has impacted on their identity.

Muslim participants' comments on the *shariah* law

There were 116 (46 males, 70 females) respondents (aged 15–30) and four Muslim adults (over 30) who discussed *shariah* law. Table 7.1 shows the pattern of the 116 responses (15–30). The four Muslim adults' (over 30) opinions have been blended throughout the chapter (all of whom held Archbishop Dr Williams in high esteem, and knew that *shariah* already existed in financial circles).

Discussion

In this section, I analyse and discuss the responses summarised in Table 7.1.

Praise for the archbishop

As Table 7.1 (overleaf) indicates, some comments were exclusively focused on Dr Williams. For example, when I asked a British-born girl, Humaira (aged 16, Pakistani background), 'Can you name any non-Muslim role model?', she promptly replied, 'I think the Archbishop [of Canterbury] is good because, like the things that he says, they're really good' (Interview, Bradford, 9 April 2008). Another British-born student, Omar (Bangladeshi background, aged 16), said, 'Credit to the Archbishop because he's actually supporting the Muslims' (Interview, London, 30 March 2008). Another student, Waheeda (female, British-born of Pakistani background, aged 16), thought:

> What he [Archbishop Dr Williams] said was right, I think, yeah, they should enforce it because obviously of the increased Muslim population within the country. When people sort of contradict him and go against him, that's when I start to get angry because I think it's a secular country with respect to all religions . . . he's not saying turn it into a *shariah* country, he's just saying about the laws those regarding the marriage stuff like that. (Interview, Bradford, 9 October 2008)

It seems that the archbishop has won the hearts of some young Muslims, as indicated by Waheeda when she said that she was hurt when people contradicted him. Another example was given by a young British-born Muslim woman of Pakistani background, Bilqis, who met the archbishop at an interfaith gathering and was impressed by his modesty. Bilqis said:

> I've met the Archbishop of Canterbury. We [the archbishop and other speakers] talked to about 500 people in the Town Hall in Manchester, and I'd never met him

Table 7.1 Key points of 116 responses, aged 15–30

Number of participants	Responses	Key points
10 (4 males, 6 females)	Praise for Archbishop	Archbishop is respectful of other religions. Archbishop is my non-Muslim role model. We think that we know Islam in the right way, but there are also non-Muslims. Archbishop was neutral and unbiased.
9 (3 males, 6 females)	This is not a Muslim country	We cannot implement the law of Islam without an Islamic setting. Not appropriate for Britain (confused with *hudud*). English and Islamic law cannot co-exist. Islam is peace but *shariah* law has too much force.
20 (4 males, 16 females)	We need *shariah* law to a certain extent	We can have *shariah* in marriage and divorce but not the whipping of people (*hudud*). We need it for the benefit of women. The Jews had their religious laws for hundreds of years so why not the Muslims? Why such a fuss? We should have some elements of it.
6 (5 males, 1 female)	*Shariah* law already exists	We already have *shariah* in finance.
4 females	Islamic laws are better than the British laws	To contain the social ills of the British societies, e.g. rape, paedophilia, Islamic law would be good. 'English law is not that much better to be honest.' 'Use *shariah* law on bike thieves.'
2 (1 male, 1 female)	Some confusion regarding the *shariah* debate	I heard it but women should have the right to wear the *niqab* (confused with Jack Straw's debate). *Shariah* people are multifaceted (also connected it with the *niqab*).
5 (1 male, 4 females)	Criticism of Muslims' behaviour	Critical of Muslims' reaction over the teddy-bear issue in Sudan. Misuse of the law, sometimes people lie even swearing on the Quran, sometimes women lie, and men are the victims. Muslims need to shape up.
1 female	Defensive of Muslims	Did not hear archbishop's debate but defensive over Muslim's reaction against Prophet Muhammad [PBUH] cartoons
19 (9 males, 10 females)	Criticism of the media	Archbishop had good intentions but the media went berserk. All the newspapers slammed him. It was blown up out of proportion. It was taken out of context.

Table 7.1 (continued)

Number of participants	Responses	Key points
		Archbishop could have been easily misinterpreted.
		The media has had a lot to do . . . now it's become like a forbidden word.
2 females	Media's indirect positive role	There were discussions on *shariah*, so it was also a learning process, quite educational.
2 females	Criticism of archbishop	Archbishop purposefully stirred up the tension.
1 female	Multicultural dilemma. *Shariah* law has been misused	English people are fearful of losing their identity. Teddy-bear incident in Sudan could have been political.
1 female	Pessimistic view	'No, they [the English people] won't do it, something like that [*shariah*].'
15 (8 males, 7 females)	Did not follow up	I did not follow up. There is still a lot to explore. I did not take much interest.
19 (11 males, 8 females)	Uninformed audience	I did not hear archbishop's *shariah* debate.

before . . . I mean he didn't really speak to me personally but he appeared like a very nice, really kind of . . . there was just something about his face, he was just glowing . . . (Interview, Bradford, 29 August 2008)

While expressing their admiration for Dr Williams, these respondents identified themselves as exclusively Muslim (rather than average British citizens) and were grateful that a non-Muslim of high standing was kind to their religious group. These were occasions when identities were revealed as they expressed feeling for their group. Also connecting with his Muslim identity, an overseas-born young Muslim, Khaled (male, Nigerian background, aged 20), pointed out why the archbishop's comments were important:

Archbishop is very open. He is very honest in a way that he is taking these issues and deals with them. And he is very impartial in these things and he has got an academic background which gives him that spirit of debate. On the other hand, the thing is, it is not about what Muslims think of the Archbishop's comments, Muslims need to hear the English people, they need to talk, that is, what we want?, or what do we want?

But again, there are other considerations because you see the hoohah that came with it and you had the Prime Minister coming out and saying, 'Yeah, whatever you do it is going to be under our laws, subservient to our law.' And at the end of the day, that would pose theological questions to us: 'Do we subject God's law to man's law?' So we have to be careful in dealing with these things, because sometimes Muslims are just being like a football and just being played in the media. So when a non-Muslim raises the issues and he deals with it and debates it, it is more effective. (Interview, London, 20 April 2008)

Khaled realised that communication and dialogue are important in address-ing Muslim needs, and he appreciated the value of support from a non-Muslim person. He also pointed out the vulnerability of Muslims when it comes to the politicians and media who are most likely to make Muslim issues into a politi-cal football for their own personal or commercial gain.

This is not a Muslim country

Some respondents thought that Britain was not a Muslim country so *shariah* law was inappropriate in an English-Christian setting. In this context, their British identity took precedence. An overseas-born student, Hamid (male, Sudanese background, aged 16), commented:

I think the *Sharia* law should only be established when there is a majority of Muslims and the thing about what archbishop said is that *shariah* law should be applied according to civil law. And many Muslims already practise it alongside the normal laws – we practise the *shariah* law like in weddings. (Interview, London, 15 April 2008)

Similarly, a British-born youth, Suraj (male, aged 16, Bangladeshi back-ground), argued:

We cannot implement the law of Islam without having an Islamic setting, an Islamic backbone, Islamic environment, and this country is in no state, it is in no fitting con-dition to put Islamic law like that . . . but I admire Archbishop Dr Rowan Williams, the Professor, for his understanding, because I think he has high understanding from a non-Muslim perspective. (Interview, London, 8 April 2008)

Both these students, Hamid and Suraj, attended different Islamic schools but they realised that Islamic laws could be inappropriate in a non-Muslim country. Hamid thought that since Muslims were already using Islamic laws in weddings alongside normal British laws, to demand more laws or give the Islamic laws an official status would be incorrect. Suraj praised the archbishop but believed that *shariah* law was not appropriate in a predominantly non-Muslim country. In effect, Hamid was saying, 'Don't ask for more concessions' and Suraj was saying, 'Don't ask at all.' In both cases, the participants' British identity overshadowed their Muslim identity, though they attended Muslim schools.

We need shariah *law to a certain extent*

Twenty respondents (4 males, 16 females) expressed the opinion that Muslims needed *shariah* law to a certain extent, and provided examples. A young woman, Mehjabeen (Pakistani background, aged 20), pointed out that some parts of *shariah* law should be introduced:

It is also a long process the English law, but with the Muslim law, it is not that easy because if the man says, 'No', or he might demand some payment and say, 'Well okay, I will divorce you if you give me XY and Z.' So in that sense, if that [Islamic] law was implemented with English law and it would come to be one law whereby women can divorce her husband just as easily as a man can divorce her. (Interview, London, 9 April 2008)

Similar views were echoed in Cardiff a few months later by another Muslim woman, Mehr (Yemeni background, aged 24):

I was just watching a documentary trying to get divorce . . . In Islam you're allowed to get divorce in special circumstances and it's really hard for a [woman] . . . Here [in Britain] a woman gets to vote but she don't get her rights that she should have from Islam. (Interview, Cardiff, 22 October 2008)

As discussed earlier in this chapter, some women wanted a divorce but found it difficult to get the approval of the existing *shariah* councils in Britain. Therefore, the 20 respondents in this section of the study (including men) thought that if some parts of *shariah* law relating to marriage and divorce were incorporated into the British legal system, it would be helpful for the Muslim community. An English convert, Abdul Hakim (male, aged 35), argued:

But certainly some of the elements of it could be very good here. I know that Rowan Williams recently came out in the press and said it . . . and got slated for it. Which is a great shame because all he was saying was: why can't we give the Muslims what the Jews have had for hundreds of years, which is their own courts where they can religiously you know practise marriage and divorce rights? (Interview, London, 2 April 2008)

Here Hakim's religious identity as a Muslim came into play. Hakim also said he regretted that the Muslim world has gone backwards since its 'Golden Age' when it was leading the world in education and its visions and now a lot of Islamic countries are known as 'Third world countries' and the extremists in Afghanistan were giving Islam a bad name. Another respondent, a British-born East African background student, Firoza (female, aged 15), expressed her Muslim identity through this interview:

> I think it could be a good idea but obviously the British would find it offending because they always argue that it's their country first and we've just come here from different countries so we can't take over. But he [Archbishop Dr Williams] needs to think about that at the moment; there's loads of Muslims in like the whole of England so it would be good if he did that [for the Muslim community]. (Interview, Leeds, 14 October 2008)

Though Firoza connected the issue with her Islamic identity, she realised that only a reputable English person such as an archbishop would have the authority to pursue it. I assume her statement recognised the power of a prominent person in the wider community, where Muslim voices do not carry the same weight (as indicated earlier by Khaled).

Shariah *law already exists*

A British-born youth worker in Leeds, Sobhan (male, Indian background, aged 27), said:

> Well, apparently I was reading an article the other day that a *shariah* council is already established in Britain but it hasn't been broadcast on the wide stream media.
> There's some sort of loophole in the British law that has actually allowed these councils to be set up but, according to [this article], they set up as, I can't remember if it was a tribunal or something like that. (Interview, Leeds, 6 October 2008)

A British-born tertiary student in Cardiff, Rubaba (female, Iraqi, aged 23), also believed *shariah* law was allowed in some financial transactions in Britain:

> Someone told me the other day, or a while ago, that like even business like non-Muslim business, some of them will implement the Islamic ruling on money and interest and stuff like that and what they'll do is that they'll go to some scholar who's studied Islam and they'll check that all the transactions fit within the Islamic law and if they don't then they won't carry out the transactions. (Interview, Cardiff, 17 October 2008)

Overall, the *shariah* law debate revealed the double standard of the British government. It suggested that Britain was keen to get financial benefit so it incorporated some parts of *shariah* law in its financial sector, while it neglected Muslim women's issues (perhaps unintentionally) by not incorporating some elements of *shariah* law into the British law to resolve family matters.

Islamic laws are better than the British laws

The young woman who earlier praised the archbishop, Bilqis (female, Pakistani background, aged 22), said:

> Personally I've not done too much research on *shariah* law but . . . I'm so conscious of paedophiles, I mean youngsters have lost their innocence, because of what's around in our societies – rapists, etc., . . . there's so much commotion within the Muslims themselves, there's so many issues, but I think I'm all for *shariah* law . . . in hindsight I think it's the best. (Interview, Bradford, 29 August 2008)

Bilqis thought that if Britain had strict laws (such as *hudud*) then there would be less crime. On the surface it may appear that Bilqis is a strictly fundamentalist woman, but I regarded her as a British citizen who deeply cared for her country. Another British-born woman in Cardiff, Tabassum (Pakistani background, aged 30), also wished Britain to be a 'safe' country.

> There was an MP and I think somebody stole his bicycle. I can't remember but it was on TV just, not too long ago . . . if you Google search you will find it. He jokingly said, 'Maybe we should bring *shariah* law', . . . so then it's alright to have Islam isn't it?
>
> *Shariah* law sounds something so dangerous and so big and so severe but it's actually what's best for us. Whereas in America, or I suppose in Britain as well, they think, 'Oh, it doesn't matter, if I steal this or rob somebody or murder somebody, I will be in life imprisonment', but you could do appeals and you'll be out soon. And prison's a luxury life you know . . . they've got TV and their own room and dinner . . . so it's easy to go into prison. So then where *shariah* law is there, it's there for a reason, to make actually people not commit any crimes. (Interview, Cardiff, 22 October 2008)

On the advice of Tabassum, I did a Google search and retrieved the information on the British Member of Parliament. On 16 March 2007, it was reported in the media that the Conservative Member of Parliament, Boris Johnson, was tired of having his bicycle stolen and wheel nuts taken away and at the Annual General Meeting of the Islington Cyclists Action Group at Islington Town Hall, he called for 'hardline "Sharia law" to be used on bicycle thieves' (*Evening Standard*, 16 March 2007: 25).

Criticism of Muslims' behaviour

Some Muslims were critical of Muslims' behaviour; for example, British-born Afroza (female, Bangladeshi background, aged 17) stated:

> I have heard of it [*shariah* debate] . . . even though if you named the teddy bear Muhammad, it doesn't mean it's the Muhammad [our Prophet, PBUH]. Also people

should not react as they did at Prophet Muhammad's [PBUH] cartoon. I think, well it is the teaching of Islam to be calm. (Interviewed, London, 25 March 2008)

In the previous chapter, Afroza (in the *niqab* debate) defended women's right to wear the *niqab* and argued that communication was possible through eye contact. She also said that people of the wider community called her 'Ninja turtle' when she wore the *niqab*, but that did not bother her as 'they don't understand the real purpose of wearing it so'.

However, in this context, she was critical of the Muslims' overreaction on certain controversial issues. Perhaps her Islamic identity (as she believed Islam means 'peace') reminded her to be calm even when some people thought that Islam was under attack. However, another respondent, Samira (female, Bangladeshi background, aged 18), differed from Afroza and defended the Muslims' reaction over Prophet Muhammad's [PBUH] cartoon controversy:

If I was to write an article about George Bush and his family, and I was to give a wrong insight of his family, I'm sure his family – his people would be angry because it's not true, it's false. At the end of the day it – it's not going to affect only him, it's going to affect the whole people who's living in his country. It's the same way. The people in this country if one writes a wrong article of one person – a specific renowned person in a Muslim religion or Christianity – it will have an effect on the whole person, the whole entire people. (Interview, London, 26 March 2008)

Samira differed from Afroza's view of non-violence, and justified the Muslims' protest over the Prophet Muhammad [PBUH] cartoons. Samira thought that if the Muslim community is vilified then their voices should be heard in protest. As Pnina Werbner (2002) observed, when the British-Pakistanis reacted against Salman Rushdie's book, *The Satanic Verses*, this could be seen as an assertion of their collective Muslim identity and it was also their right as citizens to let their voices be heard. The next participant, the British-born student Aulad (male, aged 17, Somali background), was critical of the Muslim countries:

I mean they say Saudi Arabia has *shariah* law; it doesn't have proper *shariah* law; it's bent *shariah* law, it's corrupted. The men have twisted it for their own purposes and for their own benefit. If you want *shariah* law you need a proper *khilafah*; in order to have a proper *khilafah* you need a proper leader, and not one [Muslim] country in the world has a decent leader – I don't think. (Interview, Leeds, 14 October 2008)

Aulad believed *shariah* law has been distorted by the Muslim countries. Perhaps the vivid graphics of the Taliban or Saudi regimes' extreme punishments based on *hudud* impacted on him, as it has impacted on many people of the wider community. UK-born Noori (female, Pakistan, aged 30) observed:

I think that for Muslim communities to move forward we need a much more pragmatic understanding of what religion is and how it can help us, not just achieve success in our own communities but the wider community. So far the only thing people see is the negatives of Islam on a broader scale, so the Archbishop of Canterbury's comments about the *shariah*, they wouldn't have been taken so badly if Muslims were acting in a much more Islamic way towards non-Muslim people. But you know if you turn around and you're burning this and you're doing this and you're fighting and you're being really abusive to people of different faiths and then you say and I also want to have *shariah* law. It's like [the wider community thinks] 'Why do they have to have another thing'? (Interview, Bradford, 30 August 2008)

Another participant, Nahila (female, Bangladeshi background, aged 18), concluded:

I practise Islam as thoroughly as I can but *shariah* law is something that I would not exactly favour with because I think there's too much force. Instead of you having your own will, because Islam is about free will, it seems more like force and I don't think we should make Islam look like as if it's a forced religion. It is of peace and people's views are taken into consideration, whereas *shariah* law sometimes just lumps it all on you. (Interview, Bradford, 14 October 2008)

Both respondents, Noori (aged 18) and Nahila (aged 30), wear the *hijab* and live in Bradford; many Muslims of Pakistani background live in this city. Bradford was the first place in Britain where the Muslims burned Salman Rushdie's book, *The Satanic Verses*. Nahila may have remembered news of the burning as she would have been 10 years old at that time. Both Nahila and Noori are critical of the perceived harshness of Muslims. It appears that social cohesion can be enhanced when people of different faiths and diverse backgrounds discuss the controversial sides of their communities.

Criticism of the media

As discussed in previous chapters, many young Muslims believe that the media is against them. On a discussion of the archbishop's *shariah* debate, 19 respondents (9 male; 10 female) explicitly pointed out that the media had blown up the archbishop's speech out of all proportion. A British-born student, Umbareen (Pakistani, female, aged 16), exclaimed, '*The Sun*, they talk rubbish' (Interview, Leeds, 15 October 2008), and UK-born Roshan Ara (Bangladeshi background, female, aged 16) commented:

Some of them, it's like say some of them do stand up then they would be like, it'll make more news out of it and then do you know like some newspapers' reporters they just like lie about it as well. (Interview, Leeds, 15 October 2008)

I agree with Roshan Ara's view that some media sources sensationalise the news because it sells well, but I disagree with her that they 'lie'. Their knowledge of culture and religion may be shallow, for example, when they think female circumcision or forced marriage is exclusively Islamic, though in fact these are practised by non-Muslims as well. The next interviewee, Kashfia (British-born, Pakistani background, female, aged 16), observed:

> They made a programme about *shariah* law in this country. It was Channel 4 that made the programme, we went to them, there was the producer who made it like they wanted us to talk about it, the audience, to see what we think about the programme and there was one audience [member] who asked the archbishop about introducing it [*shariah* law] but he was just completely ignored [the producer did not allow the archbishop to engage in that discussion]. And that just shows that they don't even want, like the Muslim law to be into this country, they don't want change, they want to keep it as it is. (Interview, London, 19 April, 2008)

Kashfia's observation was of a first-hand experience as a member of the audience of the TV programme. She noticed that the producers had some hidden agenda and that they did not want to promote the law. Kashfia's opinion could be interpreted as subjective, but I had a similar experience with a TV programme (Channel Nine, 'Islam in Australia', November 2006) in Australia where I was invited to be a member of the audience. The forum was on the heated debate about the former Australian Mufti Sheikh Al Hilali's 'women and meat sermon' (discussed in Chapter 6). It appeared the programme convenor had a set agenda to show that the Muslims were divided over the issue. Some members of the audience were critical of Al Hilali, while others said that his speech was taken out of context. The convenor gave opportunities to speakers on both sides but she seemed determined to emphasise the Muslim dissension. However, it was my experience that through the debate the participants were becoming more aware of Muslim issues, and reconciling some of their differences of opinion. Also through such programmes, the mainstream audiences may learn that Muslims are a diverse group of people.

Media has inadvertently been positive too

Only two respondents spoke of the positive side of the media. The British-born Nawsheen (female Pakistani background, aged 17) observed:

> The media exaggerated it . . . And there's a programme on Channel 4 called *Make Me a Muslim* which is really good. It's set here, locally, as well as in Harrogate which is not far from Bradford, sort of Leeds Harrogate area, and these people were, had to pretend, had to be Muslims for a few weeks, so they had to live the lifestyles of Muslims. So refrain from alcohol, you know going to clubs, relations outside of the

marriage and there was one man who was very vocal about *shariah* law was quite shocked, but he still obviously had a certain dislike for it because he wanted to say that Britain is Britain. If you want to have *shariah* law, have it in a Muslim country where it is, but he thought, 'I grossly misunderstood the meaning of *shariah* law'. He thought it was all you know, violence and suppression but it isn't. (Interview, Bradford, 7 October 2008)

Similarly, the UK-born Rubina (female, Pakistani background, aged 18) said:

I've noticed they [the media] have produced a lot more programmes about Muslims, trying to explain not everyone believes in *jihad,* which is to go kill people. And I think that's good because it has settled a few things, you know I'm not saying everything. It's nice to see other people looking into, about your religion trying to show people they're not all bad. So there have been some positive outcomes. (Interview, Leeds, 14 October 2008)

In my earlier research on Muslims in the Western world (Australia), I found that there was a rise in Islamophobia after the 9/11 Twin Towers tragedy but at the same time the wider community learned more about Islam and Muslims. I found heated debate (Kabir 2008a; Kabir 2008b) on controversial issues has been fruitful for both sides – Muslims had their voices heard and thereby displayed their citizenship rights, while the wider community also expressed their opinions on integration and social cohesion. Similarly, in the British context, as Nawsheen mentioned, the programme *Make Me a Muslim* (Channel 4, 2007, shown in three episodes) was also educational.

English people are fearful

A British-born woman, Nusaybah (Ugandan background, aged 25), noted:

When first everyone started immigrating to this country, there was this fear of losing our identity, losing who we are as being English and being British and being white, there was this whole worry at the beginning. And I think now, casting it [*shariah* law] with Islam, is then just bringing back this whole fear again that a lot of the people, a lot of the English people are feeling intimidated that we are losing our identity, that our culture's being taken. (Interview, London, 24 April 2008)

Fear that the mainstream British culture would be taken away is not new. However, initially it was fear of colour or race, and now it appears to be culture. As Cesari (2004: 32) noted in 1968, the Conservative politician Enoch Powell declared, 'The Indian and the Asian do not become English by being born in England.' A few decades later, colour appeared to remain an issue (Barker 1982; Bulmer and Solomas 1999). In 2000, the Parekh Report denounced the 'insidious' racism of British society and recommended that the English or British identity should be disassociated as much as possible from the notion of 'whiteness' (Cesari 2004: 32). I have observed that after the 9/11 Twin Towers tragedy, for the Muslims residing in the Western world, the issue of colour or race has been replaced by the question of their culture and religion (Kabir 2005). After the 7/7 London bombings, the *shariah* law debate has had a negative impact on the wider community because people tend to equate *shariah* law with Taliban-style ultra-conservative laws. Media caricatures have depicted Muslims as the 'Other'.

Shariah *law has been misused (teddy bear incident in Sudan)*

As demonstrated above, discussion of the *shariah* debate with the respondents of this study evoked rationality, emotion, blame and self-criticism. A British-born woman, Nusaybah (Ugandan background, aged 25), treated the use of *shariah* law in Sudan in Ms Gibbons' case with suspicion:

> I think that was definitely blown out of proportion. I don't know if you know, but in England we had a teddy bear, we called it 'Adam' [also a name of a Prophet]; and it was very popular and you'd move one arm and it would say '*Allah O Akbar*' [God is Great], you'd pinch the ear and it would say '*Ma'shallah*' [May God preserve you], you'd pinch another ear and it would say something – and we called it Adam. And if you look at it most Arabs have the name Muhammad, they name anything Muhammad. So I don't think it was just the naming of the teddy bear . . .
>
> But what I'm saying is that there must have been other issues that had added up and this may have been the final thing to certify that 'look there are no other elements there'. I don't think we were given the full picture whatever happened. (Interview, London, 24 April 2008)

Muslim scholar Dilwar Hussain, of the Islamic Foundation, Leicester, said that he had no problem with a teddy bear called Muhammad because for some years the Islamic Society sold a soft toy made for British Muslim children named Adam, the Prayer Bear (BBC 2007). It appears there are two issues arising from Nusaybah's opinion that other factors may have been involved: first, Sudan is a developing and Islamic African country which has *shariah* law (*hudud*). Their literacy level is low, and they hold their religion very dear. Therefore, they overreacted to the entire teddy bear issue; second, I assume, there prevailed an anti-US and anti-West sentiment among some people in Sudan. In the 1990s, Sudan provided a safe haven for the Al-Qaeda terrorist group. On 20 August 1998, the United States launched an attack on Khartoum in Sudan, bombing the al-Shifa pharmaceutical plant under direct orders from President Bill Clinton. The US attack was initiated a week after bomb blasts in US embassies in Kenya and Tanzania killed 260 people; these were blamed on the CIA-trained Saudi dissident and Taliban favourite, Osama bin Laden. The al-Shifa plant was totally destroyed in the American attack and many people were killed. This attack created ill-feeling between the Sudanese and the US government. Later, after the terrorist attacks of 2001, the USA reached an agreement with Sudan to contain the Al-Qaeda terrorist group. But it is alleged that the US did not keep its word. It provided limited political support to Khartoum in return for co-operation and intelligence sharing on the 'war on terror'. The US believed that Sudan's Islamist rulers knew a lot about Al-Qaeda, but at the same time, the US made a peace agreement with the Southern Sudanese rebels, the Sudan People's Liberation Army. Analysts say this was a 'bad miscalculation', so the Sudanese government was unhappy with the United States (see 'Sudan: the Pitfall of US Foreign Policy', *The Age*, 9 May 2006: 13). I assume that Britain, being a strong ally of the US, was also regarded by the Sudanese as the 'Other', and Ms Gibbons, being a Westerner, became a prime target because of the teddy bear incident. In other words, Ms Gibbons was a victim of circumstances.

Conclusion

In discussion of the 'Archbishop and the *Shariah* law' episode, I have explored the meaning of *shariah* law (the civil law and the criminal law or the *hudud*). I have examined the context that led Archbishop Dr Williams to comment on this issue, and how the British press reacted to it. Of all the newspapers, I found *The Times* and *The Sun* were most strident in their reporting and thereby conveyed criticism of the 'Muslim Other'. *The Sun*, being a tabloid newspaper, was more aggressive and declared that the archbishop was unfit for his job. The *Daily Express* (8 February 2008: 1) was also critical of Archbishop Dr Williams. In its report '137 beheadings in just one year' (8 February 2008: 5), informing readers about the 137 beheadings of people in Saudi Arabia in 2007, it associated a photo of a beheading in Saudi Arabia with Dr Williams' photo. Once again, it was a fearmongering tactic of the press. Finally, in its editorial ('Dismal Williams does not deserve to lead church'), the *Daily Express* (8 February 2008: 10) concluded, 'But it is certainly time the Church was rid of him'.

The *Guardian* was sympathetic to the archbishop's ordeal, as depicted in Steve Bell's cartoon, but the columnist Brown, in his opinion piece 'Sharia Law must not be Reduced to a Game' (*Guardian*, 8 February 2008: 39), confused *shariah* law on marriage and divorce with 'forced marriages, female circumcision, and other evils', which are cultural concerns and also practised by non-Muslims. I found the media study in this chapter relevant to the media issues raised by my interviewees. I believe the interviewees demonstrated that the media can be an influential factor in the formation of young Muslims' identity.

From the young Muslims' interviews (15–30 years), trends were revealed about how young people express themselves when they find their religious identity is in jeopardy. Admittedly some respondents were just not interested in the debate, and some did not know about it at all. It was interesting to find that both the wider British community and some Muslims have been apprehensive about the implications of *shariah* law (*hudud*) because it has been fiercely emphasised by some Muslim extremists, such as the Taliban. Certainly in some cases the Taliban have misused the law by banning Muslim women's education, and destroying the 2,000-year-old Buddhist statues. Finally I believe Archbishop Dr Williams, who has been involved in interfaith dialogue, is to be commended for voicing his opinions on behalf of the Muslim minority in Britain, who are mostly moderate Muslims. A Muslim observer, Sayeed (male, aged 40), noted:

> Archbishop Dr Rowan Williams is an academic theologian and perhaps the problem is, comes down to people who are academic theologians having to be aware that things that they say even in fairly sophisticated academic settings will be reported in ordinary newspapers. And how do you translate what gets said in an academic theological setting, something fairly complex into an article or a statement that ordinary people are going to read? And I think that in a sense that's the problem. It's not a problem about what he said, it's a problem about people in those positions having to be aware that whatever they say nowadays will get reported. (Interview, Leeds, 1 September 2008)

I assume that although the archbishop spoke to an enlightened audience in the series on Islam and English law at the foundation lecture at the Royal Courts of Justice on 7 February 2008, the word *shariah* triggered anxiety in some people (including news media reporters) as they were an uninformed audience. When this incident occurred in February 2008, I was in Australia, and I noted the indignant columnists and letter writers in the newspapers. I also wondered, 'Why is the archbishop stirring up things, and how could a non-Muslim of his position support the *hudud* (stoning to death, etc.)?' But as I interviewed Muslims in Britain I was surprised to find out they had a lot of respect for the archbishop, and as I continued questioning them, the concept of *shariah* (as intended by Dr Williams) became clearer. In the context of the *shariah* law episode, I believe, the identity of young British Muslims became more apparent.

CONCLUSION: A HUMANITARIAN WAY FORWARD

In my investigation of the identity of young British Muslims (aged 15–30), I found that most of the participants valued their British connections because they were either born in Britain or had lived there for a long time. They were also attached to their ethnic heritage, including languages other than English and their cultural celebrations. They spoke of their religious identity, which was reflected through their Muslim names, Islamic practices and celebrations, and sometimes through their dress. However, many respondents were distressed by the media practice of 'Othering' Muslims. Some felt they were the 'Other' as a result of the 7/7 London bombings, and/or because of their Islamic attire or appearance, which was not acceptable to some members of the wider society. Some Muslim women felt 'under attack' when British Foreign Minister Jack Straw pointed a finger at the *niqab*, and Muslim men felt alienated when they were 'stopped and searched'. The extreme right-wing British National Party had capitalised on the Muslim-related issue (for example, Prophet Muhammad's [PBUH] cartoon issue) with their anti-immigration propaganda, whereas other British politicians, such as the Mayor of London, Ken Livingstone, and religious leaders, for example the Archbishop of Canterbury, Dr Rowan Williams, have been sympathetic to mainstream Muslims and their issues. As Fazlul, a British-born male respondent of Bangladeshi background, aged 30 (British-Bangladeshi Muslim) remarked:

> I find it strange to see that on one hand the English BNP are trying to smash you up and get rid of you and send you back home, and the others are against your enemy! And they are also English. (Interview, London, 31 March 2008)

Though the BNP leader Nick Griffin is from Wales, Fazlul associated all BNP activists with Englishness. The Archbishop of Canterbury, Dr Williams, is also a Welshman but Fazlul considered that there were good and supportive people in the English/British society as well. Apart from racialist factors, some respondents of this study were finding it difficult to cope with their family restrictions and the broader Muslim community's expectations, for example, arranged marriage, disapproval of English music, Muslim women's denial of entry into mosques, and so on. In such cases, there was tension between the interviewees' ethnic identity and their British identity.

A person's identity appears to be always in a state of flux, and it changes shape according to their living environment, the opportunities they have for work and education, and their length of stay in the host society. Some immigrants living in a diaspora think that one day they will return to their homeland. They also expect their children will return to their imagined homeland, though these children may not necessarily know the history, people and culture of their parents' homeland.

I have reached the conclusion that the more the first-generation immigrants and the host society encourage the later generation to embrace a bicultural identity, the easier it will be for later generations to settle in a foreign land. By bicultural identity I mean that Muslims should retain some of their ethnic cultural practices and endorse some of the mainstream British culture, including English language skills and sport. Yet sometimes the later generations drift into a singular identity (single ethnic or religious) by choice when they see that they are being targeted by the wider society as the 'Other'.

In this chapter, first I discuss how the media affects social cohesion. Second, I discuss the areas that need attention within the Muslim community, such as integration, education, political participation, women, mosques and youth. Third, I examine some positive steps taken by the Muslim community, and finally, I advocate the endorsement of biculturalism.

Media

Some British media play a proactive role in 'Othering' the Muslims, for example, the tabloid newspaper, *The Sun*. But the question arises: How can Muslims counteract the stereotypes? A British-born Muslim woman of Pakistani heritage, Alizah (aged 27), noted the media stereotype of Muslims in the British press, but she emphasised the need for Muslim involvement in the media:

> For me the solution [to counter media bias] is that we encourage our children, not just to be doctors and lawyers, but also to be journalists. Encourage them to be broadcasters because when you're within something you can really create change, whereas if you're always on the outside it's difficult. So encourage our children to get into these areas, but it also takes corporations and institutions that to be honest with you can be highly racist, to open up their doors as well. That's the solution. We can't always be complaining, we can't be victims. (Interview, Bradford, 26 August 2008)

In other words, Alizah emphasises taking some responsibility for integration, including integrating into the media. In her interview, Alizah also mentioned Anila Baig, a Muslim columnist whose opinion pieces are published in the tabloid press, *The Sun*. Nevertheless, I have noticed that *The Sun* is the most sensational tabloid newspaper. For example, *The Sun* (8 February 2008) vehemently opposed Archbishop Dr Rowan Williams' views on *shariah* law. In the same issue, *The Sun* (page 9) published columnist Anila Baig's and Labour MP Khalid Mamood's comments on the *shariah* law debate, which enhanced *The Sun*'s agenda: defamed the archbishop's view and constructed a negative image of the Muslim 'Other'. However, some broadsheets such as *The Guardian* have been generous in giving space to Muslim columnists (Poole 2002), though in times of crisis even it considered the Muslims to be the 'Other' (Green and Kabir 2007). Douglas (2009: 50–60) observed that newspapers aim to promote national feeling to retain 'loyal readership', so in that context the rhetoric of 'We' and 'Us' emerges. Yet I agree with Alizah that the involvement of Muslims in the media is necessary. A simple effort can make a difference. For example, if Muslims persistently write letters to the editors of different newspapers their voices reach out to the wider community. This provides balance to generate debate and contributes to British democracy. Muslim voices (for example, Shaykh Ibrahim Mogra's views) are heard in the media, but more voices need to be disseminated thus, generating debate and citizen engagement towards cohesion.

Integration

I have advocated in my other publications that the Muslim community needs to integrate with the wider society. By integration, I mean on the one hand participating in the wider society, such as in sports, politics and engaging in community work. But as a respondent of this study, Aziz (British-born of Bangladeshi background, aged 28) in Tower Hamlets, East London pointed out:

> Yeah integration happens from both parties – both parties need to be willing to integrate. You can't force one party. If one party is willing to integrate and the other party is not then there will be no integration.
>
> And I think with the Bangladesh community, when we are a minority the white should integrate with us. Then there are the local authorities – they've divided areas as well. The Bangladeshi went to a certain area, the dark-skinned people, the African people who came here, they were put in a certain area so we were divided in the first. (Interview, London, 20 April 2008)

Of course, where there is a deliberate policy or practice which is intended to keep ethnic groups segregated, integration is difficult. But I believe that the

minorities should make an effort to integrate, starting with simple friendly gestures, for example, saying 'Hello' to one's neighbour. This might take the form
of casual conversation on the weather, or inviting people home for a cup of tea.
Sometimes, due to the media's negative publicity, the mainstream neighbour may
think that for cultural reasons, the minorities would be reluctant to integrate. So
the minorities may need to make the first move to erase that misconception fed by
the media. Of course, integration is more likely to happen if people place emphasis on their commonality rather than their differences, as a male respondent,
Jamal (British-born of Pakistani background, aged 17), in Bradford observed:

> I think the way to tackle this is don't put your differences forward, put your commo
> nality forward and from that you start friendships. And your religion is yours, so you
> don't have to enforce your religion on anybody else. Everybody's an individual and
> they believe what they believe, so I feel just to make friends with the white/non-white
> person, just be friends with what you've got in common, don't bring your differences
> which will probably create a sort of distance between you and them. (Interview,
> Bradford, 7 October 2008)

Voluntary work within the wider community – all working to help disadvantaged people – is a good way to be a part of the wider community. However,
the process of integration is hampered with the 'stop and search' practice.
Under the Anti-Terrorism Act 2000 (TACT, which came into force in 2001)
'stop and search' powers have been widely used: 10,200 in 2001/2, 32,100 in
2002/3, 33,800 in 2003/4, and 35,800 in 2004/5, but even more rigorously
used under the Criminal Justice and Public Order Act 1994: total numbers
under both Acts for England and Wales went from 29,100 in 2001/2 to
82,920 in 2002/3 (Birt 2006: 696). One government minister stated that
these powers would be excessively felt by the Muslim community' (Birt 2006:
696). A British-born respondent of Bangladeshi background, Muttaqui, aged
22, has integrated with the wider community as he does voluntary work
in a prison but because of his Islamic visibility (he has a beard and wears a
jilbab and *topi*) he has been stopped and searched a few times. Though the
police did not exert force, Muttaqui was upset because he was taken away
to be searched. However, Muttaqui's love for British football (he's a fan of
Manchester United) has helped him to retain his sanity. So Muttaqui's biculturalism (British-Bangladeshi Muslim) helped him to stay calm and cope with
occasional inhospitable behaviour.

Education

This study found that the first-generation Muslims who came to Britain in
the 1960s had few qualifications. The second and third generations have
sought education, but the 2001 Census showed that the Muslim population

in England and Wales was relatively poorly qualified. Nearly 40 per cent had no qualifications (Peach 2006: 641). Low education inevitably translates into a vicious cycle of non-participation in the formal labour market, low English-language skills and a high level of poverty. In 2001 in London, 70 per cent of Bangladeshi and Pakistani children were living in poverty (Mayor of London report 2006). A 16-year-old respondent of this study said that he lived with his family in a two-bedroom council house in London. His parents lived in one bedroom and his brother and his wife and children shared the other. The respondent slept on the floor of his parents' bedroom. It is very important that Muslims prioritise education, as this is the only way Muslims can obtain better employment and improve their standard of living. An emphasis should be given to women's education so that they can become self-sufficient and confident to look after themselves in times of crisis, such as domestic violence or marriage break-up.

Political participation

The Report of the Mayor of London (2006) pointed out that for proportional representation of Muslims in London, there would need to be 169 Muslim councillors and six Muslim MPs. But there were only 63 such councillors and one MP – Sadiq Khan, MP for Tooting (Mayor of London report 2006; also see Smit 2006). I believe this is still a very positive outcome and a great inspiration for young Muslims. However, in the UK voting is not compulsory, so some Muslims (and non-Muslims) do not exercise their voting rights, and unfortunately, some Muslims think that voting is *haram* (forbidden in Islam). In the light of the success of the right-wing British National Party at the European Parliament in June 2009, it is vital that Muslims become more politically conscious and exercise their voting rights. In 2008, on the topic of the possible rise of the BNP, the Secretary General of the Muslim Council of Britain (MCB), Dr Muhammad Abdul Bari remarked:

> That's why in the election we are asking Muslims and non-Muslims to come and vote for whoever they like so that the BNP becomes marginalised. (Interview, London, 23 April 2008)

In June 2009, British National Party Chairman, Nick Griffin, was elected a Member of the European Parliament in the northwest of England region and Andrew Brons won the BNP's first European seat in the nearby region of Yorkshire and the Humber. Mr Griffin spoke from the Manchester Town Hall, where he was awaiting the result of the Euro Elections: 'When you go to somewhere like Bradford, it is not immigration it is colonisation and it is out of control' (*Press Association National Newswire*, 8 June 2009, online). Mr Griffin told Sky News television:

This is a Christian country and Islam is not welcome, because Islam and Christianity, Islam and democracy, Islam and women's rights do not mix. That's a simple fact that the elites of Europe are going to have to get their heads round and deal with over the next few years. ('BNP wins its first seats, from Labour', *Australian*, 9 June 2009: 1)

Muslim MP for Dewsbury, Shahid Malik, said, 'It's a profoundly sad day for British politics and for our great democracy.' Former London Mayor, Ken Livingstone, now chair of campaign group Unite Against Fascism, said BNP members were '21st-century Nazis'. He added: 'Wherever the BNP win elections, racist attacks increase' (*Press Association National Newswire*, 8 June 2009, online).

The British National Party also gained three seats in the county council and unitary authority elections in February 2009 and the BNP held 55 councillor positions. Therefore, the BNP leader Nick Griffin, who was excluded from public platforms previously, began to receive frequent airtime on mainstream media channels and primetime programmes (James 2009: 7). The rise of the BNP, particularly at the European Parliament, means that Muslim leaders in Britain cannot ignore the threat it poses. There needs to be a systematic Muslim-led campaign against the BNP's anti-Muslim propaganda. Though some Muslim individuals and groups such as the Muslim Council of Britain (MCB) have issued condemnations after the BNP's victory at the European Parliament, it was not enough 'to combat the BNP's public onslaught' (James 2009: 8). There should be more awareness among the Muslim community in Britain, and more political participation in elections (exercise voting rights), so that other political parties can come to power that would confront the BNP's anti-Muslim campaigns. I repeat: it is crucial for Muslims in Britain to become politically conscious and exercise their voting rights.

Muslim women

Over 70 per cent of Muslim women in Britain aged 25 and over were economically inactive in 2001. Over 40 per cent of Muslim women in this demographic were classified as 'looking after home/family' (Peach 2006: 642), but what about the other 30 per cent? The absence of Muslim women from the formal labour force, and their preference to remain as home makers, can be attributed to both religious and cultural reasons. For the reason of *purdah* or *izzat* (women prefer to remain separate from men), some women prefer to stay at home. However, their performance as home makers should not be under-estimated as these women contribute to the upbringing of their children. If Muslim women do choose to pursue education, this should be encouraged.

A survey of 634 South Asian Muslim migrant women in the UK aged 16–60 (Dyke and James 2009) found 57 per cent of women wanted to have a paid job. About 39 per cent women did not want to find work, and 2 per cent believed that working was against their family honour (*izzat*). Generally speaking, most women thought that they could work at a paid job if they received enough support from their husband or family members. However, the lack of English-language skills was revealed to be the biggest skill-based barrier. The report (Dyke and James 2009) found that the Pakistani and the Bangladeshi Muslim women (largely economically inactive) were a huge resource for reducing socioeconomic disadvantage and poverty levels within their communities which suffered the lowest rate of unemployment in terms of both ethnicity and religion. Therefore, their desire to obtain a paid job should be taken into consideration both by the Muslim and wider communities.

Regarding the question whether Muslim women who wear the *niqab* should be permitted to work, I believe that the non-homemaking Muslim women who wear the *niqab* should work where they are permitted, for example, in Muslim institutions. However, if a Muslim woman is committed to wearing a *niqab* she must accept that this will limit her from working in areas where it becomes a barrier to communication. Just as much as a motorcycle helmet is an obstruction to communication, a *niqab* poses similar barriers. Commerce and religion are not good bedfellows and I think that employers should be permitted politely to indicate that women wearing *niqab* would not be good for their business. Surely those who wear the *niqab* would be happier in an Islamic environment?

In October 2009, it was reported that an 18-year-old Muslim female student, Shawana Bilqes, who wore a *niqab* was banned from attending the Burnley College in Britain (IslamOnline.net 2009). The principal of the college, John Smith, said:

> We do require all students of Burnley College to have their faces visible when at the college. We are determined to maintain the highest standards of teaching and learning in Burnley College. It is not possible to maintain this essential full communication if the face of any student is not fully visible. (Cited at IslamOnline.net 2009)

So *niqab* could also become a barrier to communication in mainstream educational institutions. However, Britain has generally allowed Muslim women to work while wearing the *hijab*. The Race Relations Act 1976 (as amended in 2000) is concerned with direct discrimination on the basis of 'ethnicity' or 'race'. For the purpose of that Act, Jews and Sikhs are considered ethnic groups, since each shares a common cultural tradition and history, and hence discrimination against these two groups is illegal. Religious discrimination in employment in Northern Ireland is illegal. There is also legislation that bans indirect discrimination on the basis of race, which could be used to defend Muslims who originate from predominantly Muslim societies (Hellyer 2007: 245). In 2003, the British government followed a European Commission directive which outlawed discrimination in employment (Modood 2007: 163). However, some female respondents of this study said that they faced prejudice because they wore the *hijab*. In such cases, *hijab* discrimination should be addressed.

Mosques

The Muslim community in Britain is diverse, and mosque rules and regulations differ from each other. Some mosques have very strong ethnic ties, where Muslims who are outsiders can be treated as the 'Other'; whereas other mosques have an exclusive *Ummah* feeling and treat the wider society as 'different'. A British-born male Muslim student, Shiraj, aged 18, who was involved with his family in mosque affairs in London, noted:

> It is like one Mosque is completely Bangladeshi, one Mosque is like African, one Mosque is Pakistani and no one would think of going in the other Mosque, because you would be worried about what was going to happen. (Interview, London, 18 April 2008)

Shiraj also noted that some mosques emphasise separateness:

> The Muslims, they don't try to interact and you know you go to a Mosque on an 'Open Day', and the imam will say, 'No non-Muslims [are allowed] in the Mosque, no foreigners in the Mosque'. (Interview, London, 18 April 2008)

Under the circumstances, I believe imams need to be enlightened and educated to promote integration. Towards this end, a Muslim working group concerned with imams and the mosques, chaired by the House of Lords peer Lord Ahmed of Rotherham, announced several proposals in October 2005. The main recommendation, which has received financial support from the Home Office in its developmental phase, was the setting up of the Mosques and Imams National Advisory Body (MINAB 2009). It is proposed that MINAB be an independent non-sectarian body designed to act as a national voice for imams, to facilitate the accreditation process of imams, to provide training and guidance for and promote best practice among imams and mosque committees, and to take up an intra-sectarian arbitration role. It also proposed that MINAB 'assist mosques and imams in playing their role in community cohesion and combating extremism'. The working group also recognised the need to develop *madrasah* curricula and to provide professional development for imams and mosque officials outside of the seminaries (Birt 2006: 701). However, some of the Muslims I interviewed were sceptical about whether MINAB would work as an independent body. As the Muslim Council of Britain leader, Dr Bari, noted:

So we are a part of this consultation, we are asking community to share their opinions on these so it remains an independent advisory board free from government dictation. But occasionally we see that there is an over enthusiasm by the government to try to dictate it or set agenda for it, but we are saying that if it is seen as a government sponsored body, it will lose all this creditability to the Muslim community. (Interview, London 23 April 2008)

As mentioned in Chapter 3, some mosques do not accommodate Muslim women on their premises for prayers. The Muslim leader, Shaykh Mogra, hoped that more and more mosques would open up through MINAB. Shaykh Mogra said, 'I've talked on this subject of women and youth participation in every seminar we've held. And we've tried to explain to them that they must open up and allow women to attend [the mosque] if they wish to' (Interview, Leicester, 14 April 2008).

On 10 May 2009, the MINAB general council met in Birmingham and elected an executive board consisting of members from both the Sunni and Shi'ite groups. If MINAB succeeds in overcoming the differences between the Muslim groups, it would enhance social cohesion generally and be 'a way forward'.

Muslim Youth

Some young Muslims feel alienated in both the Muslim and the wider British communities (Murtaza 2006; Lewis 2007; Rehman 2007). There can be much pressure on home duties, cultural restrictions and marginalisation from the wider community. The MCB leader Dr Bari noted that there is a generation gap within the Muslim community between the first and the later generations which contributes to the lack of communication, social deprivation, and educational and economic under-achievement among young Muslims. Dr Bari said, 'Because young people have their own risk taking adventure as well doing things, by putting them in a corner does not help'. Dr Bari further commented:

I think the best [method] should be if the establishment, politicians, media, and the people in authority just give some space to Muslim young people to flourish and don't simply bash them because they are Muslims. If you want a real social cohesion based on harmony and understanding then we should address the issues of criminality, and terrorism in a very selective way as to how it generates rather than putting the whole community in the dock. (Interview, London, 23 April 2008)

Dr Bari admitted that there are issues such as criminality and terrorism, but these issues need to be jointly addressed by the society as a whole rather than singling out young people who are suffering from social deprivation or an identity crisis. In my research, I found some young people were distressed by certain websites, which they thought were attacking their religion. As one male respondent, Faris, aged 18, said:

> There's a website, www.bombislam.com, and I think it's skinheads from America, they made the site, and it's terrible. (Interview, Leicester, 10 April 2008)

Another respondent, Khatib, aged 18, believed in conspiracy theories:

> All these terms, like Islamophobia, they were all created after 9/11 and 7/7. They weren't there before so it's all a conspiracy really. Places like America, they've got so many things to hide that they've always been trying to cover up things by doing stuff like this, it's so controlled.
>
> And the 7/7 bombings, have you seen on the internet, there's videos, I've seen on Youtube, there's different conspiracies of what happened, so if you click on the video, it explains a lot to you. (Interview, Leicester, 10 April 2008)

The belief in conspiracy theories is not new among these youths. Some Muslim adults also believe in theories such as that Al-Qaeda does not exist or that the 9/11 Twin Towers tragedy was a Jewish plot. I assume that if such preconceived notions remain in the hearts and minds of young Muslims, then it will hamper the process of their social cohesion. There should be more dialogue within the Muslim community about the real threat posed by Muslim extremists.

Some positive steps: East London

After the 7/7 London bombings some Muslim leaders, mosques and youth centres have taken positive steps to address the issues of radicalisation. Some mosques, such as the East London Mosque and the Leeds Grand Mosque, have taken initiatives towards social cohesion. In 2008, I met a couple of spokespersons from the East London Mosque and asked them about Ed Husain's (author of *The Islamist*) views on radicalisation of Muslim youths in the East London Mosque. One spokesperson denied the allegation and said:

> This guy [Ed Husain] I think he's got a hidden agenda, probably serving some people for the benefit, not for the benefit of the Muslim community but probably for somebody else. (Interview, London, 24 April 2008)

As discussed earlier, there are different groups within the Muslim community. The Deobandis tend to think they are better Muslims than the Sufis and vice versa; Husain later embraced Sufism (Husain 2007: 187–96). So there could be a 'hidden agenda' behind Ed Husain's book, *The Islamist*. Nevertheless, the factors that could lead to the radicalisation of Muslim youths, such as patriarchal families, cultural restrictions, flawed British foreign policy and encounters with extreme Muslim views, are very real. Though Husain (2007) did not suggest there was any connection between the 7/7 London bombers (three of whom originated from Leeds) and the East London Mosque, the 7/7 London bombings made him consider how a Muslim could be transformed into a bomber. I also agree with the spokesperson of the East London Mosque when he said:

> There is no evidence to suggest that any of the Islamic groups in this country had any role to play in the 7/7 bombings.
>
> Yeah they went outside the country and it was a global situation okay because of the American foreign policy, and British foreign policy. People are very angry about it and they don't know how to express themselves properly, so some people took the wrong way. Those that are ignorant, you know, they take the wrong way. (Interview, London, 24 April 2008)

After the 7/7 London bombings, some mosques in Britain opened up to the wider society in order to achieve better understanding. I attended the 'Mosque Open Day' (30 March 2008) at the East London Mosque and I was pleased to see it was open to everyone, including non-Muslims. There were many posters in the mosques that explained Islam. There were also free booklets on Islam. The Muslim volunteers spoke to interested people, and answered their questions. There were also tours of the mosque, and of course some complimentary snacks were served. The London Muslim Centre is affiliated with the East London Mosque and runs several projects with the government. A spokesperson said:

> We've got dozens of projects with the government; we are working with the mainstream you see. We are probably the only mosque who employs non-Muslims. We also have female employees, right? (Interview, London, 24 April 2008)

The London Muslim Centre also runs a school:

> We have a number of projects in this Muslim centre. One of the biggest ones is the school. The school [London East Academy] is not an independent school, it is a project of the mosque. (Interview, London, 24 April 2008)

The East London Mosque appears to be involved with the mainstream society, and works to remove misconceptions about Islam through its media officer. As the spokesperson said, the media officer's work involves:

> . . . drafting press releases, answering media queries, communicating with the public, communicating with internal staff as well, generally making sure that the mosque is

communicating the right message to the public and internally. (Interview, London, 24 April 2008)

The East London mosque is open to people of diverse backgrounds. It holds regular talks on Islam in English, Bangla and Somali and attracts both men and women. In 2007–8, the East London Academy expanded to include secondary classes from years 7 to 11. The students who took their Standard Assessment Tests (SATs) in 2007 scored well above the local and national average. Throughout the year the mosque receives organised visits. In 2007–8 it received 63 organised visits, with about 2,000 visitors in total (Annual Report, 2007–8). On 3 July 2008, Lord Chief Justice Lord Phillips gave a speech, 'Equality before law', at the London Muslim Centre.

Some positive steps: Leeds

Similar proactive initiatives were taken by organisations in other cities. For example, on 10 October 2008, I visited the 'Open Day' at the Hamara Healthy Living Centre at Tempest Road in Beeston, Leeds. After the 7/7 London bombings, Beeston attracted immense media attention as the three 7/7 bombers: Mohammed Siddique Khan, Shehzad Tanweer and Hasib Hussain, originated from Beeston. It was alleged that the three bombers used the other premises of the Hamara centre on Lodge Lane in Beeston where Siddique Khan engaged in youth work. However, Hanif Malik, chairman of the Hamara centre, said none of the three bombers was regular staff at the centre but had used it for sports facilities (*Guardian*, 15 July 2005: 3). Nevertheless, at the Hamara Healthy Living Centre Open Day (10 October 2008), I was pleased to see the presence of members of the wider community. It was a community cohesion day where a representative from the police force, people from the fire safety division, academics and local people gathered. The centre's wide range of food for the visitors was impressive.

The July 7th bombings created considerable challenges for Muslim communities in Beeston, Leeds. In 2006, the Hamara Healthy Living Centre, together with Muslim youths, Leeds Grand Mosque, Makkah Mosque and Resourcing the Community (community service) facilitated workshops in five areas in Leeds. Over 150 people attended the workshops which engaged Muslim youths and explored their views on identity, discrimination and community relations. Many youths spoke of the Islamophobia they faced after the 7/7 London bombings, while some were critical of the cultural restrictions imposed upon them by their elders (Murtuja 2006). The centre has also established initiatives to improve the well-being of its members. It is aiming to reduce inequalities in accessing health and social care, increase people's awareness of issues affecting their lives, and provide services in a culturally and religiously sensitive manner. Furthermore, it offers necessary help for individuals and their families to access support services. A survey (South et al. 2007: 54) found a high level of satisfaction with Hamara's services among users, and Hamara's initiative for community cohesion impressive. Though the events of the 7/7 London bombings were raised by the interviewees in the survey, Hamara was seen by the researchers (South et al. 2007) to have handled the situation well.

Some positive steps: Leicester and Cardiff

I collected some interviews from the people operating the youth centres in Leicester and Cardiff. The centres were also proactive in engaging young people in different activities and sports. One of the youth workers in Leicester, Zaki, aged 30, described their work:

> It's a bit of everything; it's a bit of word of mouth, we put posters up in the local shops, we work with the mentors in the schools, the community teachers in the schools.
>
> We say if you need anything come and see us. We provide activities both educational and physical, like we do football tournaments, we'll do hockey or cricket tournaments, we'll take them a day to go-karting . . . They don't want to grow up in twos and threes, they want to grow up as a group, so we try to treat them as a group and train and educate them as a group. Now individually they all come, like today someone's texted me they want me to help them fill out an application for a job. (Interview, Leicester, 12 April 2008)

A topic that frequently came up in discussion with youth workers in Britain was the lack of funding. The issue was also raised by Zaki:

> My hope is that we get a lot more funding, yeah, for ourselves and my dream is that funding continues because we need it. It's not just for disadvantaged kids, it's for normal kids. I mean I loved coming here when I was young . . . We do more than we should in fact and most of us work here for pennies to be fair. So that's our situation. (Interview, Leicester, 12 April 2008)

As indicated by his response, Zaki was very passionate about his work with young people. Regarding his dream to have more funding, I hoped this would come true, as I found their current youth centre was a very old building which looked very depressing. Initially, I was too scared to enter the youth centre as it looked like an abandoned building without a proper entrance! In Cardiff, the youth centres that I visited were attended by young people of diverse backgrounds and they were regarded by some interviewees as particularly helpful for young Muslims with a Somali background.

Some positive steps: Bradford

The youth centre in Bradford was also actively involved with young Muslims, particularly those of a Bangladeshi background. The youth worker, Tababul, aged 23, said:

> I work with a lot of young people, a lot of delinquent young people as well. This organisation itself has helped me through you know my younger days when I have been, ah what you call on the wrong track sort of thing.
>
> And it's just working with the community itself. You know being one of the young people, seeing the issues in the surrounding area; I just want to help. (Interview, Bradford, 27 August 2008)

Tababul commented that the youth centre was under-financed:

> Well, the money's not good. I don't want to continue here. Well I still want to be involved. I always give a lot of voluntary time.
>
> Yeah I do because I do a lot of courses with them [young people] and as a reward sort of thing we take them out abroad, so we've been to quite a few places . . . we have just returned from Jordan. (Interview, Bradford, 27 August 2008)

The youth centres I visited in Leicester, Bradford, Leeds and Cardiff appeared to be secular, and aimed to help young Muslims (or non-Muslims) have a healthy and successful life through the gymnasium and sports, which I thought were very important bicultural skills. They also had outdoor camps and excursions which helped young people to be responsible British citizens (and good Muslims). There were also some projects run through the mosques for young Muslims, which were also citizenship projects, for example, the school run by the London Muslim Centre (of the East London Mosque). Similarly, in Bradford, in May 2007 the Bradford Council for Mosques launched a course on practical citizenship. Through the course, young Muslims were taught to be critical of Islamic extremists such as Osama bin Laden and that his extremism was a betrayal of Islamic norms. The complex nationalism of Israel and Palestine was explained, and that the *madrasah* was meant to be a place of traditional Islamic teaching and not terrorism. Other areas of knowledge delivered to the students included English-language teaching, child protection policy and knowledge of relevant aspects of British society. The latter included appropriate general legal issues, the British political system, the culture of tolerance and free speech, how to promote a healthy and safe environment for education, and how to encourage a sense of belonging within the boundaries of Islamic teachings (Lewis 2007: 82–6).

Emphasis on biculturalism

Throughout this book, I have mentioned the importance of biculturalism because it has the potential to reduce social distance between groups. It is important that young Muslims manage the two cultures successfully. In biculturalism, a person would retain her/his parents' home culture and language and add it to the culture and language of the host society. Jim Cummins (1994) contends that minority cultures (language) should be perceived as 'additive' and not 'subtractive' to majority culture. In the context of the United States, Cummins (1994: 33) observed that in the classroom when English as Second Language (ESL) teachers are constantly changed, and the new teachers are not informed of the students' ethnic backgrounds (as to how much attention they needed in their English language), this hinders minority students' progress in education. Cummins (1994: 40) also reminded school authorities that students should be actively encouraged to preserve their ethnic language and culture because that added to their identity, power and self-esteem. Moreover, research on bilingualism has shown emphatically that proficiency in the first language is conducive to proficiency in the second.

In the British context, I argue that state schools should continue to provide support for minority language and cultures. For example, I found some schools provided subjects such as Urdu or Bengali for the Pakistani and Bangladeshi background students in Britain. The state schools also respected the minority's (Muslim) culture; for example, Muslim girls were allowed to wear *hijabs*. However, there are other aspects that need attention, for instance, Muslim girls' preference for single-sex swimming classes. In this way, young Muslims would feel more inclined to adopt the host society's culture, for example, to improve their English-language skills and be a part of the wider society.

In the American context, Amando Padilla (2006: 470) notes that some marginal people, for example the Latino-Americans, feel isolated and closed off from members of either their culture of origin or the culture of the host group or isolated from both groups. This results in a sense of inferiority and low self-esteem. On the other hand, biculturalists see a more positive image of the bicultural person, as Padilla (2006: 470–1) observes:

> The bicultural person is well adjusted, open to others, and a cultural broker between peoples of different backgrounds. The completely bicultural person is an individual who possesses two social persona and identities. The person is equally at ease with members of either culture and can easily switch from one cultural orientation to the other and does so with native-like facility. Furthermore, this comfort with two cultures extends to interactions with individuals from cultures other than those the bicultural person has competence in.

Research in the US (Padilla 2006: 472–3) has shown that immigration prior to about age 12 resulted in less acculturative stress than for a group of university students who had migrated to the United States. The ease with which young immigrants were able to adjust to a new culture depended on the support and assistance they received from their host institutions. On the other hand, children born in the US adhered to the traditional practices, values and languages, as diasporic parents imagined that one day their children would return to their country of origin. However, depending on the facilities provided to these children by the host institutions and rate of adaptation, these US-born second-generation children felt American in the wider society (Padilla 2006: 474–5).

In the context of Britain, I argue that bicultural social flexibility among young British Muslims could only be attained if the person has an equal footing in both cultures, for example, Bangladeshi-British culture, which entails having good language skills in both cultures. To be successful in Britain, a person has to have a high level of English-language skill. As revealed in Chapter 1, Tajfel (1986, cited in Jacobson 1998: 10) asserts that there are three components of group membership: first, the cognitive (knowledge that one belongs to a group); second, the evaluative (assumptions about the positive and negative value connotations of group membership); and third, the emotional (emotions towards one group and towards others who stand in particular relation to it). I would add that it is equally important for an individual to be a member of his/her ethnic group as of the wider society group. By virtue of good communication skills an individual will be recognised as a member of each group; extra facilities may be needed to improve migrants' English-language skills so that they can take their place as members of the wider British society. Their cultural and religious values should be respected by the host institutions, and young Muslims should feel obliged to appreciate the values of the host society. It is important that the host community should continue to provide heritage cultural programmes to the later-generation immigrants so that this cultural knowledge is sustained for the benefit of the whole society.

Another important factor of biculturalism that could help young Muslims to be members of the ethnic or host society is their love for music. One-quarter of the respondents in this study said that they don't listen to music by choice because 'music is *haram*', and a few others said that they were not allowed to listen to music. An example of the latter is the 16-year-old male student of Somali background, Hamid, who said, 'I don't listen to music. I have strict parents, yeah, very religious' (Interview, London, 25 March 2008). Farhana, a 15-year-old female student of Bangladeshi background, said:

> Watching TV, it's a waste of time. It has music in the background, it's [music] not allowed in Islam. And sometimes it is *zina* [a major sin] . . . we could do *zina* with our eyes, with our hands, with our ears listening to things we shouldn't, stuff like

that. And *zina* with eyes is looking at stuff you shouldn't look at, so like when you look at opposite sexes, that's a sin and plus sometimes you can get attracted and so I don't watch it. (Interview, London, 15 April 2008)

However, almost three-quarters of Muslim youths in this study (15–18 years) expressed a love of music. Most of them said they listened to Rhythm and Blues, hip-hop and pop music. The 18-year-old British-born male student of Somali background, Haroon, said, 'If I'm bored I like songs. They keep you calm' (Interview, Leeds, 13 October 2008). A 16-year-old British-born girl of Pakistani background, Saima, said, 'Yeah I like hard rock, heavy metal' (Interview, Leeds, 15 October 2008). Faris, a British-born male youth of Indian-Gujrati background, aged 18, said:

I like niche. It is a new kind of music. It's like underground version of British music, it's more of a garage-type music, it's like dance music. It's got bass. Niche gets to you and it makes you want to move and stuff like that. It doesn't make you want to sit in place. It's quite fast music, kind of calm kind of music. (Interview, Leicester, 10 April 2008)

Hamid, a 16-year-old male student of Sudanese background, said:

I only listen to one rapper and he's like my favourite artist. He is the Chicago rapper called Lupe Fiasco. I mean he never swears in any of his songs, he doesn't sit there rapping about women and sort of degrading women . . . he is Muslim. (Interview, London, 8 April 2008)

Some students spoke of other music, for example, Umair, a British-born male student of Moroccan background, aged 16, said, 'I listen to J-Rock, which is Japanese Rock. I listen to metal, speed metal, black metal, viking metal . . . I listen to a bit of classical and I totally hate pop which is the stuff you hear blaring out of people's cars everyday!' A few students of Pakistani and Bangladeshi background spoke of their liking for Indian *Bhangra* music.

The psychologist Robinson (1985: 47) suggests that adolescence is a critical juncture in high-school students' cultural identity. Too many restrictions from an immigrant student's family could be detrimental to an adolescent's development. Therefore, it is suggested that junior high school may be a particularly relevant time for cultural instruction aimed at developing positive attitudes towards and identification with other people (Robinson 1985: 47). According to Robinson (1985: 29), songs and music have always been important in the transmission and acquisition of cultural learning, and in the promotion of cultural affiliation. The use of sound, rhythm and self-expression is not a supplementary activity but rather an integral part of promoting positive affiliation among members of a culture (Robinson 1985). Many students in this study said that they listened to Rhythm and Blues, hip-hop and pop. In some cases there was particular mention of Tupac Amaru Shakur. Most of Shakur's songs are about the hardships of growing up around violence in US ghettos, poverty and racism, and sometimes his feuds with fellow rappers. Messages of political, economic and racial equality pervade his work. Adherence to cultural celebrations and musical entertainment may also contribute to a healthy mental state for Muslim youths (Kabir and Rickards 2006).

Dr John Diamond spent over 25 years working with the emotions and meridians, refining the role the unconscious plays in disease – both mental and physical. Although there are many different modalities that can be used to actuate Life Energy (or traditional healing practices), including herbs, nutrition, minerals, homoeopathy, massage, chiropractic, osteopathy and others, Dr Diamond has found that one of the most effective means of raising Life Energy is through the practice of the high creative arts, particularly music. Dr Diamond (2001–2) explains: 'For years, I have used many forms of music, including jazz, classical and folk, to help identify each person's individual and highly personal harmony.' He believes that music, performed in the right way, is highly therapeutic and that each person has his or her own individual 'song of the soul'. He found the role of music to be a life-affirming therapeutic activity.

I contend that music is not only therapeutic but it also helps youth acquire a subcultural identity. For example, the language in hip-hop provides a message against the dominant culture. It addresses racism, stereotypes and economic disadvantage. So the distressed youths find some commonalities with those lyrics because they have addressed their grievances. The songwriter Connor (2003: 51) observes that the language of the music generates an individual's subjectivity, organises his or her worldview, perception or identity and locality, and guides them through 'blatant and subtle manipulation of goals and ways of thinking', and it signifies confidence and power. The British singer and songwriter Yusuf Islam, formerly known as Cat Stevens, converted to Islam in 1977 and left his music career, though he was advised by his imam that he could continue as a musician as long as it was morally acceptable. In 2006, Yusuf Islam returned to pop music when his son 'brought him a guitar'! He released his new secular album, 'An Other Cup', after 30 years (*New York Times*, 7 January 2007: 15). Yusuf has reconciled his personal life with his creative history (music), and he had the ability to move between the two cultures. Yusuf comments, 'It's a tough time to be a Muslim with a Western fan base. But . . . music can help harmonize different outlooks.' He adds, 'I think the recent events of the world – the polarization of creative chaos, if you like – has helped create an upsurge in people wanting to mend this world and call humanity back to its senses.' He concludes:

> I think Muslims should work a little bit harder at making people a bit more at ease and to create an atmosphere of happiness which is what we need. I think that's what

this record [new CD *Roadsinger*] does, that's what my music used to do and it still does. (*Deseret Morning News* 2009: 8)

I also believe that music and sports can reconcile people of any background. People can find a common inspiration through them. However, I note that if some young Muslims do not wish to listen to music or play sports, they should be encouraged to pursue other creative activities such as art and reading. For group membership with the host society, such activities are important.

Conclusion

After the 7/7 London bombings, the British government intervened in the Muslim community's affairs to 'tackle extremism'. In the summer of 2005, the government convened a process of consultation with seven working groups to look into engaging with young people: education, Muslim women, community capacity-building, imams and mosques, community security, and radicalisation. The British government has provided a multi-faith capacity-building fund, the Faith Communities Capacity Building Fund, to push along a process of self-regulation in British society. Its 2005/6 budget of £7.5 million approved 578 out of 2016 applications (94 or 16% of the successful bids went to Muslim organisations), and its 2006/7 budget has been allocated £5 million (Birt 2006: 700). Of course, it is a good sign that the Muslim community and the British government are collectively working to address some of the social issues existing in the Muslim community. However, more effort is needed at the grass-roots level. The establishment of MINAB is another good sign of social cohesion within the Muslim community. The Mosque's 'Open Day' invitation to non-Muslims is also a good indication of community cohesion. But encouraging the optimism of young people still remains a challenge in British society.

This study finds that young Muslims speak English, support liberal democratic values and feel loyalty to Britain. There is evidence in this study that young Muslims who have integrated into the wider community through sports, working at mainstream stores, and taking part in inter-faith discussions are able to articulate and identify with a broader set of British values and behaviours. Through their schooling and community life, all young Muslims should be respectfully encouraged to engage with other British people in similar activities so that they too will come to appreciate better 'Britishness'. In the current climate of global extremism and the rise of the extreme right-wing British National Party, it is even more crucial that young Muslims are encouraged to become bicultural. This means that their parents' cultural ways should not be regarded as deficits but as valuable assets to be complemented by the absorption and appreciation of the new language and culture (art, architecture, national heroes, literature and sports) of their country of birth or host country

– Britain. It is equally important that Muslims focus on higher education, value the optimism of both the Muslim community and the wider society, exercise their citizenship rights (voting rights) and engage in dialogue both with their fellow Muslims and non-Muslims and address the misconceptions prevailing both in the Muslim and non-Muslim communities. Judging from what I have witnessed through first-hand contact with them, this sample of young British Muslims has the potential to be a tremendous asset to their home nation – Britain. It is imperative that they are encouraged to, and are able to, participate in the social cohesion-building activities outlined above.

BIBLIOGRAPHY

Abbas, T. (ed.) (2005), *Muslim Britain: Communities Under Pressure*, London: Zed Books.

ABC *Four Corners* (2009), 'Pakistan on the Brink' transcript, ABC *Four Corners*, 23 February 2009, http://www.abc.net.au/4corners/content/2008/s2499266.htm accessed 26 April 2009.

Abdel-Fattah, R. (2005), *Does my Head Look Big in This?*, Sydney: Pan Macmillan Australia.

Adams, M. and P. J. Burke (2006), 'Recollections of September 11 in three English Villages: Identifications and Self Narrations', *Journal of Ethnic and Migration Studies*, 32 (6), August: 983–1003.

Ahmed, R. (2001), *Taliban: The Story of the Afghan Warlords*, London: Pan Books.

Ahmed, T. S. (2005), 'Reading Between the Lines: Muslims and the Media', in A. Tahir (ed.), *Muslim Britain: Communities under Pressure*, London: Zed Books, pp. 109–25.

Ahsan, M. (2003), 'Introduction', in M. Seddon, D. Hussain and N. Malik (eds), *British Muslims: Loyalty and Belonging*, Leicester: The Islamic Foundation and the Citizen Organising Foundation, pp. vii–ix.

Aitchison, J. W. and H. Carter (2000), *Language, Economy and Society*, Cardiff: University of Wales Press.

Alam, M. Y. (2006), *Made in Bradford*, Pontefract: Route Publishing.

Al-Qazwini, S. M. (2000), *Inquiries about Shi'a Islam.* Costa Mesa, CA: The Islamic Educational Center of Orange County.

Ali, A. Y. (n.d.), *The Holy Quran: Translation and Commentary*, (publisher not known): The Solly Noor Group of Companies for distribution by the Islamic propagation centre international.

Ali, M. (2003), *Brick Lane*, London: Black Swan.

Ali-Karamali, S. (2008), *The Muslim Next Door: The Quran, The Media and That Veil Thing*, Ashland, OR: White Cloud Press.

Anderson, B. (1991), *Imagined Communities*, London: Verso.

Annual Report (2007/2008), East London Mosque & London Muslim Centre, 18 pages.

Ansari, H. K. (2002), 'The Woking Mosque: A Case Study of Muslim Engagement with British Society since 1889', *Immigrants and Minorities* 21(3) November: 1–24.

Ansari, H. K. (2004), *The Infidel Within: The History of Muslims in Britain, 1800 to the Present*, London: C. Hurst & Co.

Archbishop's Lecture (2008), 'Civil and Religious Law in England: a Religious Perspective', 7 February, http://www.archbishopofcanterbury.org/1575 accessed 27 February 2009.

Barker, M. (1982), *The New Racism: Conservatives and the Ideology of the Tribe*, Frederick, MD: Aletheia Books/University Publications of America.

Batrouney, T. and J. Goldlust (2005), *Unravelling Identity: Immigrants, Identity and Citizenship in Australia*, Melbourne: Common Ground.

Baxter, K. (2007), *British Muslims and the Call to Global Jihad*, Clayton: Monash University Press.

BBC (2002), 'Islam in the UK (1500s–present)', *BBC Religion & Ethics*, http://www.bbc.co.uk/religion/religions/islam/history/uk_print.html accessed 15 May 2009.

BBC (2006a), 'Brown Speech Promotes Britishness', *BBC News*, 14 January, http://news.bbc.co.uk/2/hi/uk_news/politics/4611682.stm accessed 31 January 2009.

BBC (2006b), 'Church Recalls "Prophet" Magazine', *BBC News*, 21 March, http://news.bbc.co.uk/1/hi/wales/4827294.stm accessed 27 May 2009.

BBC (2006c), 'Warning over UK Race Riot Danger', *BBC News*, 22 October, http://news.bbc.co.uk/1/hi/uk_politics/6074286.stm"http://news.bbc.co.uk/1/hi/uk_politics/6074286.stm accessed 1 February 2009.

BBC (2007), What Can't be Named Muhammad?, *BBC News*, 29 November, http://news.bbc.co.uk/1/hi/magazine/7115821.stm accessed 6 March 2009.

BBC (2008), 'In full: Rowan Williams interview', *BBC News*, 11 February, http://news.bbc.co.uk/2/hi/uk_news/7239283.stm accessed 9 February 2009.

Birt, J. (2006), 'Good Imam, Bad Imam: Civic Religion and National Integration in Britain Post-9/11', *Muslim World*, 96(4) October: 687–705.

Blair, T. (2006), 'The Duty to Integrate Shared British Values', 8 December, http://www.number10.gov.uk/Page10563 accessed 1 February 2007.

Bowlby, S. and S. Lloyd-Evans (2009), 'You seem very Westernized to me: Place, Identity and Othering of Muslim Workers in the UK Labour Market', in Hopkins, P. and R. Gale (eds), *Muslims in Britain: Race, Place and Identities*, Edinburgh: Edinburgh University Press, pp. 37–54.

Brah, A. (2007), 'Non-binarized Identities of Similarity and Difference', in Wetherell, M., M. Lafleche and R. Berkerley (eds), *Identity, Ethnic Diversity and Community Cohesion*, London: Sage Publications, pp. 136–45.

Brown, D. (2005), 'Profile: Role Economic Distress Plays in Terrorism', *Minnesota Public Radio: Marketplace*, 22 July, http://global.factiva.com.ezproxy.library.ecu.au/ha/default.aspx accessed 10 December 2008.

Bulmer, M. and J. Solomos (eds) (1999), *Racism*, New York: Oxford University Press.

Burlet, S. and H. Reid (1996), 'Riots, Representation and Responsibilities: The Role of Young Men in Pakistani-heritage Muslim Communities', in W. A. R. Shahid, and P. S. van Koningsveld, (eds), *Political Participation and Identities of Muslims in non-Muslim States*, Kampen, Netherlands: Kok Pharos Publishing House, pp. 144–57.

Cesari, J. (2004), *When Islam and Democracy Meet: Muslims in Europe and in the United States*, New York: Palgrave Macmillan.

Channel 4 (2006), 'What Muslims Want – Muslim Opinion Tx', *Dispatches: Society*, Channel 4 *Dispatches* Blog Site, 7 August, 20:00hrs, http://community.channel4. com/eve/forums/a/tpc/f/7070069631/m/3910027375 accessed 30 January 2009.

Channel 4 (2007), 'Make Me a Muslim', Faiths and Beliefs, 16–18 December, http:// www.channel4.com/culture/microsites/C/can_you_believe_it/debates/makeme. html accessed 17 March 2009.

Channel Nine (2006), 'Islam in Australia', *Sunday Morning Forum*, 12 and 18 November 2006.

Charmaz, K. (2006), *Constructing Grounded Theory: A Practical Guide through Qualitative Analysis*, London: Sage Publications.

Charsley, K. (2009), 'Risk and Ritual: The Protection of British Pakistani Women in Transnational Marriage', in V. S. Karla (ed.), *Pakistani Diasporas: Culture, Conflict and Change*, Karachi: Oxford University Press, pp. 129–49.

Chaudhry, A. A. (1996), *The Promised Messiah and Mahdi*, Islamabad and Tilford: Islam International Publications Ltd.

Cheng, Y. and A. Heath (1993), 'Ethnic Origins and Class Destination', *Oxford Review of Education*, 19(2): 151–65.

Choudhury, T. (2005), *Muslims in the UK: Policies for Engaged Citizens The Eumap Project*, Budapest: Central European University Press.

City of Bradford Metropolitan District Council (2001), 'The Ethnic Mix of the Bradford MDC Population as per Census 2001 Overview', http://www.bradford. gov.uk/employment_jobs_and_careers/equal_opportunities_and_diversity/social_ services_workforce_equalities/the_ethnic_mix_of_the_bradford_mdc_population_ as_per_census_2001 accessed 28 May 2009.

Cohen, A. P. (1982), 'Belonging: The Experience of Culture', in A. P. Cohen (ed.), *Belonging: Identity and Social Organisation in British Rural Culture*, Manchester: Manchester University Press, pp. 1–17.

Commission for Racial Equality (CRE) (1996), *We Regret to Inform You . . .*, London: Commission for Racial Equality.

Connor, B. (2003), 'Good Buddha', *Youth Studies*, 22(2): 48–54.

Cressey, G. (2006), *Diaspora Youth and Ancestral Homeland: British Pakistani/ Kashmiri Youth Visiting Kin in Pakistan and Kashmir*, Leiden and Boston: Brill.

Crown Prosecution Service (2007), 'Bradford Rioter Gets Custodial Sentence, *CPS*, 9 February', http://www.cps.gov.uk/west_yorkshire/news_events/press_releases/ bradford_rioter_gets_custodial_sentence/ accessed 17 June 2009.

Cummins, J. (1994), 'Knowledge, Power and Identity in Teaching English as a Second Language', in F. Genesee (ed.), *Educating Second Language Children: The Whole*

Child, the Whole Curriculum, the Whole Community, Cambridge: Cambridge University Press, pp. 33–58.

Daily Telegraph, (2006) 'Investigation Timeline', 8 July, http://www.telegraph.co.uk/news/1400029/Investigation-timeline.html accessed 26 April 2009.

Day, G. (2003), *Making Sense of Wales: A Sociological Perspective*, Cardiff: University of Wales.

Dench, G., K. Gavron and M. Young (2006), *The New East End: Kinship, Race and Conflict*, London: Profile Books.

Devereux, E. (2003), *Understanding the Media*, London: Sage Publications.

Diamond, Dr J. (1983), *The Life Energy in Music*, 1, New York: Zeppelin.

Diamond, Dr J. (1983), *Life Energy in Music*, 2, New York: Enhancement Books.

Diamond. Dr J. (2002), 'The Third Side of the Triangle', *The International Journal of Applied Kinesiology and Kinesiologic Medicine*, 12, Winter, http://www.drjohn-diamond.com/content.php?id=114 accessed 4 May 2009.

Douglas, F. M. (2009), *Scottish Newspaper, Language and Identity*, Edinburgh: Edinburgh University Press.

Dwyer, C. and B. Shah (2009), 'Rethinking the Identities of Young British Pakistani Muslim Women: Educational Experiences and Aspirations', in Hopkins, P. and G. Richard (eds), *Muslims in Britain: Race, Place and Identities*, Edinburgh: Edinburgh University Press, pp. 55–73.

Dyke, A. H. and James, L. (2009), 'Immigrant, Muslim, Female: Triple Paralysis?' London: Quilliam, http://www.quilliamfoundation.org/images/stories/pdfs/quilliam_immigrantmuslimfemale_triple_paralysis_july_2009.pdf accessed 26 October 2009.

Epoch Times (2008), 'London Becomes Islamic Finance Hub', 14 February, http://en.epochtimes.com/news/8-2-14/65890.html accessed 10 February 2009.

Fiaz, N. (2008), 'Muslim Scholar Warmly Welcomed at Anglican Church', *Bradford District Faiths Forum: Bridging Futures – Enhancing Friendship*, Spring/Summer, 2: 1–5.

Forsyth, F. and D. Gardener (2006), 'Geographic Diversity', in J. Dobbs, H. Green and L. Zealey (eds), *National Statistics: Focus on Ethnicity and Religion*, Basingstoke: Palgrave Macmillan, pp. 44–82.

Garbin, D. (2005), 'Bangladeshi Diaspora: Socio-cultural Dynamics, Religious Trends and Transnational Politics', in W. Menski, and B. Chanda (eds), *Proceedings of the European Human Rights Conference on Bangladesh Extremism, Intolerance and Violence*, London: CEMS-SOAS,http://www.swadhinata.org.uk/misc/DavidGarbinBangladeshidiasporaPaperDRAFT-7June%5B2%5D.doc accessed 3 February 2009.

Gardner, K. (1993), 'Mullahs, Migrants, Miracles: Travel and Transformation in Sylhet', *Contributions to Indian Sociology*, 27(2): 213–34.

Geaves, R. (2005), 'Negotiating British citizenship and Muslim Identity', in Tahir Abbas (ed.), *Muslim Britain: Communities Under Pressure*, London: Zed Books, pp. 67–77.

Gentleman, A. (2009), 'Legal Threat to Councils over Rape Victims', *Guardian*, 30 January, http://www.guardian.co.uk/society/2009/jan/30/council-action-support-services accessed 20 April 2009, p. 1.

GFK NOP Social Research (2006), 'Dispatches Muslim Survey: Attitudes to Living in Britain, GFK (Growth from Knowledge) NOP (National Opinion Poll) Social Research', 14 March–9 April, http://www.imaginate.uk.com/MCC01_SURVEY/index.htm accessed 1 February 2009.

Giddens, A. and S. Griffiths (2006), *Sociology*, 5th edition, London: Polity Press.

Gilliat-Ray, S. (2005/6), 'Shattering Misconceptions', *Agenda*, Winter: 4–7.

Gillespie, M. (2006), 'Transnational Television Audiences after September 11', *Journal of Ethnic and Migration Studies*, 32(6), August: 903–21.

Gilroy, P. (1997), 'Diaspora and the Detours of Identity', in K. Woodward (ed.), *Identity and Difference*, London: Sage/Open University, pp. 299–343.

Glynn, S. (2002), 'Bengali Muslims: the New East End Radicals?', *Ethnic and Racial Studies*, 25(6) November: 969–88.

Green, L. and N. Kabir (2007), 'What the British Papers Said on the First Anniversary of the London Bombing', in John Tebbutt (ed.), *Communication, Civics, Industry*, ANZCA and La Trobe University, 5–6 July, http://www.latrobe.edu.au/ANZCA2007/proceedings/Green%20and%20Kabir.pdf accessed 3 February 2009.

Guardian (2006), 'British Muslims Protest over Cartoons', 3 February, http://www.guardian.co.uk/world/2006/feb/03/religion.uk accessed 7 April 2009.

Haddad, Y., J. Smith and K. Moore (2006), *Muslim Women in America*, Oxford: Oxford University Press.

Hall, S. (1992), 'The Question of Cultural Identity', in S. Hall, D. Held, and T. McGrew (eds), *Modernity and its Futures*, London: Polity Press, pp. 273–316.

Hall, S. (1994), *Polity Reader in Cultural Theory*, Cambridge: Polity Press.

Hall, T. (2005), *Salam Brick Lane*, London: John Murray.

Hamid, S. (2007), 'Islamic Political Radicalism in Britain', in Tahir Abbas (ed.), *Islamic Political Radicalism: A European Perspective*, Edinburgh University Press, pp. 145–59.

Hansen, R. (2000), *Citizenship and Immigration in Post-War Britain: The Institutional Origins of a Multicultural Nation*, Oxford: Oxford University Press.

Harb, Z. and E. Bessaiso (2006), 'British Arab Muslim Audiences and Television after September 11', *Journal of Ethnic and Migration Studies*, 32(6), August: 1063–76.

Hellyer, H. A. (2007), 'British Muslims: Past, Present and Future', *The Muslim World*, 97(2), 1 April: 225–57.

Heneghan, T. (2008), 'Sharia Laws, Theories Vary Among World's Muslims', *Reuter News*, 12 February, http://global.factiva.com.ezproxy.library.ecu.au/ha/default.aspx accessed 1 December 2008.

Herbert, D. (2005), 'Media Publics, Culture and Democracy', in Marie Gillespie (ed.), *Media Audiences*, Maidenhead: Open University Press, pp. 97–136.

Hobsbawm, E. J. (1992), *Nations and Nationalism since 1780: Propaganda, Myth, Reality*, 2nd edition, Cambridge: Cambridge University Press.

Hopkins, P. (2004), 'Young Muslim Men in Scotland: Inclusions and Exclusions', *Children's Geographies*, 2(2): 257–72.

Hopkins, P. (2007a), '"Blue Square", "Proper" Muslims and Transnational Networks: Narratives of National and Religious Identities Amongst Young Muslim Men Living in Scotland', *Ethnicities*, 7(1): 61–81.

Hopkins, P. (2007b), 'Young Muslim Men's Experiences of Local Landscapes after 11 September 2001', in C. Aitchinson, P. Hopkins and M. Kwan (eds), *Geographies of Muslim Identities: Diaspora, Gender and Belonging*, Aldershot: Ashgate, pp. 189–200.

Husain, E. (2007), *The Islamist: Why I Joined Radical Islam in Britain, What I saw Inside and Why I left*, London: Penguin.

Hussain, D. (2007), 'Identity Formation and Change in British Muslim Communities', in M. Wetherell, L. Michelynn, and B. Robert (eds), *Identity, Ethnic Diversity and Community Cohesion*, Los Angeles and London: Sage Publications, pp. 34–9.

IslamOnline.net (2009), 'UK College Bans Muslim Student over Burka', 24 October, http://www.islamonline.net/servlet/Satellite?c=Article_C&cid=1256033936512& pagename=Zone-English-News/NWELayout accessed 30 October 2009.

Jacobson, J. (1998), *Islam in Transition: Religion and Identity among British Pakistani Youth*, London and New York: Routledge.

Jamal, N. and Chandab, T. (2005), *The Glory Garage: Growing Up Lebanese Muslim in Australia*, Sydney: Allen and Unwin.

James, L. (2009), 'In Defence of British Muslims: A Response to BNP Racist Propaganda. Quilliam, August', http://www.quilliamfoundation.org/images/stories/pdfs/in_ defence_of_british_muslims_09.pdf accessed 26 October 2009.

Jenkins, R. (2008), *Social Identity*, 3rd edition, London and New York: Routledge.

Johnes, M. (2004), 'Everyday When I Wakeup I Thank the Lord I'm Welsh', in Smith, A. and D. Porter (eds), *Sport and National Identity in the Post-War World*, London and New York: Routledge, pp. 52–68.

Johnson, N. (2007), 'Building an Integrated Society', in M. Wetherell, L. Michelynn and B. Robert (eds), *Identity, Ethnic Diversity and Community Cohesion*, Los Angeles and London: Sage Publications, pp. 24–33.

Julios, C. (2008), *Contemporary British Identity: English Language, Migrants and Public Discourse*, Aldershot: Ashgate.

Kabbani, S. M. H. (2007), *Illuminations Compiled Lectures on Sagariah and Rasawwuf*, Fenton, MI: Islamic Supreme Council of America.

Kabir, N. (2005), *Muslims in Australia: Immigration, Race Relations and Cultural History*, London: Routledge.

Kabir, N. (2006), 'Representation of Islam and Muslims in the Australian Media, 2001–2005', *Journal of Muslim Minority Affairs*, 26(3), December: 313–28.

Kabir, N. (2007a), 'What does it Mean to be Un-Australian?: Views of Australian Muslim Students in 2006', *People and Place*, 15(1): 51–68.

Kabir, N. (2007b), 'Why I Call Australia 'Home'?: A Transmigrant's Perspective',

M/C Journal 10(4), August, http://journal.media-culture.org.au/0708/15-kabir. php accessed 4 February 2009.

Kabir, N. (2008a), 'Globalised Islam: Does it Have any Impact on Australian Muslim Youth?', *The International Journal of Diversity in Organisations, Communities & Nations*, 8(2): 37–46.

Kabir, N. (2008b), 'Media is One-sided in Australia: Views of Australian Muslim Youth', *Journal of Children and Media*, 2(2): 267–81.

Kabir, N. (2008c), 'To be or Not to be an Australian: Focus on Muslim Youth', *National Identities*, 10(4): 399–419.

Kabir, N. and L. Green (2008), 'What the British Papers Said on the Second Anniversary of the London Bombing', in Elspeth Tilley (ed.), *Power and Place: Refereed Proceedings of the Australian New Zealand Communication Association Conference*, Wellington, 9–11 July, http://anzca08.massey.ac.nz/massey/depart/ cob/conferences/anzca-2008/anzca08-refereed-proceedings.cfm accessed 4 March 2009.

Kabir, N. and T. Rickards (2006), 'Students At Risk: Can Connections Make a Difference?, *Youth Studies Australia*, 25(4): 17–24.

Keily, R., F. Bechhofer, R. Stewart and D. McCrone (2001), 'The Markers and Rules of Scottish Identity', *Sociological Review*, 49(1): 33–55.

Kettani, A. M. (1986), *Muslim Minorities in the World Today*, London and New York: Mansell Publishing Limited.

Knightly, P. (2001), 'The Disinformation Campaign', *The Guardian*, 4 October, no page number.

Kolig, E. and Kabir, N. (2008), 'Not Friend, not Foe: The Rocky Road of Enfranchisement of Muslims into Multicultural Nationhood in Australia and New Zealand', *Immigrants and Minorities*, 26(3), November: 266–300.

Kowalski, R. (2004), '"Cry for us Argentina": Sports and National Identity in the Late Twentieth-century Scotland', in Adrian S. and P. Dilwyn (eds), *Sport and National Identity in the Post-War World*, London and New York: Routledge, pp. 69–87.

Kristianasen, W. (2006), 'Britain's Multiculturalism Falters', 1 November, *Le Monde Diplomatique*, http://mondediplo.com/2006/11/02ukmuslims#nb11 accessed 9 February 2009.

Lee, B. (2007), *Cardiff's Vanished Docklands*, revised edition, Stroud: Sutton Publishing.

Lewis, P. (1994), *Islamic Britain: Religion, Politics and Identity among Muslims*, London: I. B. Tauris.

Lewis, P. (2002), *Islamic Britain: Religion, Politics and Identity among British Muslims*, second edition, London: I. B. Tauris.

Lewis, P. (2007), *Young British and Muslim*, London: Continuum.

Lichtenstein, R. (2007), *On Brick Lane*, London: Hamish Hamilton.

Los Angeles Times (2008), 'Islamic Law Plays a Role in British Legal System', 20 June, http://articles.latimes.com/2008/jun/20/world/fg-sharia20 accessed 4 April 2009.

Mail Online (2005), 'Sick BNP produce bus blast leaflets', 12 July, http://www.daily-mail.co.uk/news/article-355518/Sick-BNP-produce-bus-blast-leaflet.html accessed 20 April 2008.

Mail Online (2008), 'Sharia Law SHOULD be used in Britain, Says UK's Top Judge', 4 July, http://www.dailymail.co.uk/news/article-1031611/Sharia-law-SHOULD-used-Britain-says-UKs-judge.html accessed 9 February 2009.

Mail Online (2009), 'Doctor Cleared of Glasgow Bomb Plot Works in NHS Hospital after Home Office Dropped Bid to Deport Him', 10 August, http://www.dailymail.co.uk/news/article-1205473/Doctor-cleared-Glasgow-bomb-plot-works-NHS-hospital-Home-Office-dropped-bid-deport-him.html accessed 16 September 2009.

Malik, S. (2007), 'My Brother the Bomber', *Prospect*, Issue 135, http://www.prospect-magazine.co.uk/article_details.php?id=9635 accessed 25 May 2009.

Matar, D. (2006), 'Diverse Diasporas, One Meta-narrative: Palestinians in the UK talking about September 11 2001', *Journal of Ethnic and Migration Studies*, 32(6): 1027–40.

Mayor of London (2006), 'Muslims in London, Report', October, http://www.london.gov.uk/gla/publications/equalities/muslims-in-london.pdf accessed 28 May 2009.

Mernissi, F. (1987), *Beyond the Veil: Male-Female Dynamics in Modern Muslim Society*, revised edition, Bloomington and Indianapolis: Indiana University Press.

MINAB (2009), 'Mosque and Imams National Advisory Board. The Minab General Council', http://www.minab.org.uk accessed 8 June 2009.

Mir, S. (2007), '"The Other within the Same": Some Aspects of Scottish-Pakistani Identity in Suburban Glasgow', in C. Aitchinson, P. Hopkins and M. Kwan (eds), *Geographies of Muslim Identities: Diaspora, Gender and Belonging*, Aldershot: Ashgate, pp. 57–77.

Modood, T. (1997), 'Culture and Identity', in Madrid T. and R. Berthoud (eds), *Ethnic Minorities in Britain: Diversity and Disadvantage*, London: Policy Studies Institute, pp. 290–338.

Modood, T. (2005), *Multicultural Politics: Racism, Ethnicity and Muslims in Britain*, Edinburgh: Edinburgh University Press.

Modood, T. (2007), *Multiculturalism: A Civic Idea*, Cambridge: Polity Press.

Mohammad, R. (2005), 'Negotiating Space of the Home, the Education System and the Labour Market: the Case of Young, Working-class, British Pakistani Muslim Women', in F. Gazhi, and N. Caroline (eds), *Geographies of Muslim Women: Gender, Religion and Space*, London: Guilford Press, pp. 178–202.

Morning Star Online (2006), 'Livingstone Publishes Report on Barriers Facing London Muslims', 24 October, http://global.factiva.com.ezproxy.library.ecu.au/ha/default.aspx accessed 28 May 2009.

Murtaza, B. (2006), 'Muslim Youth Speak: A Strategy to Work with and Engage Young Muslim People in Leeds', Lancashire: Vis-à-vis Research Consultancy Limited.

Nairn, T. (1981), *The Break-up of Britain*, London: Verso.

Nasr, S. H. (2002), *The Heart of Islam: Enduring Values for Humanity*, New York: HarperOne.

National Public Radio: Talk of the Nation (2008), 'Religious Courts and Civil Law', 18 February, http://www.npr.org/templates/transcript/transcript.php?story Id=19147891 accessed February 2009.

NMA (Newspaper Marketing Agency) (2007), 'Facts and Figures', *The Sun*, http://www. nmauk.co.uk/nma/do/live/factsAndFigures?newspaperID=17 accessed 17 May 2007.

National Youth Agency (2004), 'UK Muslim Community Statistics', *The National Youth Agency*, http://www.nya.org.uk/information/100582/109652/100630/108761/uk muslimcommunitystatistics/ accessed 27 February 2009.

Office for National Statistics (2001) 'Census', http://www.ons.gov.uk/census/index. html accessed 28 May 2009.

Office for National Statistics (2004), 'Muslim Unemployment Rate Highest', *Annual Population Survey*, January 2004 to December 2004, http://www.statistics.gov.uk/ cci/nugget.asp?id=979 accessed 21 May 2009.

Oliver, H. J. (2004), *The 'Wahhabi' Myth*, Second Edition, Toronto: TROID Publications.

O'Neill, S. and D. McGrory (2006), *The Suicide Factory: Abu Hamza and the Finsbury Park Mosque*, London, New York: Harper Perennial.

O'Shaughnessy, M. and J. Stadler (2002), *Media and Society: An Introduction,* 2nd edition, Oxford: Oxford University Press.

Padilla, A. M. (2006), 'Bicultural Social Development', *Hispanic Journal of Behavioral Sciences*, 28(4), November: 467–97.

Parekh, B. (2007), 'Reasoned Identities: A Committed Relationship', in Margaret W., L. Michelynn and R. Berkeley (eds), *Identity, Ethnic Diversity and Community Cohesion*, Los Angeles and London: Sage Publications, pp. 130–5.

Parekh Report (2000), 'Published by Runnymede Trust', http://www.new-diaspora. com/Culture&Identity/2-Parekh%20Report%202000.html accessed 6 May 2009.

Peach, C. (2006), 'Muslims in the 2001 Census of England and Wales: Gender and Economic Disadvantage', *Ethnic and Racial Studies*, 29(6): 629–55.

Polley, M. (2004), 'Sports and National Identity in Contemporary England', in Adrian S. and P. Dilwyn (eds), *Sport and National Identity in the Post-War World*, London and New York: Routledge, pp. 10–30.

Poole, E. (2002), *Reporting Islam: Media Representations of British Muslims*, London: I. B. Tauris.

Poole, E. and Richardson, J. E. (2004), *Muslims and the News Media*, London: I. B. Tauris.

Poynting, S. and Mason, V. (2006), '"Tolerance, Freedom, Justice and Peace"? Britain, Australia and Anti-Muslim Racism since 11 September 2001', *Journal of Intercultural Studies*, 27(4), November: 365–91.

Powell, E. (1968), 'The Man himself, Enoch Powell, Enoch Powell's famous "Rivers of Blood" speech, as delivered in Birmingham on 20 April 1968', http://www. natfront.org.uk/powell.html. accessed 12 April 2009.

Press Association National Newswire (2006), 'Muslims Feeling Targeted – Cameron', 20 October, http://global.factiva.com.ezproxy.library.ecu.au/ha/default.aspx accessed 10 December 2008.

Press Association National Newswire (2007), 'Veil Controversy Sparks Debate on Religious Integration', 20 March, http://global.factiva.com.ezproxy.library.ecu.au/ha/default.aspx accessed 10 December 2008.

Press Association National Newswire (2009), 'BNP Wins First Euro Seat', 8 June, http://global.factiva.com.ezproxy.library.ecu.au/ha/default.aspx accessed 8 June 2009.

Press Association Regional Newswire – Yorkshire and Humberside (2007) 'Veil "Mark of Separation", says First Muslim Peer', 20 February, http://global.factiva.com.ezproxy.library.uwa.edu.au/ha/default.aspx accessed 8 June 2009.

Ramadan, T. (2004), *Western Muslims and the Future of Islam*, Oxford and New York: Oxford University Press.

Rehman, J. (2007), 'Islam, "War on Terror" and the Future of Muslim Minorities in the United Kingdom: Dilemmas of Multiculturalism in the Aftermath of the London Bombings', *Human Rights Quarterly*, 29(4): 831–78.

Richards, J. (2005), *Cardiff: A Maritime History*, Stroud: Tempus.

Robinson, G. L. N. (1985), *Crosscultural Understanding: Processes and Approaches for Foreign Language, English as a Second Language and Bilingual Educators*, Oxford: Pergamon Press Ltd.

Rogler, L. H., D. E. Cortes and R. G. Malgady (1991), 'Acculturation and Mental Health Status among Hispanics: Convergence and New Directions for Research', *American Psychologist*, 46(6): 585–97.

Runnymede Trust: Commission on British Muslims and Islamophobia (1997), *Islamophobia: A Challenge to Us All*, London: Runnymede Trust.

Ruthven, M. (2004), *Fundamentalism: The Search for Meaning*, Oxford and New York: Oxford University Press.

Said, E. (1995), *Orientalism: Western Perceptions of the Orient*, London: Penguin.

Said, E. (1997), *Covering Islam: How the Media and the Experts Determine How We See the Rest of the World*, London: Vintage.

Salam (2009), 'Muslims in Britain: Who's Who Men', http://www.salaam.co.uk/theme-ofthemonth/september03_index.php?l=9#hamid accessed 29 May 2009.

Shaw, Alison (2000), *Kinship and Continuity: Pakistani Families in Britain*, London and New York: Routledge, Taylor and Francis.

Sheddon, M. S., D. Hussain and N. Malik (2004), *British Muslims between Assimilation and Segregation*, Markfield: The Islamic Foundation.

Smit, M. (2006), 'Muslims Worst off in London', *Newsquest Media Group Newspapers*, 25 October, http://global.factiva.com.ezproxy.library.ecu.au/ha/default.aspx accessed 10 December 2008.

Straw, Jack (2006), 'I want to Unveil my Views on an Important Issue', *Lancashire Telegraph*, 5 October, http://www.telegraph.co.uk/news/1530718/%22I-want-to-unveil-my-views-on-an-important-issue%22.htm accessed 13 Feb 2009.

Smith, A. D. (1991), *National Identity*, Reno and Las Vegas: University of Nevada Press.

Smith, A. and D. Porter (eds) (2004), *Sport and National Identity in the Post-War World*, London and New York: Routledge.

Smith, T. (2008), *Coal, Frankincense and Myrrh: Yemen and British Yemenis*, Stockport: Dewi Lewis Publishing.

South, J., K. Akhionbare, M. Farrar, L. Gomez, C. Newell and S. Titford (2007), 'Hamara Healthy Living Centre – An Evaluation', Leeds: Centre for Health Promotion Research, November.

Tajfel, H. (ed.) (1978), *Differentiation between Social Groups: Studies in the Social Psychology of Intergroup Relations*, London: Academic Press.

Tajfel, H. (1981), 'The Experimental Social Psychology of Intergroup Relations, in J. C. Turner and H. Giles (eds), *Intergroup Behavior*, Oxford: Blackwell, pp. 66–101.

Tajfel, H. (1986), 'The Social Identity Theory of Intergroup Behaviour', in S. Worchel and W. G. Austin (eds), *Psychology of Intergroup Relations*, Chicago, IL: Nelson Hall, pp. 7–24.

Thorne, J. (2004), 'British Muslims Push to Integrate', *The Christian Science Monitor*, from 24 November 2004 edition, p. 6. http://www.csmonitor.com/2004/1124/p06s01-woeu.html accessed 4 February 2009.

Tohon (2010), *The Jihadi*, London: Athena Press.

Turner, J. (1984), 'Social Categorization and the Self-concept: A Social Cognitive Theory of Group Behaviour', *Advances in Group Processes: Theory and Research*, 2: 77–122.

Turner, J., C. Hogg, M. A. Oakes, S. D. Reicher and M. Wetherell (1987), *Rediscovering the Social Group: A Self Categorization Theory*, Oxford: Blackwell.

Van Dijk, T. A. (1991), *Racism and the Press*, London: Routledge.

Ward, P. (2004), *Britishness since 1870*, London: Routledge, Taylor and Francis Group.

Werbner, P. (2002), *Imagined Diasporas among Manchester Muslims*, Oxford: James Currey, and Santa Fe: School of American Research Press.

Werbner, P. (2004a), 'The Predicament of Diaspora and Millennial Islam: Reflections on September 11, 2001', *Ethnicities* 4(4): 451–76.

Werbner, P. (2004b), 'Theorising Complex Diasporas: Purity and Hybridity in the South Asian Public Sphere in Britain', *Journal of Ethnic and Migration Studies*, 30(5), September: 895–911.

Williams, C. (2003), 'Social Inclusion and Race Equality', in C. Williams, N. Evans and P. O'Leary (eds), *A Tolerant Nation? Exploring Ethnic Diversity in Wales*, Cardiff: University of Wales Press, pp. 139–59.

Wilson, II, C. and F. Gutierrez (1995), *Race, Multiculturalism, and the Media*, London: Sage Publications.

Yaqoob, S. (2007), 'British Islamic Political Radicalism', in Tahir Abbas (ed.), *Islamic Political Radicalism: A European Perspective*, Edinburgh: Edinburgh University Press, pp. 279–94.

Yorkshire Post (2005), 'Archbishop Joins other Faith Leaders in Condemning "Evil"', 8 July, http://0global.factiva.com.library.ecu.edu.au/ha/default.aspx accessed 25 January 2009.

Yorkshire Post (2007), 'Yorkshire Muslims Pray as Bhutto Laid to Rest', 28 December

http://global.factiva.com.ezproxy.library.ecu.au/ha/default.aspx   accessed   12
December 2008.

Yorkshire Post (2008), 'Man Guilty over "Honour" Killing', 25 June, http://global.
factiva.com.ezproxy.library.ecu.au/ha/default.aspx accessed 5 June 2009.

Yorkshire Evening Post (2004), 'Muslims Fear Rise in Racial Attacks', 8 June, http://
global.factiva.com.ezproxy.library.ecu.au/ha/default.aspx accessed 1 December
2008.

Young, R. J. C. (2007), *The Idea of English Ethnicity*, London: Wiley-Blackwell.

INDEX